# The Big
# Green Apple

Advance praise for *The Big Green Apple*

"By most accounts, New York is already America's greenest city, simply because people live in smaller homes and rely on public transit. But with the help of Ben Jervey's comprehensive guide, New Yorkers can now take that unconscious environmentalism and extend it with a few powerful modifications of their ways of life. If they do, then someday Gotham will join places like Oslo and Stockholm as truly ecological metropolises."

—Bill McKibben, author *The End of Nature*

## Help Keep This Guide Up to Date

Considering the dynamic nature of this town, particularly of the businesses and organizations that operate here, some of the information found within this book is subject to change. I ask all readers to send along updated info, along with questions, suggestions, and even criticisms, to: author@greenappleguide.com.

Furthermore, the website www.greenappleguide.com will serve as a forum to discuss, commend, or critique the ideas presented in this book, or you can share your own ideas and solutions with others. So check out the site and plug into a dynamic, public-service oriented forum for all things green in New York City. Thanks!

The book's publisher would also value your input and would love to hear from you directly concerning your experiences with this guide. Please send your comments and suggestions to:

The Globe Pequot Press
Reader Response/Editorial Department
P.O. Box 480
Guilford, CT 06437

Or you can e-mail the publisher at: editorial@GlobePequot.com. When you e-mail, please put the book title (*The Big Green Apple*) in the subject line of your message.

Thanks for your input!

# The Big Green Apple

**Your Guide to Eco-Friendly Living in New York City**

Ben Jervey

**INSIDERS'** GUIDE®

GUILFORD, CONNECTICUT
AN IMPRINT OF THE GLOBE PEQUOT PRESS

**INSIDERS' GUIDE**®

Copyright © 2006 by Benjamin Jervey

Text design: LeAnna Weller Smith

**Library of Congress Cataloging-in-Publication Data**

Jervey, Benjamin.
 The big green apple : your guide to eco-friendly living in New York City / Benjamin
Jervey.
  p. cm.
 Includes bibliographical references and index.
 ISBN 0-7627-3835-9
 1. Green marketing—New York (State)—New York. 2. Environmentalism—New York
(State)—New York. 3. Conservation of natural resources—New York (State)—New York. I.
Title.
 HF5413.J47 2006
 646.7—dc22                                                       2005023413

 Printed on 100 percent recycled paper

Manufactured in the United States of America
First Edition/First Printing

To my parents—lifelong teachers of whom I was
fortunate enough to be a full-time student

# Acknowledgments

First and foremost, without the endless support—inspirational, editorial, and motivational—of my parents, these words never would have found the page. Few are the parents who will smile encouragingly when their child tells them he turned down yet another benefits-loaded job to spend time working on a book.

I am also enormously indebted to my editors at The Globe Pequot Press—Laura Strom, who brought me on board and helped steer early drafts away from the shoals of tedium, and Mimi Egan, whose enthusiasm and vision for this project mirrored and emboldened my own. Also to my copy editor, Laura Jorstad, whose gentle touch has improved this text immeasurably.

All of us New Yorkers should be grateful for the work of the various organizations, businesses, and individuals whose endeavors make for a greener New York cityscape. I regard all such enterprises and green entrepreneurs with complete admiration and gratitude. I am particularly grateful to those individuals who went well out of their way to open their offices and schedules to accommodate my investigations. Always generous with time and information were: Ruth Katz of Just Food; Ian Marvy of Added Value; Karen Washington of La Familia Verde; Allen Katz of Slow Food NYC; Jonathan Cramer at the Community Environment Center at Stuyvesant Cove; Margaret Lydecker of GreenDrinks NYC; Sarah Johnston of the Northeast Organic Farming Association of New York; Steve Hindy of the Brooklyn Brewery; Bari Franklin of Renewable Brooklyn; Kate Zidar at the Lower East Side Ecology Center; and the very helpful folks at the New York City Department of Parks and Recreation, especially John Mattera and Laura LaVelle.

Information contained herein was also generously made available by the Natural Resource Defense Council, Transportation Alternatives, Consolidated Edison, the New York City Department of Sanitation,

Sustainable-Table.com, and the New York City Department of Parks and Recreation.

I'd be remiss not to recognize the great support provided to me by the faculty of the Environmental Studies Department at Middlebury College, in particular professors and thesis advisors John Elder and Christopher McGrory Klyza, who helped me understand the importance of clearly communicating environmental issues; by my uncle, Bill Jervey, who lent many hours and spent many red pens on my earliest drafts; and by Bill McKibben, who has always been enormously generous with his time, experience, and vast expertise in the environmental writing field. For this I am dearly grateful.

Finally, I owe a great deal of thanks to my friends and roommates—especially Cara, Matt, Jeff and Jeffie, Pace (for his particular style of motivation), Patxi, Harriet, Jake, and Stacy—who have patiently put up with my irrational behavior and peculiar schedules while working on this book. All of them have been dynamic motivators, remarkably effective critics, and—perhaps most importantly—alleviators of stress. This process wouldn't have been nearly as gratifying without them.

# Contents

# Preface

A City, like a living thing, is a united and continuous whole.
—PLUTARCH, Molaria

Right now, right here in New York City, somebody is cultivating a garden. Around the corner somebody is pocketing a set of car keys and hopping onto a bicycle. In some nearby kitchen locally grown, organic produce is being kept cool in a refrigerator plugged into wind power energy. Somewhere in New York City, a street tree is being cared for by a concerned local resident, while a sanitation worker on an adjacent street is dutifully keeping the recyclable paper and plastics separate.

Although difficult for many to believe, all over the city of New York acts of sustainable, low-impact living are being performed by a hearty bunch of citizens. Indeed, green living is possible here in New York City. You can harbor personal philosophies of sustainability and environmentally low-impact living in the Big Apple and survive. In doing so, you can create for yourself a healthier, more rewarding life.

I know this because I have lived this.

Like so many New Yorkers, I'm a transplant. In fact, my arrival in New York City marked the beginning of my first true urban experience. What can possibly prepare you for that? After growing up in a small town in Massachusetts, I went off to pastoral Vermont to study and then work, all the while developing an appreciation and concern for the fragile state of the world's ecology. But as easy as it is to don a green hat up in Vermont, the beast that is New York City has the tendency to tear that noble lid off and throw it into a puddle of mud. Upon arriving in the big city, I struggled to reconcile the environmentally concerned mind-set that comes so effortlessly in a place like Vermont with my new urban lifestyle. Of course sustainable living is easier in a Vermont township, where local produce is plentiful and nearly every backyard is equipped with a compost bin. In the city such conveniences are harder to come by; however, that's not to say they're nonexistent.

As I hope to make clear throughout this book, by spending some time exploring and by making a bit of an extra effort, it is more than possible to live an environmentally responsible life here in New York City . . . and have a good time, too. If you've purchased this book, you've already taken the first step toward such a life. Or perhaps you've been working toward it for some time and are just looking for some new ideas. In either case you've made a noble and important choice, and one that promises rewards large and small. It is also a choice that will let you rediscover this fine city and get to know it through new eyes. Here you have the opportunity to envision the city anew, and to offer yourself, your decisions, and your actions to its ultimate well-being. A greener New York is within our reach.

# New York, New York:

## The City as an Organism

W hether you've just recently unpacked here or you've been around the city for decades, there are plenty of reasons for calling New York City home. Of course almost all New Yorkers would agree that theirs is a love–hate relationship with the city. For all the wonderful benefits—the cultural opportunities, the interesting jobs, the people, the music, the food, even the feeling of being in the center of it *all*—there are enough negative aspects to drive some of us right out of town. The city's ecological health is rarely, if ever, considered one of its stronger points. Not a day passes that I don't have moments of disgust over the city's assault on its own ecology, let alone its impact on global systems. From the mountains of waste that linger on the streets to the dirty air that hangs so low over the heat-absorbent asphalt streets in the summer, there's quite a bit to grow weary of.

Fortunately, we live in a time when more and more efforts are being made to redeem our city's relationship with the natural world. While the urban sustainability movement in this country might have its roots on the West Coast, New Yorkers are waking up to this trend, and an abundance of progressive politicians, entrepreneurs, activists, and citizens alike are bringing about some wonderful changes. In the actions of these conscientious New Yorkers—in their policy shifts and public services, their educational movements and private decisions—we find a veritable catalog of diverse ingredients that make up the slow but steady process of New York City's greening.

## Why Go Green?

In *Green Urbanism: Learning from European Cities,* Timothy Beatley wrote that "the first and most obvious thing about cities is that they are like organisms, sucking in resources and emitting wastes." His analogy is worth considering carefully. For once we being to think about New York City as an organism in its own right, it's easier to understand why decisions made and actions taken individually and locally affect the overall health of our hometown. And considering the enormity of our organism as compared to others around the world, it also becomes clear that our behavior definitely affects the well-being of others. As depicted in Saul Steinberg's famous cover for the *New Yorker, A View of the World from Ninth Avenue,* in which the bird's-eye view looking west doesn't show much beyond the Hudson River, folks here certainly have a reputation for indifference to the world outside the five boroughs. But residents of New York are proving ever more frequently that they *are* concerned with the overall health and well-being of the world. And here you are, reading this book, living proof.

Considering that resources such as food, water, and energy from nonrenewable sources are finite, the more of these resources that New York City as a whole consumes, the less they are available for others outside of the metropolis. Conversely, the more waste that New York City puts out into the world (hardly any of which, it is worth noting, remains here within the city limits), the less space there is for the waste of others. The reigning model for a city's system of resource consumption and waste production is primarily a linear one: Input resources; output waste. Energy, food, water, and miscellaneous materials come in; trash and pollution go out. For most environmentalists, social thinkers, and urban planners, however, this linear system is proving to be an inefficient and eventually dangerous one. Consequently, the benefits of working toward a more circular system, whereby what comes into a system is reduced and what goes out is recycled or reused, are becoming obvious on a local, regional, and even global scale. A more circular system is a more sustainable system, and by reducing dependence on others, a city can put itself in a position to be healthier not only from an ecological standpoint, but also in terms of quality of life and economics.

Completely closing the circuit of intake and output is an impossible undertaking in any city, let alone one as enormous and cosmopolitan as New York. And all organisms consume resources from outside their own system and produce some sort of waste. But this is not to say that an ecological balance is unattainable. And reducing resource consumption and wasteful output should be of paramount concern. Sustainability, from a human standpoint, is reached when an activity or a system can be sustained over the long term, without harming, degrading, or diminishing the conditions—environmental, economic, or other—necessary to support those same activities or systems. In terms of New York City, this means consuming less energy and fewer resources while at the same time emitting less pollution and waste.

Nowhere on earth could a change in attitude have such profound, wide-reaching effects. Aside from being America's most populous city, New York's role as a global business, cultural, and diplomatic hub puts it in the world's spotlight. Any shift in cultural or lifestyle trends here would be recognized by cosmopolitan centers the world over. Such shifts would also be hailed and trumpeted by environmentalists everywhere. To paraphrase the Kauder and Ebb song made famous by Frank Sinatra more than twenty-five years ago, if we can fix it here, we can fix it anywhere.

The major predicament is this: Green living in New York City isn't terribly easy. Or, if you'll pardon another paraphrase, I give you Kermit: "It ain't easy living green." At the very least it's seldom convenient.

Separating recyclables is space consuming and labor-intensive if you've got a small apartment on the fifth floor of a walk-up. Ordering delivery is easier than preparing your own meal. Surviving a New York City August without an air conditioner is considered by many to be impossible. But many New Yorkers *are* questioning these seductively convenient though environmentally restrictive behaviors. They are more than willing to put in a bit of extra time and effort to ensure that the decisions made and the actions taken contribute to the health, rather than the detriment, of the local *and* global environment.

Furthermore, working toward a more sustainable life here in New York City can be as rewarding as it is productive and positive. Who wouldn't prefer an open, smooth riverside bike path to an FDR traffic jam? Or a sweet, succulent peach picked that very week from a local orchard to one as hard as a rock, without any flavor, whose origins are unknown? Who wouldn't prefer cleaner air and cleaner water and cleaner streets? A greener life *is* a better life.

This book aims to be a practical, useful guide. Some of the tips for arriving at a greener life you may already know, but many may come as sweet surprises. I invite you to peruse these pages, considering their ideas and strategies, so that you can develop your own personal program for bringing a greener shade to life here in this wonderful city.

*The Big Green Apple* is divided into four main sections, each representing an important aspect of life here in New York City—home, food, transportation, and work and recreation. The first section, "A Greener Apple Begins at Home," takes a look at the energy and resource demands of a typical New York City household and considers a variety of ways to reduce their environmental impact. It focuses on issues such as lighting, appliance use, water consumption, climate control, and waste management. Section 2, "The Green Plate Special," discusses some of the hidden environmental costs of food, including industrialized agriculture's ever-increasing dependence on ecosystem-threatening pesticides, unnatural growth supplements and antibiotics, energy-intensive shipping processes, and a score of other environmentally unsound production practices. Sensible, eco-friendly alternatives available right here in the city are then offered. Much has been written and reported about the harmful effects of gasoline-powered vehicles. In "Gettin' Around Green," section 3, a number of viable alternatives to automobiles are discussed, as are the rewards of using alternative forms of transportation. Section 4, "Work Green, Play Green," focuses on these essential aspects of your city life and covers everything from the office to stores to city parks. It includes a chapter on greening your workplace, and another on turning shopping into an environmentally redeeming activity. Also included is advice on how best to get outside and how to be more actively involved in the city's open spaces and in environmental causes. You'll find descriptions of and ruminations on the city's elaborate parks system, information about green-friendly special events, and profiles of organizations whose services and programs you can take advantage of or work with for the betterment of New York's ecological health. Finally, "The Green Pages"—an appendix to *The Big Green Apple*—offers a comprehensive directory of contact information for groups, organizations, and businesses that share the ultimate goal of a New York City that is not only more environmentally friendly but also a better citizen of the world.

Without further delay, let's go green!

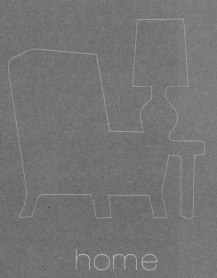

home

# A Greener Apple Begins at Home

Nobody made a greater mistake than he who did nothing because he could do only a little.—EDMUND BURKE

Homes in New York City come in all shapes and sizes—from the minuscule studios of SoHo to the cavernous lofts of Williamsburg, from the converted tenements in Chinatown to the spacious condos of the Upper East Side, and from the crowded housing projects in the Bronx to the stand-alone one-families of Flushing and Staten Island. No matter what 'hood you represent, no matter what type of building, no matter if you rent or own, there's no doubt about it: there is no place like home.

As New Yorkers our homes are our sanctuaries, our bastions of peace, and a retreat from the city's constant shuffle. For green New Yorkers, our homes are probably one of the only elements of this city life where we feel we have complete control. It's easy, though, for even the most environmentally committed of us to feel that our own homes are irrelevant to the city's overall ecological health, what with more than three *million* other housing units in the city, not to mention the vast arenas of office and commercial space, entertainment and sporting venues, and massive industrial facilities.

Indeed, we pass through a crackling Times Square and can almost feel the voltaics; we see the office buildings of Downtown or Midtown aglow throughout the night and hear the incessant whir of their climate control systems twenty-four hours a day. But even amid these mega displays of waste and excess, if you think that your home's impact on the environment is insignificant, think again.

For nowhere is the total impact of your own personal resource consumption and waste production more significant than in your home. New York City is an enormous consumer of energy, born of all possible sources—from petroleum to natural gas to coal to nuclear to wind and biomass—and residential consumers are responsible for a very significant slice of that pie. How significant? Without getting too bogged down in pages of dry and depressing figures, a few statistics make clear just how much impact residential life in this city has. Numbers are tough to come by on a city-specific level, but throughout New York State, home heating needs alone gobble nearly forty-five million barrels of petroleum annually (85 percent of which, it is worth mentioning in this day and age, is imported from foreign lands). Residences are also responsible for nearly one-third of all of the electricity consumed here in New York. And while the Department of Sanitation doesn't have figures specific to residences, when walking around a residentially zoned neighborhood on trash collection day, it doesn't take a mathematician's mind to imagine the staggering volume of waste produced in homes throughout this city.

So, yes, the decisions you make in your home are extremely important and, furthermore, are representative of the way you choose to live your urban life. Throughout this section, you'll find suggestions for a variety of ways to make your home life less taxing on our resources and the environment as a whole. Chapters 1 and 2 go over ways to limit the total energy consumed in your home, by reducing how much electricity is flowing into your home and how much petroleum is being burned to heat the space. Chapter 3 gets into the standard source of the electricity flowing into New York City's homes, then evaluates alternatives on the market, particularly renewable energy. Moving on to water consumption, and with a concerned nod to past droughts, you'll find in chapter 4 a wealth of simple strategies for conserving this valuable resource. Waste management and reduction on the home front take chapter 5's center stage, streamlining the city's seemingly ever-changing recycling program to ensure that the majority of your home's refuse will find itself useful again. Finally, chapter 6 offers ideas for keeping your home clean by the most eco-friendly means.

Hopefully by the section's end, you'll have a much clearer idea of what can be done to make your home a lower-impact environment, and you'll know that you needn't live a reduced life to accomplish it. Trust me, I'm not suggesting that anyone re-create Thoreau's Walden Pond retreat. I like a nice, comfortable home as much as the next fellow, and over the course of this section, you'll learn how to have just that, without compromising your green sensibilities.

## CHAPTER ONE

# The Juice Is Loose:

## Conserving Electricity at Home

Turn off the lights; in the silence of your
darkened home you can hear a thousand rivers
whispering their thanks.—**CLEAR CREEK**

Besides air and water, there isn't much we take more for granted than electricity. Who thinks about where it comes from when they flip a light switch or turn on an air conditioner? Most of the time, I certainly don't. Flip a switch—let there be light! Hit a button—cool air! Aside from grade school images of Benjamin Franklin maniacally flying his kite during a lightning storm, most of us don't really picture electricity in any tangible way at all. Interestingly enough, the blackout of 2003, while frightening to many and inconvenient to even more, did to some degree change all that. It forced New Yorkers to think outside our five-borough bubble and realize that electricity is not some ambiguous force that automatically powers computers, charges cell phones, and keeps food cold.

So where does it come from? New York City relies on a complex, state-governed system of energy production and distribution that, in turn, relies heavily on a number of environmentally compromising and severely polluting nonrenewable resources. The city's electricity comes from the same pool as the majority of the state, and the behemoth Consolidated Edison is the lone distributor.

New York City's share of the pool is largely provided by three coal- and oil-burning plants within city limits; a number of natural gas plants, some in the city; a handful of enormous coal plants in the Hudson Valley; and the Indian Point Nuclear Plant, a mere 20 miles from New York City limits. Coal, oil, and nuclear all give the green mind the jitters, but what exactly do they mean to the environment and greater ecological well-being? The coal and oil plants—known as "brown" in environmental circles because of their unsustainable and polluting ways of energy production—are a major source of the pollution that causes global warming, acid rain, mercury poisoning, and ozone-smog, as well as generally dirty air laden with particulate matter. Without sounding too alarmist, here are some facts compiled by the New York Public Research Interest Group (NYPIRG), which show that the local effects of these pollutants aren't anything to scoff at, and in some cases are quite dire. Electricity generation throughout New York State releases an average of 129 billion pounds of carbon dioxide annually, the most notorious of greenhouse gases. Con Ed's emissions are higher than the state average, meaning that New York City's contribution to that total is disproportionately high.

Global warming, at its current rate, is expected to cause a 3-foot rise in sea level along the coasts of

> **tip**
>
> In 2003, 61 percent of Con Ed electricity flowing into New York City was being generated by power plants using nonrenewable resources such as coal, petroleum, and natural gas.

Long Island, New York City, and up the Hudson Valley as far as Albany by the year 2100. The numbers are one thing, but consider the reality: A great deal of Manhattan sits well within this 3-foot elevation level. If these levels continue to rise unabated, city planners might spend the second half of the twenty-first century studying the Dutch system of dikes; Long Island may then need to be renamed a more appropriate Short Island. With the rising seas will come rising temperatures. Since New York City is what climatologists call an "urban heat island" that is exceptionally capable of absorbing and retaining the summer sun's heat, the increases in temperatures—estimated between 4.4 and 10.2 degrees Fahrenheit by the end of the century—will have particularly dire effects on air quality and human health. In June 2004 the *New York Times* went so far as to warn: "It will not happen the day after tomorrow. Nor a decade from now. But well before this century ends, global warming will make New York City and the metropolitan area that surrounds it a hotter, wetter, and significantly less healthy place to live and work." Over the same time period, experts are predicting up to a 40 percent reduction in agricultural yield due to climate change and sea level rise. Bad news for farmers, and bad news for those of us who enjoy the fruits of their labor.

Meanwhile, acid rain has already poisoned water sources in the Adirondacks and Catskills: One-quarter of the Adirondacks' lakes are unable to

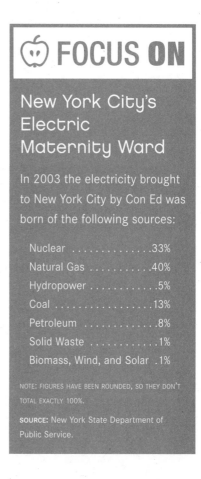

# 🍎 FOCUS ON

## New York City's Electric Maternity Ward

In 2003 the electricity brought to New York City by Con Ed was born of the following sources:

| | |
|---|---|
| Nuclear | .33% |
| Natural Gas | .40% |
| Hydropower | .5% |
| Coal | .13% |
| Petroleum | .8% |
| Solid Waste | .1% |
| Biomass, Wind, and Solar | .1% |

NOTE: FIGURES HAVE BEEN ROUNDED, SO THEY DON'T TOTAL EXACTLY 100%.

**SOURCE:** New York State Department of Public Service.

support fish, rendering this once healthy and vibrant city escape one of the most ecologically fragile regions in the country. Mercury poisoning from power plants has left the surviving fish populations in 17 percent of New York State's water bodies unsafe for human consumption. Ozone-smog has been blamed for more than half a million asthma attacks and over 12,300 emergency room visits throughout New York State over the course of one summer alone. Fine particulate matter, otherwise known as soot, has caused an estimated 1,800 residents of the state to die prematurely each year.

This is just a sampling of the bad news concerning those "brown" power plants that provide a majority of our city's electricity.

How about the 33 percent that is born in the "cleaner" Indian Point Nuclear Plant? While nuclear power plants were once upon a time heralded as the environmentalists' great hope for replacing dirty coal-burning plants nationwide, their operation has proven costly and unable to keep up with market trends over the years. More disappointing to environmentalists was the realization that the technically "cleaner" solution presented an even more vexing problem—the spent rods remain radioactive and very dangerous for centuries after their work is done. Disposing of nuclear waste has become one of the greatest environmental and political challenges of our time.

As dismal as this may seem—and, indeed, *is*—there are alternatives. There have been some wonderful developments recently in bringing alternative energy to market, and in chapter 3 you'll learn how to selectively shop around for the best source of your own electricity. Of course, using less energy in the first place is the best solution, regardless of where your electricity is born. After all, we are fortunate to live in a time where technological advances in appliance and household electronic efficiency are making it significantly easier to get more from less.

## Let There Be Compact Fluorescent Light!

Ah, the typical New York City apartment, cramped and cluttered but always with an astonishing view of—a brick wall! All right, not always. But the densely packed nature of the city—even in the less crowded boroughs—combined with an abundance of high-rises and the close proximity of neighboring buildings typically results in apartments devoid of much, if any, natural light. Natural light has become in New York City homes a valuable—and therefore expensive—commodity, and the odds are usually against any given apartment space having enough of it. Bringing illumination to your home can result in a serious expenditure of energy that becomes obvious when your Con Ed bill arrives every month. Fortunately, technological advances have worked wonders in the field of lighting. Alas, many New Yorkers remain ignorant of these advances.

Odds are, the lights in your apartment use standard incandescent bulbs. The problem is that these bulbs are literally tiny space heaters that happen to give off light as a by-product. Indeed, more than 90 percent of the energy sucked up by an incandescent light bulb ends up as heat.

Even thirstier for juice are halogen lamps. A standard 500-watt halogen floor lamp consumes more than five times as much electricity as an incandescent, and burns so hot that colleges and universities around the country are banning them for fear of dormitory inferno. The heat generated by incandescents and halogens must in summer be removed by an air conditioner; in winter it's far less efficiently generated than is standard home heat. Fortunately, recent technology has produced a practical and money-saving alternative: the compact fluorescent lamp (CFL). CFLs are a wondrous innovation, yet the majority of people I talk to don't even know what they are. CFLs use only about 25 percent as much electricity as their incandescent older siblings, are compatible with virtually all conventional lighting fixtures, and come in a variety of shapes, sizes, and wattages to suit any illumination need. And if you

> ## tip
>
> It only takes a dozen hundred-watt incandescent bulbs burning to generate the same amount of heat as a typical plug-in space heater.

despise—as I do—the process of climbing up on a chair or step stool to awkwardly balance and change a ceiling lightbulb, CFLs typically last about ten times as long as a quick-burning incandescent. Need more incentive? By most estimates a CFL will save you anywhere from $30 to $50 in electricity costs over the course of its lifetime, dwarfing the initial expense (approximately $8 to $10 more up front per bulb). As Amory Lovins, co-founder of the Rocky Mountain Institute, often says, "Efficient lighting is not just a free lunch; it's a lunch you're paid to eat!"

Some consumers complain that fluorescent (compact or not) lights generate too bright and invasive a white light, and that they can't be used with dimmer switches. To the dismay of many an environmentalist, the early models of fluorescents that hit the market turned consumers off for these very reasons. Times have changed, however, and CFLs can now be bought in a variety of colors and tones to best match your illumination desires.

If you're simply too attached to the softer golden glow of incandescents and can't find a CFL that re-creates it perfectly, you can still switch out your bulb to lower-wattage incandescents and save energy. The most commonly used bulbs are in the 75- to 125-watt range, even though a 60-watt bulb is reasonable for a moderate-size room, and 40 watts should be plenty for a desk or bedside lamp.

It's well worth the extra effort and initial cost to search out compact fluorescents for most, if not all, of your home's light fixtures. They're common in most hardware or houseware stores these days and typically cost around $10 each—an amount easily recovered through energy savings and their long lives. If you have trouble finding these bulbs, check out the lighting section on Energy Star's website (www.energystar.gov), which offers (among many other things, as you'll discover throughout this section) a store locator for energy-efficient products, including CFLs. After installing the new lamps, you'll thank yourself not only when writing your check to Con Ed every month, but also whenever you realize that your step stool hasn't come out of the closet for a long time.

# Green Machines: Energy Star in Your Home

I know what you're thinking. You don't just replace a large appliance like you do a lightbulb. What with cost, availability, and rental agreements, New Yorkers tend to take whatever appliances they can get. But occasionally you might find yourself in a situation where you need to replace a refrigerator or dishwasher, and most of us choose our own smaller home appliances such as toasters and blenders. When this is the case, you simply must know about Energy Star.

Energy Star itself is a government-backed program that helps businesses and individuals protect the environment through superior energy efficiency. It's probably best known for offering certification—*the* Energy Star—of household appliances and business products that meet strict energy-efficiency standards set by the Environmental Protection Agency (EPA) and the Department of Energy. On a larger scale it offers certifications for efficient homes and buildings in their entirety, as well as tools and resources to help plan and undertake home improvement projects to reduce energy use and improve home comfort.

There have been radical advances in the efficiencies of large appliances over the past decade or so, which means it's crucial to find those that have earned the Energy Star. A quick example: Refrigerators are the single highest energy consumer in most households, yet replacing a decade-old refrigerator with a new Energy Star–certified model would reduce energy use by a full 50 percent—that's enough energy annually to light the average household for more than three months. This savings amounts to a reduction of over 300 pounds of pollution each year, not to mention the hundreds of dollars of savings.

Similar advances in electricity and water (more on water later in chapter 4) consumption are found across the board. Consult and pay close attention to the Energy Star energy-efficiency numbers if you're fortunate enough to be picking out a new unit. On the website (www.energystar.gov), you can compare the various efficiencies of a whole slew of products, including large appliances, lighting fixtures, electronics, and home heating and cooling systems.

# FOCUS ON

# Community Environmental Center

**I**f you want to see alternative energy being efficiently employed to its maximum potential, check out the Community Environmental Center (CEC) in Stuyvesant Cove Park on Manhattan's East River. Here the CEC has constructed New York City's first stand-alone solar-powered building, with the fitting name of Solar 1. The first phase of an ambitious project to develop a larger and comprehensive Environmental Learning Center on the same site, Solar 1 serves as a multifaceted resource for the neighborhood and the city at large where students and residents can learn firsthand the reasons for and principles of sustainable living. The 500-square-foot classroom embodies the principles it promotes; a rundown of Solar 1's features reads like a text to Green Building 101. Aside from the public services it provides, the building itself uses passive and active (using photovoltaic, or PV, panels) solar energy for heating and electricity; combines natural and efficient lighting systems; was constructed with "structurally insulated panels" (SIPs), which are used for floors, walls, and roof, and combine structural framing and insulation into one element, produce no CFCs when produced, and reduce heating and cooling demands considerably; features Energy Star–certified windows, doors, and appliances; employs a "heat recovery ventilator" that extracts heat from exhaust to warm incoming fresh air; wears a sheath of recycled aluminum siding; is equipped entirely with water-saving fixtures and a water-conserving toilet; features "low-embodied energy" interior finishes—the list goes on and on.

Solar 1 manages to exist entirely off the electrical grid—all lights, computers, a television, slide projectors, phones, and assorted other equipment operate off power generated by the sun and captured by the PV panels on the building's roof. In fact, during the blackout of 2003, Solar 1 was up and running, its three kilowatts worth of power effectively keeping all systems go for the event's duration.

Looking beyond Solar 1, the CEC has ambitious plans for the further development of the site. The logically named successor, Solar 2, aims to be "a permanent icon of environmentally responsible living," while offering its space to the increased promotion and understanding of environmentally sustainable products and practices. Plans for Solar 2 call for a two-story, 8,000-square-foot structure constructed with the latest in green building technology. The majority of the power will be generated by state-of-the-art PV solar panels, supplemented by geothermal or hydroelectric sources. It will feature a "green screen" of deciduous vegetation on the building's shell that will help naturally shade and cool the rooms in summer while allowing for substantial passive solar heating through direct sunlight in winter. The ground floor promises a lobby that could potentially host exhibits—from artistic to scientific—and will offer a view of the "living machine," a natural wastewater treatment system. In the Eco-Basement visitors will be able to view various elements of the building's system in action. Ever wonder how a small-scale renewable energy system could be integrated for use in a stand-alone building? Or care to watch a heat recovery ventilator in action? Solar 2 will allow you a look at the inner workings of an operational green building.

The second floor will feature a handful of educational and cultural spaces—another exhibit hall, a classroom, an auditorium for public lectures, artistic programs, and musical performances, and the Eco-Neighborhood, which will use interactive technology to teach visitors about sustainability in everyday life—but perhaps most interesting is the Eco-Apartment. This room will be arranged and laid out like a typical New York City studio, but one that incorporates many essentials of the low-impact home. Using Energy Star–certified appliances and a water-conserving toilet, low-flow showerheads and faucets, compact fluorescent lightbulbs, and other conservation features, the apartment will clearly show just how easy it can be to incorporate an environmental ethic into your home, without suffering any reduction or change in lifestyle.

Because education and community involvement are paramount to the organization's goals, there will be more info about the CEC and the future of the Environmental Learning Center in section 4. In the meantime feel free to visit the CEC's website (www.cecenter.org) or call (718) 784–1444 and arrange a visit.

A five-minute test—the "Home Energy Yardstick"—on the site's "Home Improvement" page allows you to compare your home's energy consumption with similar homes. All you'll need is some very basic info about your home (age, square footage, number of occupants) and your utility bills. A tad more revealing is the site's "Home Energy Advisor" tool, which takes only about fifteen minutes to work through. This page inventories your home's energy needs, then offers a list of customized energy improvements and their estimated savings. Suggestions range from replacing windows to installing storm panels in winter months, installing of ceiling fans, replacing light fixtures with CFLs, or even carpeting hardwood floors to help passively insulate rooms. The site is also armed with a very useful "Savings Calculator" that will show you exactly how much energy and money you can save using products that have earned the certification.

It's important to remember, however, that simply possessing the technologically advanced lighting systems and appliances is only part of the battle. These systems yield even greater energy savings when used properly and with regard for conservation. Many folks shudder—literally—at the thought of such energy conservation, because it conjures up images of shivering in a dark, cold apartment. Not so. I don't intend to prescribe anything uncomfortable or extreme, but rather a practical, livable set of guidelines that can help reduce both electricity consumption and costs in your home. Some of these ideas may be new to you, while others seem obvious—but you'd be surprised to see how many are regularly neglected. My roommates and I—all self-proclaimed sloths—still manage to shape our home life around these easy tips:

✳ It should go without saying that lights should be turned off when not in use. An empty room doesn't need illumination.

✳ If you're able to install dimmer switches for your home's lights, you can better dispense the appropriate amount of energy necessary for different lighting needs, rather than letting the lights burn full tilt whenever they're switched on.

✳ Like lights, ceiling fans, ACs, dehumidifiers, and so on should be used only when necessary.

✳ Computer monitors are enormous propagators of energy waste— but they use up to 90 percent less energy when they're in sleep mode. (And 100 percent less when they're turned off!)

✳ Unplug your chargers when you're not charging. Every home is full of little plastic power boxes to charge cell phones, PDAs, digital cameras, laptops, cordless tools, and other personal gadgets, and these suck up power even when they're not charging the devices. Keep them unplugged until you need them.

✳ Use power strips to switch off televisions, home theater equip- ment, and stereos when you're not using them. Even when you think these products are turned off, their standby consumption can together be equivalent to that of a seventy-five- or hundred- watt lightbulb running continuously. By switching off the power strip, no energy at all flows through the machines.

✳ Set your refrigerator temperature at 38 to 42 degrees Fahrenheit and your freezer between 0 and 5 degrees. Use the power-save switch if your fridge has one, and make sure the doors seal tightly. You can check this by making sure that a dollar bill closed in between the door gaskets is difficult to pull out. If it slides easily between the gaskets, replace them.

✳ Defrost your freezer on a regular basis. It'll use less electricity to maintain a cool temperature.

✳ Don't preheat or peek inside the oven more than necessary. Check the seal on the oven door, and use a microwave for cooking or reheating small items.

✳ Make sure your home is furnished with enough table settings to last until the dishwasher is filled, and only run it when it reaches that point. Use short cycles for all but the dirtiest dishes. This conserves not only water, but also the electricity used to pump and heat it. Also, avoid using the "heat-dry," "rinse-hold," and "pre-rinse" settings, or anything comparable that your machine may offer. "Heat-dry" requires a bundle of energy to pump hot air through the machine in order to dry dishes, but it's superfluous. If there isn't an "air-dry" setting, prop the door open after the final rinse, a tactic that works perfectly fine with no energy expenditure. "Rinse-hold" and "pre-rinse" settings demand extra water and extra energy to heat and pump the water, and are generally excessive for all but the dirtiest dishes.

✳ If you do your laundry at home, switching your washing machine's temperature setting from "hot" to "warm" will cut the electrical load in half, and—unless you're dealing with heavy, oily stains—will be just as effective. Even a "cold" wash is generally more than adequate.

✳ It's also important to wait until you have a full load of laundry before running the cycle—smaller loads (even when you're using a machine's "small load" setting) use close to the same amount of energy. Fill the tank with clothes rather than washing half loads more frequently.

✳ Clean the lint filter in the dryer after each use. Dry heavy and light fabrics separately and don't add wet items to a load that's already partly dry. If available, use a moisture sensor setting. (And of course a clothesline is the most energy-efficient clothes dryer of all!)

CHAPTER TWO

# Natural Comfort:

## Climate Control in the Green Home

Man shapes himself through decisions that
shape his environment.—**RENEE DUBOS**

Many of us hesitate when it comes to changing our home climate control patterns. New York City, firmly planted in the temperate zone, can experience all sorts of climatic extremes—from debilitating heat in summer to core-chilling cold in winter. Since green design doesn't grace most of New York's residential buildings, artificial methods of heating and cooling must be employed. Most cooling systems (air conditioners, fans, and so forth) run off the same electrical resources as the rest of your apartment's appliances, and by now we all understand the ramifications of using this power. An apartment building's heat, however, can be generated by electricity, natural gas, and—most often—oil. You will remember that oil, a terribly dirty-burning fossil fuel, is one of the leading perpetrators of acid rain and air pollution, and releases significant amounts of greenhouse gases when burned. Natural gas, while heralded as being the cleanest burning of energy fuels, still emits considerable amounts of methane and other greenhouse gases when burned, and thus is far from exempt from responsibility in the case of global warming. So while the different systems of heating and cooling your home use different resources and generate different types and amounts of pollution, the general importance of conserving is the same across the board.

## The Colder Months

Let's face it: There's only so much that the typical apartment renter in New York City can do to conserve heat. Many New Yorkers are at the mercy of someone else when it comes to a building's heating system, so the decisions we make inside our homes are largely symbolic. If you rent and are fortunate enough to have a thermostatic control over your home's climate, or if you own your home, consider installing a programmable thermostat. These nifty devices can be set to automatically turn down the heat at night and raise it again before you wake up in the morning. This can reduce heating energy consumed by roughly 6 to 16 percent. And just in case I haven't mentioned it enough already, the tireless folks at Energy Star have certified a number of programmable thermostats; check out their increasingly necessary website (www.energy star.gov). Programmable unit or not, by keeping your thermostat no higher than 68 degrees Fahrenheit during the day and 55 degrees overnight or when you're not home, you should stay perfectly comfortable.

> **tip**
>
> Insulating curtains or blinds effectively trap more heat indoors. They're commonly available just about anywhere draperies are sold.

Whether or not you wield the thermostatic control, some very simple and basic ideas can help keep you cozy during long, blustery January nights. Check all your windows on a particularly chilly autumn day. Any window that seems to be letting in an excessive amount of cold air should be reported to the building's superintendent. It's your legal right as a tenant to have properly sealed windows. Remember that holiday tip, and your super should be more than happy to have those windows airtight. If you'd rather not deal with the super, or if you own your home, many strategies for fixing window leaks are easily accomplished by even the least crafty. Gaps of less than $\frac{1}{2}$ inch can be easily filled with caulk, available at any hardware store; the staff there can also show you how to use it, a remarkably simple procedure that cuts drafts and prevents warm air from escaping considerably. (Important: Caulk should only be used around the frame of a window, not on any movable parts, such as the base, where you'd want it to open.) Weatherstripping can be used on the movable components of windows and doors. There are a number of different materials used for weatherstripping, so it's worth talking to an expert at a hardware store for what specifically will work best for your needs. Go prepared with information about the area to be sealed—the size of the gap and the type and material of the window or door in question. Self-adhesive weatherstripping is certainly the easiest to install, so unless you've a penchant for screwdrivers and hammers, choose the simple stuff.

Of course, more reliable than any super or do-it-yourself project is the good old sun. Use it: The sun's ability to warm your home is often underestimated. In the cooler months open the curtains and blinds on sun-exposed windows when they're receiving direct sunlight. (Here in New York, this generally means south-facing windows, but also east and west facing for mornings and afternoons, respectively, depending on your building's setting amid trees, other buildings, and any other sun obstructions.) Then close the same curtains or blinds at night to help trap the heat.

## The Warmer Months

For my money, keeping the home comfortable in the summer months is a more severe challenge than heating it in winter. You can always throw on another sweater or blanket, but when your apartment feels like a

# Green Roofs

I magine investing in a large-scale climate control renovation that not only helps regulate your home's temperature but also contributes significantly to moderating the city's overall heat burden in the sweltering summer months. Well, you can, and with the help from Greening Gotham—a project of Earth Pledge's Green Roofs Initative—your roof could become a natural cooling device. Curious? It's relatively common knowledge that natural, vegetated surfaces moderate temperature, whereas constructed surfaces such as concrete, brick, and tar absorb and retain heat. Vegetated surfaces collect water in their soils, which then evaporates while the plants transpire, and provide natural shade, the entire system efficiently reflecting and moderating heat. Built surfaces are impervious to water—it simply runs off—and have low albedos (or reflectivity) combined with high heat capacities, meaning they absorb and retain much of the sun's radiation. This is why New York City is considered by climatologists as an "urban heat island" and regularly registers summer temperatures much higher (between 3.6 and 5.4 degrees Fahrenheit, according to the Columbia Earth Institute) than surrounding areas.

Green roofs—also sometimes referred to as eco-roofs, rooftop gardens, vegetated rooftops, and sky gardens—effectively act to ease this heat burden, creating a vegetated (rather than built) surface that reduces outdoor air temperature. Then, because a green roof is much cooler than a nonvegetated roof, less heat is transferred on hot days into the building below. Logically, fewer artificial, energy-demanding cooling methods are necessary within the building.

The environmental benefits of green roofs don't end there. Aside from helping to insulate the building, a green roof absorbs and retains—until evaporation—a good deal of rainwater. This is a good thing, because New York City regularly experiences overflows in its "combined sewage overflow" (CSO) system. This system attempts to transport all the city's rainwater runoff and household sewage to treatment plants, but half of the time, when it rains here, the pipes overflow and untreated wastewater (thirty billion gallons a year) spills into the city's waterways. This regularly results in beach closures, wreaks havoc on fish habitats, and propagates viral and bacterial diseases such as West Nile.

While some cynics argue that New York's buildings aren't structurally sound enough for green roofs, one of the two common systems—the "extensive" green roof—is lightweight, relatively cheap to construct, and requires minimal maintenance. Extensive green roofs, or green meadows, are indeed practical for application on most city rooftops. Greening Gotham lists thirty-five green roof projects within the five boroughs on its website. It also provides detailed explanations of both green roof systems, as well as a comprehensive "Toolbox" that walks anyone—"whether you're an architect, landscaper, building owner, or just an interested resident"—through the process of designing and implementing a green roof. Visit www.greeninggotham.org or call (212) 725-6611, and start planning your first rooftop garden party.

Guatemalan rain forest, there's only so much you can take off before your neighbors across the alley break out their binoculars.

The question on any green's mind as summer approaches seems to be: *Can I justify using an AC to relieve myself from this maddening heat?* I lasted through the heat wave of 2005 without an AC, but I'll admit that I made plenty of excuses to visit friends who had one, and I understand it's a must for many.

But before committing to an air conditioner, try out any of a number of passive methods for cooling even the most broilerlike top-floor apartment in the dog days of August. Blocking out direct sunlight with heavy shades is a surprisingly effective means of keeping down a room's temperature. If you still haven't switched your lighting to compact fluorescent bulbs, now is definitely the time—the fiery little incandescent (or, even worse, halogen) bulbs that they replace produce a disproportionately staggering amount of heat. Often an efficient, modern dehumidifier (remember Energy Star!) can relieve the stickiness of summer's heat by reducing the uncomfortable moisture content in your apartment's air. Also, and perhaps most effective, is the creation of air currents through a space. Most modern fans are fairly efficient devices, whether they're window, freestanding, or desk fans. Avoid commercial fans, which are excessive for a home. Ceiling fans are a luxury, and they demand a tricky bit of installation, but they're unparalleled at efficiently creating air currents through a space. Energy Star, again, offers certifications and tips for choosing the right model and installing it. With a few open windows and a strategically placed fan or two, cool, refreshing drafts can be created and directed to where they are needed most in your home—your favorite reading chair, bed, or sweltering kitchen.

If this is still not enough to make your place bearable (or safe, if the case is dire) and you do need an AC, it's time again to find the Energy Star. Replacing a ten-year-old AC with a new Energy Star–qualified model effectively reduces the electric load by more than 10 percent.

Choosing the right-size AC for your space, and placing it appropriately in your apartment, is more important than you might realize. Try to limit any AC's range to one "cool" room to maximize the effectiveness of the unit. Choose a model with the lowest number of BTUs (British thermal units—the measuring standard for AC strength) that can effectively cool that particular space. This will require pulling out the tape measure and doing some easy calculations; think *high school geometry.* The Energy Star website offers a chart (see below) suggesting reasonable BTU levels for different spaces. For example, an 18-by-12-foot living room is 216 square feet. Consulting the chart, we see that a 6,000-BTU unit should be sufficient for that space alone.

| AREA TO BE COOLED (SQUARE FEET) | CAPACITY NEEDED (BTUS PER HOUR) |
| --- | --- |
| 100–150 | 5,000 |
| 150–250 | 6,000 |
| 250–300 | 7,000 |
| 300–350 | 8,000 |
| 350–400 | 9,000 |
| 400–450 | 10,000 |
| 450–550 | 12,000 |
| 550–700 | 14,000 |
| 700–1,000 | 18,000 |
| 1,000–1,200 | 21,000 |
| 1,200–1,400 | 23,000 |
| 1,400–1,500 | 24,000 |
| 1,500–2,000 | 30,000 |
| 2,000–2,500 | 34,000 |

Source: Energy Star (www.energystar.gov)

## ⓐ FOCUS **ON**

# Basics of Efficient Climate Control in Your Home

### When It's Cold

Heating your home accounts for the majority of energy you use. And whether you wield thermostatic control over your home or not, working to minimize heat loss and the demand for more heat is of utmost importance to an environmentally responsible life. Here are a few tips to help maximize energy efficiency in winter.

✻ Check all exterior doors and windows for gaps, and seal with caulking and/or weatherstripping.

✻ Put up storm windows, and consider covering them with plastic on the inside to keep any cold air from leaking in.

✻ Keep your thermostat no higher than 68 degrees Fahrenheit during the day and 55 degrees Fahrenheit overnight or when you're not home.

✻ Close doors and any heating vents in unoccupied rooms.

✻ Use sunlight wisely. Leave shades and blinds open on sunny days and then close them at night to help trap the heat in your home.

## When It's Hot

Keeping your home comfortable in the summer months can be a tough—and energy-demanding—battle. But with some thought and resourcefulness, there are plenty of energy-efficient ways to keep your home cool, even when the streets outside are blazing.

✳ Check your air conditioner's setting in the window for a tight, snug fit. Seal around the edges with weatherstripping or insulation. Vacuum its filter weekly during periods of high use, and replace it when it shows signs of heavy wear or is extremely clogged.

✳ A strong fan will help circulate the cool air throughout your living space and will consume much less energy than lowering the temperature on your AC's thermostat.

✳ If you rely on a cooling unit inside your home, check all windows and doors for a tight seal, and help keep the cool air in and the hot air out by weatherstripping or caulking any gaps. Counterintuitive as it may seem, keeping storm windows in place during warmer months will help insulate against the heat and will keep cold air inside.

✳ Keep the sun out. Use shades, blinds, or curtains to keep the sun's heat out in the daytime.

✳ Turn your AC off when you leave home. Leaving it on all day and night does not save any energy. Even when operating on a lower setting, a proper-size AC burns more electricity when running nonstop than it would to restore a room to a comfortable temperature when you are there and actually need it.

✳ Use discretion—don't get in the habit of turning your AC on automatically. Try a fan if it's not unbearably hot, or open the windows when there's a nice breeze.

There are a few more factors to consider, however, before you settle on a unit. As suggested by Energy Star, if the room in question is heavily shaded, or doesn't receive much natural sunlight, you can reduce the unit's BTU capacity by 10 percent. Conversely, if the room is exceptionally sunny, increase the number by 10 percent. These numbers are also estimated for a room with two regular occupants, so if *more* than two people regularly occupy the room, you should add 600 BTUs for each extra person. It's also wise to increase the capacity by a full 4,000 BTUs if you're using an AC in the kitchen, which is probably a luxury most of us don't need, unless you're running a catering business out of your home!

Once you have an air conditioner, make sure it's properly maintained. Here's a pretty simple idea that is often forgotten. Routine maintenance—much of which you can do yourself—will dramatically improve the electrical efficiency of your machine. Basic maintenance includes cleaning all indoor and outdoor coils, cleaning the blower, and replacing filters, all of which should be done annually, and all of which should be described in the machine's manual. It doesn't hurt to have a certified technician check the levels of the refrigerant every couple of years; efficiency drops sharply when these levels are off. This step may seem like a huge hassle, but keeping your AC's inner workings up to snuff will quell its appetite for Con Ed's kilowatt hours (or kWhs, the standard billing unit of electricity consumption). If you limit your appliance's range and use it conservatively, your monthly bill won't be ridiculous and your green mind can rest at relative ease.

## CHAPTER THREE

# Bringing Alternative Energy Home

First there is the power of the Wind, constantly
exerted over the globe.... Here is an almost incalculable
power at our disposal, yet how trifling the use we
make of it! What a poor compliment do we pay to
our indefatigable and energetic servant!

—**HENRY DAVID THOREAU,** *Paradise (To Be) Regained,* 1843

Ask New Yorkers where their power comes from and they'll
almost always answer: Con Ed. Indeed, Consolidated Edison
is the default and only distributor of electricity to New York
City's buildings, but what most folks don't realize is that Con Ed dishes
out power that it collects from a whole slew of suppliers.

It wasn't always this way. The energy market in New York State—as
well as a bundle of other states across the Union—was deregulated in
1998, and this brought about major changes in the ways that energy
flowed to the city. Once upon a time Con Ed produced a majority of the

energy that it then distributed around the state. With the implementa-
tion of deregulation, Con Ed was forced to sell off almost all of its generating assets. This book is certainly not the place for trying to explain
the complex and confusing process of deregulation, but it is important
to have a basic understanding of exactly what deregulation is and how
it has affected the process of delivering power to the city.

Traditionally, a regulated utility provider, such as Con Ed, generated
most of the electricity and distributed it through the grid to consumers at
prices that the state regulated. Since deregulation, the price of electricity
is allowed to fluctuate with the forces of supply and demand, and new
companies have been permitted to build or take over electricity-generating
facilities and to market their power directly to the consumers. These new
companies are known as energy service companies (ESCOs); as of March
2005 there were six ESCOs serving power to New York City residential
customers. The electricity that these new companies generate is distributed over the same grid system, and the same utility company, Con Ed,
still governs that distribution, subsequently profiting from a standard distribution charge. Con Ed is not itself an ESCO; rather, the company that
distributes the power. (Although Con Ed does run one ESCO called ConEd
Solutions, which will be discussed later.) The ESCOs then compete for
customers by setting attractive prices or by generating electricity in a
particular manner that some consumers find desirable.

It is at this point that Green Power enters the equation, and for those
of us with environmental concerns, *Green Power* is a term that deserves
our full attention. Dan Harris wrote in an article for *GreenHome NYC*,
"'Green Power' is a delightful phrase, full of promise and hope for the
future—as if we will plug our appliances into a smiling oak tree with a rainbow glistening in the background." Obviously, he wrote with a sense of
irony, but the reality of Green Power's revolutionary introduction to the
New York City power grid is one that is, in fact, "full of promise and hope."
A working definition of *Green Power* is: electricity that has been generated
solely from clean, renewable resources that can include any combination
of wind, biomass, hydroelectric, and geothermal. A couple of uplifting

figures: If 10 percent of New York City's residents were to switch to Green Power, it would prevent more than 900 million pounds of carbon dioxide from being released into the atmosphere each year. That's roughly the equivalent of an average car driving over 850 million miles, or the same number of New York residents driving more than 1,000 miles each. And that's only to speak of the carbon dioxide! For such dramatic reductions of emissions and pollution of all sorts, it's remarkably easy and not tough on the wallet to switch your home to Green Power. At the moment, there are a few different routes you can take.

But first, it's important to understand that in no circumstance—save an unlikely coincidence—is the electricity flowing into your home going to be the actual Green Power that you purchased. To power your apartment by those means would require installing solar panels on the roof—an expensive, but definitely feasible undertaking (see the "Big Apple Solar" sidebar). Through either of the options that I'm about to mention, you are merely buying power—or the production of power—from a renewable source, which will then enter the grid to be dispersed alongside the rest of the electricity. This is not the easiest concept to grasp. It took me a number of phone calls, e-mails, and altogether too much time poring over literature from various companies and organizations to come to a good understanding of how the system works. So consider this a disclaimer: While the purchasing of Green Power in New York City is remarkably simple, understanding exactly what your money is paying for is not.

That said, the motivation for purchasing Green Power through any venue can be broken down to one truth: The Green Power that you purchase is beneficial to the environment, because it represents a certain amount of electricity—however much you use in your home or decide to fund—that is now unnecessary for the Indian Point nuclear facility, the Lovett coal-burning plant in the Hudson Valley, or any of the three loud, unsightly, and polluting plants scattered around the city to produce.

There are two methods for powering your home with green-generated electricity. The first uses ESCOs, and is a system that promises to soon offer plenty of choices for the consumer. The second, certificates, is a

# Big Apple Solar Installation Commitment

**I**f you own your building and are eager to make a stable, long-term commitment to alternative energy, then you may want to consider solar panels. The Big Apple Solar Installation Commitment (BASIC) is a not-for-profit organization dedicated to promoting the use of solar power throughout New York City, primarily in the form of rooftop photovoltaic panels. If your roof is more than 250 square feet, is flat or south facing, and is unshaded so that it gets direct sunlight for the greater part of the day, then your home is a great candidate for solar PV panels.

The upfront investment is formidable. After tax incentives and rebates from the government, a three-kilowatt system—sufficient for a typical New York City home—will cost $10,000 to $15,000. But keep in mind that you're purchasing electricity for the life of your home, and that having such a system generally increases a home's value by $5,000. Still, it will take twenty years on average for the system to pay for itself, so it's certainly not for the transient at heart. Many people fear that using PV panels will leave them powerless at night or in times of prolonged overcast skies, but BASIC reassures us that solar electricity users stay on Con Ed's grid and can tap into the standard energy pool when the panels don't provide enough juice. Furthermore, when the panels produce more electricity than you're using in your home, the extra energy is channeled back into Con Ed's pool, effectively crediting your account (called net metering) for use at night and cloudy times.

The BASIC website (www.basicsolar.org) is full of information on everything from common misconceptions about solar panels to technical details to resources for purchasing and installing. Certainly, PV panels aren't for everyone, but if you're resolute about reducing your demand on fossil fuels, and have the luxury of owning your home and some spare cash to invest, it's well worth taking a look at the wealth of information provided by BASIC.

system that grew as an alternative to the ESCO program and is already being capitalized on by a number of companies. Along with the information to follow, I'd like to refer you to the user-friendly and very comprehensive website www.green-e.org, where you can search for all available Green Power products in any area of the country.

## Option One: Power Your Way

Green Power can be marketed to consumers by an ESCO, a program Con Ed refers to as Power Your Way, because you're free to decide where you'd like to purchase your energy from. While many ESCOs are developing the Green Power option, as of May 2005 there are only two offering it to residential consumers—ConEd Solutions (www.coned solutions.com; 888-320-8991) and ECONergy (www.econergy.com; 800-805-8586). This is, however, a market that is fast evolving and difficult to keep up with. The best source for information about new Green Power services is the New York State Public Service Commission (NYS PSC). Its website (www.askpsc.com) is constantly updated with developments on the city's Green Power options. The commission can also be reached at (866) GRN-POWR. To actually sign up for Green Power from an ESCO, visit Con Ed's Power Your Way site (www.poweryour way.com), where you'll also find an abundance of information and a form that will steer you to the best options currently available in your area.

Purchasing Green Power through an ESCO is probably the most straightforward and undemanding method of powering your home with renewable resources. The greatest benefits lie in the simplicity of conversion, the process of billing, and the straightforward paperwork. In most cases you'll receive only one bill from Con Ed at the end of the month, with two statements enclosed. The normal Con Ed rates for distribution apply. The first statement in the bill will be from Con Ed the distributor, featuring the standard distribution charges for the electricity, as well as for any natural gas as is standard on the Con Ed statement. The second statement comes from the ESCO and clearly shows the total amount of green electricity supplied to your home, alongside the cost of the power.

One minor deterrent from Green Power is that it must be purchased at a premium cost—typically about 1 to 2 cents more per kWh—because the facilities to generate this power are typically more expensive to develop and run than traditional, dirtier electricity-generating plants, which often have government subsidies to assist in their development. At the current premium rates, an average monthly bill of $60.40—representing a typical three-bedroom apartment using 400 kWhs of electricity per month—rises to $66.40, an increase that most environmentally minded New Yorkers would find a very reasonable price to pay for sustainable power. Try calculating the costs for your own home's average bill and doing your own cost–benefit analysis. Be sure to consider the fossil fuel–burning plants that are currently powering your home, spewing greenhouse gases and smog into the atmosphere, poisoning local watersheds, and forming acid rain. Remember the proximity of the Indian Point Nuclear Plant, currently being kept in operation by New York City's electrical load. If enough New Yorkers were to make the switch to renewable energy sources, it would represent a landmark victory for environmentalism.

## Option Two: Renewable Energy Certificates

If purchasing Green Power through an ESCO such as ConEd Solutions is relatively simple to comprehend, the certificate program offered by a handful of different Green Power companies is considerably more difficult. In other words, this is the sticky bit.

Let's start with the names. *Renewable Energy Certificates, Green Tags, Green Assurance Certificates*—all are essentially referring to the same product, and are used interchangeably in a confusing enough manner in the various companies' literature. For the sake of simplicity, I'll call them "certificates."

As a consumer of electricity, you have the option to purchase a certificate, which represents a certain amount of power that will be generated and delivered to the standard power grid by the company to which you send your check. Certificates are typically available in blocks, each of which represents a certain number of kWhs (in most cases, one hundred) that will be produced and delivered to the grid as a result of your purchase. The system is a bit more ambiguous than the ESCO programs in that Con Ed doesn't ever know of your purchase, and it will continue to treat your particular home unit as it always has. Con Ed does see, however, that whichever company you've bought your certificate from is generating that much more electricity and loading it into the pool. It, in turn, reduces its demand from ESCOs that use traditional "brown" power plants.

With certificates your contract is directly with the producers of the Green Power, and aids them in the disproportionately high costs of developing and maintaining wind or alternative power plants. You will now receive two separate bills—one from Con Ed that shows no signs of your purchase, and one from the power-generating company reflecting the premium you've chosen to pay to ensure that the demand for electricity from renewable energy sources is present—and ultimately to help displace a certain amount of the "brown" energy flowing into the grid.

The actual certificates that you receive are symbolic in a sense; they are described by one provider as representing "all of the environmental attributes or benefits of a specific quantity of renewable generation, namely the benefits that everyone receives when conventional fuels, such as coal, nuclear,

## ConEd Solutions

One of the energy service companies currently offering Green Power is Con Ed's own subsidiary, ConEd Solutions. ConEd Solutions offers electricity that has been produced by wind power (25 percent) and by run-of-the-river hydroelectric power (75 percent). A run-of-the-river hydroelectric project is one that does not interfere significantly with the flow of the river—in other words, it doesn't use massive dams to generate electricity—and is generally considered a much more ecologically considerate option to its dam-dependent cousin. Green Power from ConEd Solutions costs only a couple of cents more a day (the rate fluctuates), and features the convenience of one simple bill.

oil, or gas, are displaced." Still, your purchase ensures that a certain amount of Green Power will enter the grid and displace that amount of demand from traditional plants.

A handful of companies are offering certificate programs, two of which have established themselves as being the most reliable and accessible to residents of the city of New York. Community Energy, Inc. (CEI), generates what it calls "NewWind Energy," which is available in "wind blocks" of one hundred kWhs at the cost of $2.50 per block per month. If you live in a 400-kWh-per-month apartment, you would choose to purchase four of these wind blocks at a total cost of $10. To purchase certificates of NewWind Energy directly from CEI, visit its website (www.newwindenergy.com/regional/mid-atlantic/certificates.html) or call (866) WIND-123 (866-946-3123). A testament to the excellence of CEI is its recent contract with ConEd Solutions to provide all 25 percent of this ESCO's wind-generated allotment with NewWind Energy.

Also, the New York Public Interest Research Group's Fuel Buyers Group has created a Clean & Green Energy Program, which recently teamed up with and sponsored CEI. Through NYPIRG, consumers are able to purchase NewWind Energy at the discounted rate of $2.25 per hundred-kWh block. Using the above example, four wind blocks would cost an extra of $9.00 per month. Forms can be found for these discounted rates at NYPIRG's website (www.nypirg.org/fbg/wind1.html) or by calling (800) 695-4645.

> ## tip
>
> Methane is a trace gas that is twenty-three times more detrimental than $CO_2$ in global warming potential.

Another certificate outlet is Sterling Planet, a nationwide green electricity certificate program. A giant producer and provider of renewable power, Sterling Planet has, under its Green America program, created a Green for Homes utility partnering program that includes a certificate outlet. Signing up for certificates from Sterling Planet is simple through its website (www.sterlingplanet.com/sp

/buygreenamerica.jsp), where you'll be walked through the process of purchasing enough wind energy to ensure that your home's entire electrical use is, in essence, green. Sterling Planet doesn't strictly use wind power, but rather combines renewable energy resources: solar (5 percent), wind (45 percent), and bioenergy (50 percent). The bioenergy component is produced by clean wood waste—described by Sterling Planet as "logging and milling residues that would otherwise be unused"—and by landfill gas, the natural by-product of organic decay. While this landfill gas is mostly methane, the adverse effects are mitigated by harvesting the gas and using it to generate electricity. It's important to note that a purchase of Sterling Planet's certificates is supporting the production of renewable energy on a nationwide level, and is not specific to New York State or even to the Northeast.

When choosing among Sterling Planet, Community Energy's NewWind Energy, or any of the other certificate-offering power companies that you can find in the appendix, it's worth considering where you would like your dollar to make its impact. If local development of renewable power is your primary concern, CEI is probably your best bet. If you'd like to see your money going to a nationwide system of Green Power, perhaps Sterling Planet is your candidate. The wonderful and important lesson here is that you do have a choice—abstract as it may seem. Individual research is crucial. I'll again steer you to Green-E.org (www.green-e.org/your_e_choices/ny_home.html), where you'll find up-to-date listings of what's currently available to New Yorkers.

It is, of course, feasible to both purchase energy directly from an ESCO like ConEd Solutions and to buy a certificate offered by a Green Power company such as CEI or Sterling Planet. Superfluous as it may seem, you would, in essence, be doubling the positive impact of your power use. Think of it as powering your own home with the energy directly from the ESCO and then, with the purchase of a certificate, amending your share of the power that you use when outside of your home: at work, in restaurants and stores, or when visiting other people's homes. This is, of course, well above and beyond any environmentalist's call of duty, but well worth consideration.

# The Brooklyn Brewery

**O**n September 8, 2003, the Brooklyn Brewery announced a historic decision: to convert its entire plant and headquarters operation to 100 percent wind power. The electricity supplied, entirely by windmills in Fenner, New York, is NewWind Energy produced by Community Energy, Inc.. With this five-year wind power purchase, Brooklyn Brewing is not only the first brewery in the eastern United States to convert to wind power, but it is also the first commercial building in New York City to convert all its electrical load to this clean, renewable resource.

Speaking to both immediate, local issues and a greater global concern, Brooklyn Brewery president Steve Hindy made it clear that corporate responsibility is the brewery's governing ethic: "It is no secret that the Brooklyn Brewery is opposed to plans to develop another Goliath-size power plant on the Brooklyn waterfront [referring to the existing sixty-megawatt plant on Hudson Avenue and proposals to build another, larger plant on the Williamsburg/Greenpoint waterfront]. We wanted to demonstrate that there are viable, clean alternatives to building another polluting power plant. We also wanted to take a significant step in demonstrating a needed reduction in dependence on Middle East oil."

Compared with the average generational mix in New York's power pool, the brewery's commitment of 284,960 kWh per year is equivalent to annually reducing approximately 335,000 pounds of $CO_2$, 1,500 pounds of sulfur dioxide, and 500 pounds of nitrogen oxides that would otherwise be emitted into the atmosphere annually. It's the equivalent of refraining from driving 290,000 miles or of planting 22,000 trees each year. Brent Alderfer, the president of CEI, heralded: "Brooklyn Brewery is leading the way to clean energy for New York City. This purchase means New

York-based electric power with no fuel and no pollution. The more customers that follow Brooklyn Brewery's lead, the more wind farms come online in New York."

The Brooklyn Brewery has recently developed plans to relocate its entire operation to the waterfront at Pier 7 between Brooklyn Heights and Red Hook. This new facility promises to be even more environmentally sensitive than the current setup, with plans to integrate wind *and* solar power and to consolidate operations with distributors, requiring less transport of materials and goods. In the meantime the brewery is helping to develop and host regular forums on alternative energy use in the local urban environment, and continues to advance its involvement in community and development issues. Through this impressively evolving and ongoing display of caring capitalism, the company is making good on Hindy's promise that the Brooklyn Brewery must be "a good citizen in our community."

## CHAPTER FOUR

# Water, Water Everywhere, Leaking from a Sink

When the well's dry, we know the worth of water.
—**BENJAMIN FRANKLIN**

Ever wonder where your water comes from? Sure, the five boroughs are sliced up by rivers and sprawled around a harbor, but the water that runs out of your taps and showerheads is gathered dozens of miles away. The vast majority of the water that runs through New York City's taps collects in two vast watersheds that reach as far as 125 miles upstate—the larger Catskill/Delaware watershed and the (relatively) smaller Croton watershed. The water travels to the city through an elaborate system of reservoirs, aqueducts, and tunnels, which deliver it eventually to the municipal system. This vast system and its history are much too large a subject to get into here, but are described in brilliant and elaborate detail in Diane Galusha's book *Liquid Assets: A History of New York City's Water*—definitely worth perusing if you're curious.

New York City, as a whole, uses an enormous amount of water. We shower; we wash dishes; we do laundry; we hose down the sidewalk. Toilets are flushed tens of millions of times a day around the city. Our overactive dependence on water becomes alarmingly clear whenever the city is forced to endure one of its periodic droughts. In the summer of 2002, the time of the last major drought, the average New Yorker used 142 gallons of water per day. Citywide, this total amounts to well over one billion gallons per day.

Over the course of the twentieth century, diminishing freshwater levels became one of the world's paramount environmental issues. Paul Hawken, Amory Lovins, and L. Hunter Lovins noted: "Of all the world's water, only 3% is fresh and all but one-thousandth of that is locked up in glaciers and ice caps or is too deep in the Earth to retrieve." States and even countries are coming to conflict over rights to that fixed and increasingly scarce amount of fresh, clean water that remains. While New York City isn't in as dire a water-supply predicament as many of the world's cities, if 2002's drought was any indication, we certainly aren't exempt. On top of the supply-side issues, the water that flows down your drain then combines with the wastewater of all eight million New Yorkers, the volume so great that the combined sewage overflow (CSO) system often can't handle the load, the pipes overflowing and contaminating local waters with sewage so badly that public beaches must be closed. This pollution disrupts aquatic ecosystems, killing or fouling tens of thousands of fish, and also creates breeding grounds for insect- and water-borne diseases such as West Nile virus.

It is in some ways then relieving and in other ways frustrating to look at how easy it can be to save considerable amounts of water in your daily routine. While these techniques aren't necessarily unique to New York City,

Even a slow leak can waste up to 36 gallons of water per day, and a steady drip can spill as much as 180 gallons in that time!

they are universally practicable and are critical for anyone concerned with reducing water consumption.

More than 50 percent (and in some homes as much as 75 percent) of all residential water use occurs in the bathroom, so it's particularly important to pay close attention to how much is flowing when you're going about your daily bathroom routines. Recent design innovations in faucets, showerheads, and toilets have resulted in an incredible increase in water-use efficiency, and in many cases the costs of upgrading to such systems are insignificant compared with the cost of the water being wasted. Similarly, kitchen and laundry appliances have also benefited from such advances. Whenever possible, consider upgrading the systems in your home.

Of paramount importance in both kitchens and bathrooms is avoiding leaks. Most of us would be surprised to find out that a full 20 percent of toilets leak, and since the leaks are typically silent, you have no idea of the malfunction. Even more incredible is that a leaking toilet can waste anywhere between 30 and 500 (!) gallons of water a day—and an audible leak is wasting much more. (There will be discussion on how to check for toilet leaks, as well as a good number of other tips for water conservation, later in the chapter.) Now, those who don't fall into the handyperson category may be intimidated by the thought of do-it-yourself leak repair, particularly when it comes to the toilet, but these problems are typically quite easy to patch up. An instructive website created by the California Urban Water Conservation Council (www.h2ouse.org) offers detailed tutorials on how to repair leaks in all areas of your home, along with an incredibly comprehensive array of water-use facts and water-saving tips specific to different rooms. Perusing the site, you'll also find room-specific sections that offer a vast array of information on all

tip

The third highest consumer of indoor water use is bathing, and because most of us like hot showers, it also represents the second highest use of energy in the average home.

# Free Water Services in New York City

The New York City Department of Environmental Protection (DEP) offers free water-conservation seminars to building managers on a regular basis. These seminars cover topics ranging from the basics of water/sewer billing (flat rate versus metered), the transition to metered billing, and how to measure and account for water/sewer costs, as well as providing information on toilets, showers, boilers, hot-water heaters, and other equipment. The events are held in all five boroughs; a schedule can be found on the DEP's website (www.nyc.gov/html/dep/html/news/depnewsframeset.html) or by calling (212) 863–8830.

The city also offers free water-efficiency surveys to homeowners. City inspectors will actually come to your home, check your plumbing for leaks, provide customized water-conservation tips, and offer advice on retrofitting your faucets with water-efficient fixtures. They also generously distribute (absolutely free!) two faucet aerators and two low-flow showerheads per household, which will save you money in water costs if you pay for your water separately. It's hard to find a better deal than that in a town like New York, so I highly recommend you take advantage of this program. An application form is available for download from the DEP (www.ci.nyc.ny.us/html/dep/pdf/survey.pdf) or upon request by calling 311.

aspects of water conservation, from available incentives and rebates on water-saving devices to installation tips and research into environmental and cost benefits. Indeed, h2ouse.org is a priceless resource that certainly deserves a gander. It might even give you the confidence to plunge into your toilet tank or wrestle with your sink.

Of course, many of us apartment dwellers in New York City have water bills that are included in rent or building fees. Thus the immediate incentive for saving water—saving money—isn't as obvious. In most cases, conscientious water consumers would benefit economically if their individual water use were monitored by a meter and billed accordingly, rather than being grouped in collectively with a building full of folks who let water flow recklessly. Many buildings around the city are begining to switch to such a system.

## Stemming the Flow: Water-Conservation Tips

### IN THE BATHROOM

✳ Take shorter showers and save five to seven gallons a minute from regular showerheads.

✳ Replace standard showerheads with low-flow models, which use an average of 2.5 gallons per minute (compared with the five to seven gallons listed above). A good test to see if your showerhead sprays an excessive amount of water is to place a gallon bucket under the flow. If the bucket fills in less than twenty seconds, you should replace the head.

✳ If you're particularly shrewd about water conservation, turn off the shower while soaping up and shampooing, a method commonly practiced in Europe.

✳ And if you're incredibly shrewd, keep a bucket in the back of the shower to collect excess water, which can then be used to water plants!

✳ New low-consumption toilets on the market use only 1.6 gallons per flush, compared with the 3.5 gallons per flush used by a toilet manufactured in the 1980s and the 4.5 to 7 gallons per flush used by a pre-1980 toilet.

✳ If you're unable to purchase and install a new toilet, there are ways to reduce the volume of water used per flush in any toilet. Using good old-fashioned Yankee ingenuity, a good friend of mine fills a one-liter bottle with water and places it inside the toilet's tank. Less water is then needed to fill the tank, thereby reducing the amount used per flush.

✳ Check toilets periodically for leaks and repair them promptly. A nifty way to check for leaks is to place a few drops of food coloring in the toilet's tank. If the dye shows up in the bowl after fifteen minutes or so, the toilet has a leak. Such a leak can usually be attributed to an old or misfit flapper, which can easily be replaced by even the most amateur plumber.

✳ Avoid using caustic toilet bowl cleaners (such as tank tablets). These alter the pH of the water and damage plastic and rubber parts, eventually causing severe leaks.

✳ As ridiculous as it may seem, don't use your toilet as a trash can.

✳ Install aerators in your bathroom sink's faucet. An aerator will reduce your faucet's flow by 30 to 50 percent.

✳ Don't leave water running continuously while shaving or brushing your teeth.

> **tip**
>
> Studies show that dripping faucets and leaky toilets account for as much as 14 percent of all indoor water use in the average home, or about ten gallons per person per day.

## IN THE KITCHEN

✳ Again, install faucet aerators. They come as cheap as $5.00 to $10.00 and reduce water flow by a gallon per minute.

✳ Keep your eyes and ears open for leaky faucets. A dripping faucet can usually be repaired by replacing the rubber O-ring or washer inside the valve. The part's packaging should have installation instructions—it's really quite simple—or you can consult www.h2ouse.org.

✳ Dishwashers typically use less water to wash a full load than would be used when washing all the dishes by hand. Also, try to run the dishwasher only when it's fully loaded, and avoid using the "pots and pans" or "heavy wash" cycles unless the grime on your dishes and utensils is terrible.

✳ "Pre-rinse" and "rinse-hold" cycles are generally excessive and waste water, unless the dishes are really dirty.

✳ With the strength of modern dishwashers, it's redundant to rinse dishes before loading them. That said, it's important to properly load the machine without overlapping plates and dishes so that the powerful jets can effectively do their work.

✳ When washing dishes without a dishwasher, fill the basin rather than allowing the water to run during the entire process. Filling the average sink basin only takes about ten gallons, whereas a standard faucet spews two to three gallons per minute.

✳ Clean vegetables in a sink or pot partially filled with water rather than running it from the tap. (Feel free to reuse this water for irrigating houseplants or cleaning dishes.)

✳ While it's not the most common practice, some people defrost frozen foods by running them under hot water in the sink. Instead, simply plan ahead and defrost frozen foods in the refrigerator or at room temperature.

✳ Rather than running the faucet until the water gets cold enough to drink, use a pitcher to chill water in the refrigerator.

## IN THE LAUNDRY

✳ Only wash full loads of laundry, and set the dial for the shortest cycle that is practical for the particular load. For example, seriously grubby work clothes or the remnants from a muddy soccer game may need the highest setting, but a load of once-worn T-shirts and slacks will clean perfectly fine with a lesser setting. These settings vary from machine to machine, so it's worth consulting the manual to achieve ultimate efficiency. If you go to a Laundromat, you're largely at the mercy of standardized controls.

✳ If your washer has a variable water volume setting, select the minimum amount required per load.

✳ Pretreat stains to avoid rewashing.

✳ Check the machine's hoses regularly for cracks that could soon result in leaks.

**tip**

The average washing machine load uses about forty-one gallons of water, and is the second most consumptive use of water in an average American home.

## CHAPTER FIVE

# The Space of Waste

Waste is a tax on the whole people.
—**ALBERT W. ATWOOD**

L et's start with a few harsh truths: Residents of New York City produce four pounds of waste per person every day. This is more per capita than any other city in the world and totals no less than twenty-four million pounds of trash daily. Of this veritable mountain of refuse, 65 percent goes to landfills, half of which will fill to capacity and be forced to close within the next five years. With the recent closing of the Fresh Kills landfill in Staten Island, New York City is increasingly reliant on shipping—at the current premium rate of $70 per ton—this trash to out-of-state landfills in New Jersey, Pennsylvania, and Ohio. The recycling program here in the city—originally adopted to help curtail the flow of waste into these landfills—has been notoriously unreliable, with repeated changes in policy for what should and shouldn't be separated from our trash. Furthermore, while 4 percent of the city's waste is compostable, the compost collection program—NYC Compost Project—was suspended for two years and only had its funding restored as recently as fall 2004.

This loss of a composting program is certainly a drag, but the ongoing state of flux in the city's recycling program was, until recently, a long-standing problem. A voluntary program through 1989, weekly collections of recyclables finally covered the entire city of New York by 1999. Policies over what would and would not be collected roadside by the Department of Sanitation flip-flopped a handful of times over the years. The most infamous of these policy shifts came in summer 2002, as residents were finally getting accustomed to the process of separating glass from paper from metal and plastic. Soon after taking office, Mayor Bloomberg's administration deemed the recycling of glass and plastic to be too expensive for the municipal budget and reverted to collecting only paper and metal—sending millions of pounds of recyclable glass and plastic to the landfill every day.

Fortunately, fall 2004 saw the Bloomberg administration radically reposition itself on this issue. After serious pressure from the public and a timely new economic feasibility report, the mayor has committed to an ambitious, long-term, and comprehensive recycling program, the ultimate ramifications of which promise to be staggering. In September 2004 Mayor Bloomberg signed a twenty-year contract with Hugo Neu—a Manhattan-based salvage company—that features a program for the consistent separate collection of glass, plastic, and metal to supplement the existing collection of paper. The plan also involves the construction of a modern, high-tech recycling plant at the South Brooklyn Marine Terminal in Sunset Park.

The plan benefits more than the environment. The cost of sending trash to out-of-state landfills has risen 46 percent over the past three years,

> **tip**
>
> Every year New Yorkers throw out approximately 800 million glass bottles and jars, many of which could be reused, and all of which are now recyclable.

resulting in the current $70-per-ton rate to rid ourselves of our refuse. Conversely, the security provided by such a long-term, twenty-year contract has allowed Hugo Neu to set its price at $50 per ton, a rate that—under the terms of the contract—will fall even lower when the new plant is completed in 2007 and the cost of transporting the waste declines. This new deal is similar to the one the city struck in 1997 to secure the Australian recycling company Visy Industries into a twenty-year contract for recycling the city's paper waste.

All in all, this represents a landmark decision by New York City—one that champions the virtues of recycling and commits to a comprehensive and consistent program for decades to come. Finally, New Yorkers can be confident in the permanence of the city's recycling program, can condition themselves to follow its protocol, and can settle comfortably into their role in the system.

While this exciting evolution of the city's recycling program seems to have taken firm hold, having the system available is only part of the battle. It's now important that New Yorkers use the system appropriately to ensure that it operates as cost-efficiently as possible, as well as helping to "close the circuit" of resource use.

## Waste Not, Want Not: The Three R's

There's a wholesome sense of pleasure and pride that accompanies the act of filling your building's recycling bins with significantly more material than the true waste barrel. And as more and more New Yorkers learn to take full advantage of our revamped recycling program, its efficiency will improve and it will prove to be an environmentally and economically beneficial vehicle.

Fortunately, recycling is relatively easy. The city collects trash separately from recyclable goods, so you must

> **tip**
>
> Paper and paperboard constitute 36 percent of the total amount of solid waste produced in the United States.

start by setting up different bins or containers in your home. Paper products are to be kept separate from glass, metal, and plastic (which can be tossed together). As New Yorkers, most of us have developed an appreciation for the value of space in our cramped homes. But setting up a home recycling system of bins and containers needn't be too space consuming if you approach its design with a bit of creativity. These certainly don't need to be specialized products—I use plain cardboard boxes in the base of my small hallway closet—but there are places such as The Container Store or Bed, Bath, and Beyond that have specially designed bins.

Once your system is established, learn what materials should land where. At the moment not all types of plastic are recyclable, and some materials in the paper or cardboard family are a bit ambiguous, so be sure to check exactly what can go and what can't. This info can be found on the Department of Sanitation's website (www.ci.nyc.ny.us/html/dos/home.html), which also features flyers that can be downloaded or ordered for free. Or you can call 311 to order the materials. For items that aren't accepted by the city DOS, a great and comprehensive resource is provided by the staff of Earth 911. They maintain a website (http://newyork.earth911.org) that features local information of environmental services, including a recycling section that lists groups and locations for the most eco-friendly disposal of all your waste. If you live in a building where you cart your own trash out to the street, make sure that the barrels outside are clearly labeled. Mixing recyclables with true trash or mixing different types of recyclables makes the entire program less efficient and more expensive. Weatherproof labels for the various containers can also be ordered for free from the Department of Sanitation (same website), but should already be furnished by the owner or manager of a building. Also, the city asks that recyclables be left out in clear or translucent bags, while true,

> **tip**
>
> New Yorkers go through almost two million plastic bottles per day.

nonrecyclable trash should be put out in opaque bags. The schedule for pickup varies by neighborhood; check that same web address or call 311 to figure out your recycling days.

As important as the practice of separating recyclables is reducing how much you drop on the roadside to begin with. Much of what is "recyclable" need not be recycled. Plenty of the containers from which we get our goods—food, cleaning supplies, housewares, and so on—can be reused for a number of purposes. Empty glass and plastic jars can be brought to farmers markets or natural food stores and filled with grains, beans, or whatever dry goods you purchase, or can be used creatively for any number of small needs. Plastic Chinese food containers common in delivery and takeout make great storage for leftovers—just think, you may never have to buy plastic food-storage containers again!

Moreover, plenty of old household items that have run their course in your life may still be desirable by others. As the maxim goes, "One man's trash is another man's treasure," and here in New York, there's certainly no shortage of treasure hunters. So don't even think about throwing out usable furniture, electronics, clothing, books, sporting goods, small appliances, or any other random household items that might find renewed life in someone else's home. There are plenty of charities or homeless shelters—not to mention secondhand and thrift stores—that'd be thrilled to accept your donations. There are also a couple of free online materials exchange services such as www.newyork.craigslist.org and www.freecycle.org where you can find people who may be looking for exactly what you're tossing.

## Not in My House: Keeping Waste from Reaching Your Home

By subtly shifting your shopping and consumer habits, you can prevent a great deal of waste from ever reaching your home. Take-out food restaurants and delis typically overpackage your purchase. Do you really need a full paper bag and two dozen napkins for a lone bagel? Lots of cleaning supplies can be bought in bulk packaging and used to refill smaller, more sightly, and easier-to-manipulate containers. As for news-papers, consider sharing one paper with co-workers, roommates, or friends, or maybe reading it online. Almost all New York papers—includ-ing the *Times*, *Daily News*, *Post*, *New York Newsday*, *Wall Street Journal*, *Financial Times*, and *Village Voice*—offer all their daily content for free through their websites.

Speaking of paper waste that needn't ever cross your threshold, consider the annoying junk mail that clutters your mailbox every day. The average American mailbox sees as much as one-third of its incom-ing mail in the form of advertisements, catalogs, credit card offers, coupons, and other items that you never asked for. Almost everyone has come to accept junk mail as a fact of life, mindlessly tossing it unopened into the trash, but advertisers call it direct mail and it is big business, overseen by one organization, the Direct Marketing Association (DMA). Fortunately, though unbeknownst to most folks, you can significantly reduce the volume of junk mail land-ing in your mailbox by registering with the DMA's free "Mail Preference Service" at its website (www.dma consumers.org/privacy.html), thereby removing your name from most national mailing lists. If you don't have Internet access, you can simply write your full name and address on a postcard and send it to:

Mail Preference Service
Direct Marketing Association
P.O. Box 643
Carmel, NY 10512-0643

> **tip**
>
> It takes nineteen times more energy to manufacture an alu-minum can from raw ore than from recy-cled aluminum.

> **tip**
>
> The average alu-minum can goes from the supermarket shelf to scrap and back to the shelf in a mere forty-two days.

# Reduce, *Reuse*, Recycle

## Ideas for Donating Household Goods

✳ Books and current (less than a year old or so) magazines are eagerly accepted by after-school programs, hospitals, nursing homes, and homeless shelters.

✳ Your old sporting goods can find new life in a local children's after-school sports program.

✳ Extra paint or leftover building supplies can be used by school or community theater programs. Give the local public school a call to see if they'd appreciate the materials.

✳ Old cell phones can be donated to domestic violence prevention organizations through the Donate a Phone program. Check out: www.wirelessfoundation.org/DonateAPhone/index.cfm.

✳ Local secondhand and thrift shops, homeless shelters, and non-profit organizations that accept donations can be located by calling the NYC Stuff Exchange toll-free at (877) NYC–STUFF. The NYC Wastele$$ organization also provides on its website (www.nycwasteless.org/indiv/donations.html) a list of some non-profit groups that are currently accepting donations.

✳ Log on to http://newyork.craigslist.org or www.freecycle.org to use these goods exchange programs and find someone to take the old stuff off your hands.

The mail preference service only works for national mailings, so local direct marketers can still find your home, but mailings typically have a phone number (often buried deep in the fine print) that you can call and ask to be removed from the list, curtailing the spread of your address to other lists. The DMA's Mail Preference Service is also only good for five years, and each time you order from a catalog, sign up for a random contest or sweepstakes, or fill out a warranty card, your name can end up right back on the list. So be sure to deliberately tell companies not to share your name and address, and be very selective about whom you give it out to.

Those annoying credit card offers are another story, because the monstrous national consumer credit bureaus Equifax, Experian, and TransUnion—not the DMA—administer those lists. The good news is that one toll-free phone call to (888) 5-OPTOUT will remove your name from all those solicitation lists. So through a quick phone call and a short postcard or web form, you can relieve your mailbox of a hefty portion of its load. Considering how much unsolicited mail reaches the average home, these simple actions can have a dramatic impact on the world's dwindling supply of harvestable trees.

One last seemingly inevitable flow of paper into the typical New York City home are those menus and advertisements that pile up in your doorway. In fact, the average four-family apartment building here is inundated with two pounds of such paper waste every week! While it may feel as if this is beyond prevention, the Waste Free NYC website (www.wastefreenyc.org) has a downloadable sign with the polite message, NO MENUS, CIRCULARS, OR ADVERTISEMENTS PLEASE. This plea is offered in three languages (English, Chinese, and Spanish) and is sized to fit nicely and visibly on windows and doors.

**tip**

If all New Yorkers recycled only their Sunday newspaper every week, nearly 750,000 trees would be saved within a year.

## FOCUS ON

# Reduce, Reuse, *Recycle*

Until you order yourself a chart from the Department of Sanitation, use this guide to help separate your goods. Remember that many items the DoS won't take are still recyclable through local groups that organize collections, and a directory for all of these is provided by Earth 911 (http://newyork.earth911.org).

### Mixed Paper and Cardboard

Place these items in a translucent bag or in green recycling bins:

- Newspapers, magazines, catalogs.
- Paper, mail, and envelopes.
- Telephone books and soft-cover books.
- Paper bags.
- Smooth cardboard (such as shoe boxes, cereal boxes with liners removed, and cardboard tubes).
- Pizza boxes.
- Paper/cardboard egg cartons (no Styrofoam).
- Corrugated cardboard boxes (flattened and tied in bundles).

### Glass, Plastic, and Metal

Place these items in a translucent bag or in blue recycling bins:

- Glass bottles and jars.
- Plastic bottles and jugs (including detergent, shampoo, and lotion bottles).

- ☼ Beverage cartons and drink boxes (milk and juice cartons, juice boxes).

- ☼ Metal cans (including empty aerosol cans).

- ☼ Aluminum foil wrap and trays.

- ☼ Household metal (such as wire hangers, pots and pans, and dried-out paint cans with lids removed).

## Do Not Recycle

- ☼ Any other types of glass (lightbulbs, mirrors, ceramics, and glassware).

- ☼ Other kinds of plastics (such as deli containers, plastic bags, plastic toys, salad bar containers, and furniture).

- ☼ Soiled paper cups, plates, towels, and napkins.

- ☼ Batteries.

- ☼ Plastic and wood hangers.

- ☼ Chinese take-out containers.

- ☼ Styrofoam.

- ☼ Caps and lids from glass and plastic bottles and jars.

- ☼ Plastic six-pack rings.

Source: City of New York, Department of Sanitation, *With Your Help, It's All Falling into Place* flyer.

Of course, you can't prevent all waste from entering your home. Waste, even in blessedly small quantities, is a fact of life, and must be dealt with. But with the broad and comprehensive new recycling program, a great deal of this rubbish will find a new and functional life, so long as you take the nominal time and energy to set up a little recycling center of your own. And if you focus on reducing excess packaging, pointless mailings, and other sorts of trash, you can save yourself more than a few trips out to the curb.

## Recycling by Nature: Composting

"Composting is nature's way of recycling," reads a brochure published by the Department of Sanitation. If you're really serious about waste reduction, you can't beat composting. The average New York City household throws away two pounds of organic waste each day. This adds up to more than a million tons of organic waste citywide every year, all of which must now be shipped and sold to rapidly filling landfills. Organic waste is, in a nutshell, made up of materials that were once living, whether they be banana peels, broccoli stems, eggshells, leaves, grass clippings, or even coffee grounds. When organic waste is buried in a landfill, not only is that precious space lost, but so is a natural and valuable resource that can help beautify our parks, gardens, lawn, and even windowboxes and houseplants. You see, most organic materials can be made into compost—a dark, crumbly soil conditioner that is naturally formed when organic material decomposes. Compost is a great source of minerals and nutrients that fortify plant health.

tip

The average American uses about forty-two pounds of aluminum each year, while the average Chinese or Mexican citizen uses less than two.

Despite common perceptions, composting isn't just for the countryside! Many New Yorkers are turning their organic waste into rich compost

FOCUS **ON**

## *Reduce*, Reuse, Recycle

- Buy products made with recycled content and packaged in recyclable materials.
- Buy goods in returnable or recyclable containers.
- Politely refuse excessive bags and napkins when ordering takeout.
- Bring your own cloth bags to local stores to avoid the "paper or plastic?" dilemma.
- If you drink coffee on the go, bring your own reusable mug to be filled.
- When it's reasonable, buy food and home products in bulk to avoid overpackaged individual goods.
- Bring glass jars or other sturdy containers to farmer's markets and natural food stores to fill with ingredients.
- Share newspapers and magazines, or read them online.
- Avoid junk mail lists at all costs. Register with the Mail Preference Service online (www.dmaconsumers.org/privacy.html), at the address listed earlier, or by calling (888) 5-OPTOUT, and be diligent in keeping your name off of future lists. (Your local mail carrier will thank you, too!)
- Download and print a colorful sign from Waste Free NYC (www.wastefreenyc.org) asking that no menus, circulars, or advertisements be left on your doorstep.

every day. Whether by bringing organic waste to community drop-spots or by setting up composting systems at home, there are better ways for green New Yorkers to get rid of organic waste. A great reference, for starters, is the NYC Compost Project, an organization funded by the Department of Sanitation. While the project sat dormant for two years, it recently had its funding restored and is offering information and services around the city.

The group currently features leaf-collection services in the leafier outer boroughs (sorry, Manhattan!) where lawns and tree-lined streets are more prevalent. Call 311 or check www.nyccompost.org for details. The Department of Sanitation asks that you use clear plastic or—preferably—large paper bags to bundle the leaves. Paper bags eventually decompose with the leaves, saving the time, effort, and cost of removing and discarding the plastic. Hardware stores and large home-improvement centers typically sell thirty-gallon brown paper yard bags, and they're also available for free from the Queens Botanical Garden.

At this writing, plans for the DOS to start picking up other organic waste from the roadside on a regular schedule remained up in the air. Still, a few local groups provide drop-spots and a variety of compost-related services and activities. Expect to see more such groups forming—with the help of the NYC Compost Project—in coming months, and stay tuned to the project's website for updates. Also, check the appendix for a current list of compost-friendly organizations and any available details of their services, drop-spots, and contact information. Not surprisingly, some of these organizations are involved with a variety of ecologically focused activities in their communities, and will be discussed in greater detail in later chapters.

## tip

Making new paper from old paper uses up to 55 percent less energy than making paper from trees, and subsequently produces much less air and water pollution.

If you don't realistically see yourself dragging kitchen scraps to organized drop-spots but are still keen on the idea of composting and using the resulting rich mixture for your own garden or plants, then setting up your own home compost center is entirely feasible. In fact, the process is relatively simple—the only ingredients necessary are food scraps, air, water, and a base material such as dry leaves or soil. The experts at the NYC Compost Project have a detailed description (at www.nyccompost.org/how/index) of how to start a compost system in or outside your home.

By utilizing a composting system for your kitchen scraps and placing recyclable goods in their proper bins, you'll be well on your way to reducing your home's contribution to the city's enormous waste problem. Combine these tactics with a sensible and thrifty approach to reusing goods and take the simple steps to reduce the amount of excessive, unnecessary waste entering your home to begin with, and you'll be pleased to find how long it takes to fill your trash barrel.

# The Lower East Side Ecology Center

**P**erhaps the organization that has done the most to actively culti-
vate a compost-friendly environment in New York City is the Lower
East Side Ecology Center (LESEC), the public interface of Outstanding
Renewal Enterprises (ORE). Founded in 1990, the LESEC has worked
tirelessly to assist communities in the development of recycling and
composting programs. It has currently arranged for organic waste drop-
spots at all of the city's Greenmarkets, as well as at its home garden on
East 7th Street between Avenues B and C. This garden also offers a
Compost Education Center, featuring workshops and information on
home and worm bin composting. Alongside these public services, the
LESEC conducts extensive research on urban composting options and
community participation. It recently initiated a program in a low-income
housing project in the Lower East Side, featuring a compost drop-spot
and an extensive educational program to help encourage participation.
Unique to the city, this model has the potential for an enormous impact.

But the LESEC doesn't work with compost alone. In fact, its stated
goals are to "foster the environmentally sound management of New York
City's solid waste, to inspire New York City residents to take responsibility for their environment, and to make the City a cleaner and greener
place." This mission has spurred three chief areas of operation: the
development of community-based recycling programs (of which the
compost work is part), environmental education, and stewardship for
public open space. Aside from its admirable work with compost, LESEC
has been helping communities deal with other solid waste that the city
won't touch. Before the revamping of the city's recycling program, it
worked extensively with communities to help them deal with glass,
metal, and plastic waste. Since the permanent integration of these

materials into standard recycling, the center has been able to focus on compost issues and also incorporate systems for dealing with electronic goods, which tend to be laden with harmful chemicals that really shouldn't be set free, even in landfills.

On the environmental education front, the LESEC conducts programs for school groups and neighborhood residents to heighten environmental awareness in urbanites. These vary from waste-prevention seminars and pamphlets to ecology lessons that use the East River and its wildlife to put children and adults alike in touch with the natural world that can so easily be forgotten in the city. It's an obvious connection, then, to the group's work as stewards for public open space. Advocating for the health and resurrection of the East River waterfront, the LESEC works to mobilize locals to fight for their valuable open space. Through volunteer days in local parks to meetings with the Community Board's Waterfront Task Force, the LESEC works both in the present and for the future development of neglected public space. To get involved with any aspect of LESEC's work, call (212) 420-0621.

## CHAPTER SIX

# The Green Clean

We are molded, we say, by the conditions and
the surroundings in which we live; but too often we forget
that the environment is largely what we make it.

—**BLISS CARMAN,** *The Kinship of Nature*

N obody likes to clean. Unfortunately, modern life hasn't yet
reached the point where homes can clean themselves.
And adding to the angst of keeping a home sparkling is the
fact that most cleaning products on the market are dangerous to both
our health and the environment.

A full inventory of the toxic chemicals commonly found in household cleaners would be frighteningly long. So this chapter will look more
generally at the environment and health issues of common commercial
household cleaners that give cause for concern. Some common ingredients that pose a great threat to humans and the environment will be
examined in some detail. From a health standpoint cleaning supplies
can be the most toxic products in the home, with risks ranging from skin
irritation and burns to long-term development of respiratory illness,
nervous system damage, and cancer. Environmentally, they commonly

pose a threat to aquatic ecosystems and overall water quality. After cleaners swirl down your drain, they mix with the rest of the city's wastewater, often overflowing within the system before reaching municipal facilities, or resisting treatment upon arrival.

## The Greenest Commercial Cleaners

What should you look for, then, when choosing a cleaner? And what should you look out for? It's tricky, since many products aren't adequately labeled with the potential dangers of the ingredients within, but here's a collection of tips.

※ **Heed the warnings:** It might seem obvious enough, but it's best to avoid products with labels such as DANGER, POISON, WARNING, or CAUTION. Also check for a warning section with such phrases as *may cause skin irritation, flammable, harmful if swallowed, corrosive,* or *may cause burns.* All of these terms indicate the inclusion of ingredients dangerous to both human health and the environment.

※ **False claims:** Be careful about environmental claims like *natural* or *ecologically friendly.* There's no legal definition for either of these terms, so some companies try to dupe us by labeling their products as such. More descriptive terms such as *no solvents, no phosphates,* and *plant-based* are much more reliable.

※ **Nontoxic:** Stick with products explicitly termed *nontoxic.* Federal laws mandate that "nontoxic" products are not harmful to humans or aquatic life when used as described and in appropriate concentrations.

※ **Plant over petrol:** Opt for plant-based rather than petroleum-based products. Pine oils and

> **tip**
>
> Many cleaning supplies are packaged in plastics that often are not recyclable and wind up further cluttering landfills.

citrus-based solvents do the best work and are made of renewable agricultural by-products, rather than nonrenewable and polluting petroleum.

✳ **Biodegradable:** This term means that the surfactants, or active cleansing ingredients, break down and cause no harm when released into the environment. *Readily biodegradable* products break down quickly and harmlessly, with the least environmental impact. If something isn't labeled as biodegradable at all, assume that the surfactants break down slowly, increasing the likelihood that other chemicals can penetrate plant and animal tissues.

✳ **Chlorine bleach:** Although it's a popular and effective cleaning agent, chlorine bleach is probably best avoided. Aside from being an eye and lung irritant on its own, it also releases the extremely toxic gas chloramine when it's mixed with ammonia or any acid-based liquid (including vinegar). You may be careful at home, but when the bleach goes down the drain, there's a good chance it'll find some of these other fluids, endangering whatever human or wildlife is near the water body. A preferred substitute for chlorine bleach is sodium percarbonate.

✳ **Beware VOCs:** Volatile organic compounds—benzyne, toluene, xylene, and trichloroethane, to name a few—react in the sunlight with nitrous oxides and produce ground-level ozone and smog. VOC emissions enter the air when you use the product or after flowing down the drain.

✳ **Phosphates:** These water-softening agents act as fertilizers upon reaching bodies of water. In lakes and rivers especially, phosphates spawn plant and algal growth, leading to the depletion of oxygen in the water and ultimately the death of aquatic wildlife.

✳ **Buy bulk:** Try to buy products in the largest containers available and, when possible, stick to packaging made with recycled materials.

✳ **Concentrate:** By choosing concentrated formulas and adding the water base at home, you can initiate a number of environmental benefits. Up to 90 percent of general-purpose cleaners is water. When all of this extra fluid is shipped, energy and packaging materials are wasted, and the excess material, depending on the type of plastic, often winds up in landfills.

A list of products that meet those guidelines is provided in the appendix. Many can be found in natural food stores, holistic markets, and even some supermarkets, and all are available by mail order through the websites or numbers listed.

## Eco-friendly Cleaner Alternatives

If you feel like getting even craftier, consider "brewing" your own eco-friendly, effective cleaning supplies. Remarkably, most of your home's cleaning needs can be met by basic, safe ingredients including soap, water, baking soda, vinegar, lemon juice, and borax, combined with a little elbow grease.

Environmental Media Services offers a number of "recipes" for eco-friendly alternatives to commercial cleaning products; most are provided below, or you can find them at www.ems.org/household_cleaners/alternatives.html.

### ALL-PURPOSE CLEANER

Mix 2 tablespoons baking soda with 1 quart warm water in a spray bottle. Add a squeeze of lemon juice or a splash of vinegar to cut grease.

### SURFACE CLEANER

Mix 1 quart warm water, 1 teaspoon borax, 2 tablespoons vinegar, and 1 teaspoon vegetable oil–based soap. (Vinegar cuts grease, and borax is a water softener.) Store in a spray bottle.

## NO-STREAK GLASS AND WINDOW CLEANER

Mix 1/4 cup white vinegar and 1 quart warm water. Apply with a spray bottle or sponge, then wipe with crumpled newspaper—not paper towels—for lint-free results.

## OVEN CLEANER

Mix 2 tablespoons vinegar, 2 teaspoon borax, and enough warm water to fill a spray bottle. Spray this mixture onto a cool oven surface. Scrub with a steel wool pad. For stubborn spots you can use a paste of baking soda and water.

## NONTOXIC TOILET BOWL CLEANER

Flush to wet the sides of the bowl. Pour in 1 cup borax and 1/2 cup white vinegar and leave overnight. Scrub with a toilet brush. For stains try applying a paste of lemon juice and borax, letting this sit for twenty minutes, then scrubbing.

## FLOOR OR FURNITURE POLISH

Use 1 part lemon juice to 2 parts olive oil. Apply a thin coat, then rub in well with a soft cloth.

## CARPET DEODORIZER

Sprinkle the carpet liberally with baking soda, wait fifteen minutes, then vacuum.

## METAL POLISHING

**Brass:** Mix 1/2 teaspoon salt and 1/2 cup white vinegar with enough flour to make a paste. Apply thickly. Let sit for thirty minutes. Rinse thoroughly with water to avoid corrosion.

**Copper:** Polish with a paste of lemon juice and salt.

**Silver:** Boil silver for three minutes in a quart of water containing 1 teaspoon baking soda, 1 teaspoon salt, and a piece of aluminum foil.

**Chrome:** Wipe with vinegar, rinse with water, then dry.

food

section two

# The Green Plate Special

Change could happen if people who eat—and I don't know too many who don't—would think about how the food got to their fork, about whom they bought it from, and about what impact this food has on the environment, on farmers, on their own nutrition. Eating is a moral act.—**BROTHER DAVID ANDREWS,** quoted in *U.S. Catholic,* March 2002

Oh, the culinary delight that is New York City! A gastronomic tour of the five boroughs can take you from Argentina to Vietnam, with stops in Mexico and Mississippi, in Italy and Ethiopia, in India and Japan. From takeout fare to meals lovingly prepared at home, from four-star restaurants to pizza joints, from chic bistros to street vendors, New York City boasts a culinary lineup as diverse as its population.

Thankfully, this dazzling abundance of markets, restaurants, delis, and eateries also caters to New Yorkers of a greener persuasion. We can eat great in this town without much added effort or cost. It does take a certain degree of diligence, however. It takes some knowledge and awareness of how food is produced, and of what to look for in the food you buy and in the establishments you frequent.

Alas, the majority of establishments don't give two hoots about the sustainable production of food. But there are plenty that embrace and welcome environmentally and socially conscious food practices. By supporting these businesses—and, just as important, by not patronizing the others—your dollars are making the very persuasive point that the greater health of the planet and its people matter.

When it comes to eating green, New York is, blessedly, one of the more progressive cities in the world. Markets, delis, even menus are inundated with "organic," "all-natural," "free-range," and "hormone-free" offerings. So what's all this buzz about, and why should we care? How does the food we eat here in New York City affect the greater ecological sphere? And what's so bad about the food found in your typical Pathmark, at your average deli or lunch buffet, at a plain old restaurant or—oh no!—a McDonald's? Let's spend some time exploring the food production industry and arming ourselves with the knowledge necessary to make informed and conscientious decisions about what we eat.

## CHAPTER SEVEN

# What's Wrong with Our Food

This may be the only time in history when humans have had complete strangers ... growing and preparing all our food.—**ANONYMOUS,** quoted by Joan Gussow, *Mother Earth News*

So long as there's food on our tables, does it matter how it gets there? Many experts say yes. Paul Hawken, Amory Lovins, and L. Hunter Lovins argued in *Natural Capitalism: Creating the Next Industrial Revolution*, "The superficial success of America's farms masks other underlying problems." These problems—and they are legion—include the economy, the environment, and human health. To understand the problems inherent in the industrialized production of crops and meat is to form the argument for conscientious consumption in New York City.

# American Agriculture: A Very Concise History

This nation was founded on agriculture. For its first few centuries, settlers tended farms and produced crops using horse and human labor while livestock grazed on grass and grains. By the 1950s, however, engine-powered machines had basically supplanted all muscular labor across the nation's farms. Displaced workers moved to cities, and newly minted suburbs started slicing up productive land. Hybrid corns and grains replaced well-established varieties across the Great Plains. The new crops were easier to grow with less human labor, but required synthetic fertilizers and pesticides to prosper. With government-funded irrigation projects changing the landscape, sunlight replaced soil quality as the most valuable factor in the location of a farm, whether the crop be wheat, oranges, corn, or avocados. Despite its relatively dry climate, California became the nation's largest source of produce. The southern states beefed up their irrigation systems. Local farms were bought out by larger companies, often based in distant parts of the country. Regional growing traditions and their inherent variety gave way to single, productive cash crops. Money and capital flowed out of rural farms into urban centers where the owner companies were based. Meanwhile, meat production moved indoors as factory farms began cramming livestock—cattle, hogs, and poultry—into buildings, filling the animals with specialized feeds, and pumping them full of antibiotics and hormones.

Since the middle of the twentieth century, traditional agrarian culture has been essentially plowed off the plains. Today most farms, for crops and meat alike, exist as factories run by corporations. In an economically efficient prevalent business model called "vertical integration," the same companies that own the farms also own enterprises both up- and downstream from the production of meat and crops: seed, feed, and chemical manufacturers, meatpackers, grain distributors, and so on.

The most productive farms keep growing—physically, economically, and politically—taking over enormous swaths of the landscape, the market, and lobbying power while minimizing the need for local human labor. Legislation catering to Big Ag creates market conditions that force smaller, independently owned farms to limit production to specialized niche products, while large-scale operations can easily profit from excessive single-cropping. Although only 0.9 percent of the U.S. gross domestic product is represented by farm production, more than 13 percent is generated by businesses (usually owned by the same corporations, remember) that buy from and sell to farms.

Proponents of this agricultural industrialization point to increased efficiencies in food production and the ability to feed more people with less work. They also tout the importance of the chemical and seed industries to the gross domestic product. And so this method of food production plugs along, continually demanding more pesticides, high-yield genetically modified seed, nitrogen-based fertilizers, and vast irrigation systems. This is no problem at all to the corporations that own not only the farms but also the seeds and the chemicals. But it is a problem for independent family farms, for rural communities, for the greater environmental good, and it's even a problem for you, the consumer.

## The Economy of Food

There is no denying the connection between food production and the entire ecological sphere. The dominance of Big Ag and Big Meat over the food industry creates an economic structure in which the environment and individual human health can be compromised. The industrial food complex spends plenty of energy and money lobbying the federal government. Hundreds of billions of dollars each year are granted to farming corporations, with 71 percent of the money going to 10 percent of the largest corporate farms. These subsidies—your tax dollars, remember—allow corporations to sell food at low prices while profiting off the manu-

> **tip**
>
> Today 1 percent of the American population grows food for the rest of us; 87 percent of our food comes from 18 percent of the farms.

facturing and sale of seeds, feed, pesticides, and fertilizer, as well as from the eventual processing and distribution of the food.

Organic foods are generally more expensive than conventional foods, it's true, but it's important to include in the price tag of industrial foods the hidden costs of subsidies along with the regulation and testing of pesticides, hazardous waste disposal, water purification, and the yet-unseen costs of environmental degradation.

The worldwide degradation of the natural capital—soil, water quality and quantity—that is the foundation for farming has been well documented. Despite the constant application of more advanced technologies, this loss continues. Hawken, Lovins, and Lovins noted that "in many areas, tripled fertilizer use and new crop breeds have been necessary just to hold modern rice varieties' yields constant." Thus, the ultimate costs of producing a constant amount of food are increasing. When a system consistently demands greater inputs of energy and resources to produce the same amount, it represents the antithesis of sustainability.

Jumping from macro- to microeconomics, decisions you make at the market or restaurant directly affect farmers: As corporations seek to profit from food production (from seed to shelf), considerably less money finds its way back to farmers. Try to get your mind around this: Of every dollar you spend at a typical market, only 9 cents goes to the farmer; the other 91 cents is split among suppliers, processors, marketers, and various other middlemen. This forces farmers to cut corners and compromise their methods, jeopardizing their farms' future productivity *and* the environmental well-being of the area. The corporations collecting at the top are usually disinclined to invest in the communities, so local economies suffer, as do the residents' health and environment.

## The Environment and Food

And what happens to the environment under industrialized farming? For starters, consider the effects of our growing pesticide dependence and genetic engineering on soil, water, and biodiversity. Consider, too, the widespread use of hormones and antibiotics on livestock whose waste output is now plaguing farmlands, water supplies, and neighboring communities. Consider the outrageous amounts of energy used up in farm operations themselves, from the processing of chemicals and genetically engineered seeds and fertilizer to the food, which must be preserved and packaged so as to look perfect for consumption a couple of weeks down the line on the other side of the country. Consider these incredible distances food travels from the fields or livestock shacks to your plate, and the vast quantities of fossil fuels burned to get them there.

If you're not sure how to consider all this, read on.

The industrial food complex depends on the high-volume production of a choice few crops, and of similarly high volumes of animals. How, exactly, does this affect our environment? In a number of ways, it turns out, all tightly woven in an interconnected web that feels—when looking at it comprehensively—like an ecologically dangerous downward spiral.

Before the twentieth-century agricultural revolution, farmers worldwide produced roughly 80,000 species of plants. Today they focus on about 150. Three-quarters of the world's food comes from only seven crop species, and the top three—wheat, rice, and corn—account for nearly half of the world's calorie and protein intake. Genetic diversity is rapidly disappearing in every one of these key crops as the most productive and least specialized strains become mass-produced for maximum profit. Single cash crops, with their potential for enormous yields, are supplanting local, agriculturally diverse subsistence traditions.

This "single crop mentality," as Hawkens, Lovins, and Lovins put it, "both ignores nature's tendency to foster diversity and worsens the ancient battle against pests." You see, good soil needs to be rich in nutrients and replete with bacteria, fungi, and other organisms that fight disease and create the proper texture and composition to protect roots and hold water. The biota that live in soil are a diverse bunch, and many simply won't be compatible with the choice few crops planted in a monoculture farm. These biota don't adapt, they die, leaving the soil barren—now more closely resembling dirt—and susceptible to pathogens and insects with no competition at all. While traditional subsistence farming relied on the annual rotation of crops, enriching soil by replacing nutrients, a single, permanent crop has the opposite effect. The monocultures created on factory farms are thus breeding grounds for plant diseases and insects. Agriculture expert Janine Benyus has written that it's like "equipping a burglar with the keys to every house in the neighborhood; they're an all-you-can-eat restaurant for pests." Without the soil's organic guards, any pest or disease that takes a liking to a monoculture farm can take the place over. And how does the typical monoculture farm deal with this increased susceptibility to pests? By beefing up on pesticides, of course! Speaking to the power of these modern chemicals, James Whorton, in *Before Silent Spring,* called that notorious pesticides DDT "the atomic bomb of the insect world." These chemicals do torch insects and pests, but they also deplete the soil by burning out even more organic content, perpetuating the loss of nutrients.

Compounding this soil degradation is the loss of soil altogether. Once boasting some of the best, most nutrient-rich, and highly productive soil in the world, the United States has lost a full one-third of its original topsoil. A result of negligent farming practices with increased reliance on machines and pesticides, good-quality soil has literally been flowing off the farm. Traditionally, some amount of topsoil was always lost during seasonal rains and the harvesting of crops, but

## tip

More than 17 percent of all of the energy consumed in the United States is used by the food sector. Two-fifths of this amount is used in processing, packaging, and distributing the food. Another two-fifths is used in storage refrigeration and cooking. The last fifth is actually used on the farms, but more than half of that is tied up in the production and application of chemicals to the land.

it was typically regenerated through natural processes at a rate similar to that at which it was lost. But today more than 90 percent of this nation's farmland is losing topsoil faster than it is being formed—seventeen times faster, on average.

Carrying away the soil is water, and it also carries residues from pesticides and nitrogen-based fertilizer into rivers, streams, and lakes. In fact, the Environmental Protecton Agency (EPA) has determined that pesticides have contaminated the groundwater—the water stored *below* the earth's surface in vast reservoirs essential to ecological balance—in thirty-eight states, including New York and New Jersey, thereby polluting the primary source of drinking water for more than half the country's people.

The dead, barren soil that remains has lost its natural and optimum texture and composition. Because it's unable to effectively soak up and hold rainwater, more irrigation is necessary; as the nutrients are depleted, more fertilizer is necessary; because the roots are left unprotected in this dead soil, and crops are more susceptible to disease, more pesticides are crucial.

## tip

Two-fifths of the world's harvest is lost in the field: 13 percent is damaged or destroyed by disease, 15 percent by insects, and 12 percent by weeds. All this is a direct result of soil degradation and monoculture.

As part of this culture of monoculture, genetically modified crops have become a staple on American farms. Genetic engineering (GE) is, technically, the process of transferring specific traits, or genes, from one organism to a different plant or animal. Today the majority of genetically modified crops (GMOs) are engineered to be resistant to pesticides, or able to endure the heavy dosage of weed and pest killer sprayed on the crops. Proponents of GMOs claim that they require less pesticide volume than non-GE crops, but in fact, studies have shown that

GMO spread has enhanced weed resistance, contributing to an *increase* in pesticide use on GMO farms by seventy million pounds between 1996 and 2003.

As if this weren't enough, many scientists are severely concerned with the growing ability of farm pests to develop a resistance to the chemicals. Insects are able to adapt to even the most powerful poisons more quickly than scientists can invent new ones. The industrial food complex's resistance to diversity creates a dangerous climate for farms, a frighteningly post-agrarian environment where chemicals are the only solution to ceaseless crop crises. On the bright side alternatives to industrialized agriculture exist, and the products of sustainable farming are available right here in New York City. The next chapter will help you navigate the city's produce aisles and menus to find such offerings.

It's no prettier in the world of Big Meat, which again has focused on high-volume production for profit, dismantling the traditional family farm and replacing it with the economically efficient—if ecologically insensitive—factory farm.

## FOCUS ON

### Taking 'Cides

Pesticide, herbicide, insecticide, fungicide . . . so what, you ask, is the difference? It's fairly simple, actually, despite the sometimes overwhelming nomenclature. According to the EPA, a *pesticide* is "any substance or mixture of substances intended for: preventing, destroying, repelling, or mitigating any pest." All of the other - *cides* fall into this category, with the prefix typically describing which "pest" the substance is intended to combat. An *herbicide* kills weeds and other unwanted plants, a *biocide* combats microorganisms that threaten crops, while an *insecticide*, obviously enough, kills insects. You may also see fungicides, miticides, ovicides, and rodenticides. Other products under the "pesticide" umbrellas include: *defoliants*, which cause leaves or other foliage to drop from a plant to facilitate harvest; *desiccants*, which promote the drying of living tissues such as unwanted plant tops; *insect growth regulators*, used to disrupt the maturation of insects from pupal stage to adult; and *plant growth regulators*, which are highly engineered substances that alter the natural growth, flowering, and reproduction rates of plants.

The problems with factory-farmed meats are manifold. Perhaps the most dramatic shift in meat production over the past half century or so has been the move indoors and the illogically inverse increase in total animal volume. As the areas allotted to cattle, pigs, and poultry have gotten smaller and smaller, the numbers of animals in a typical factory farm have risen. Both of these elements, particularly both *together,* wreak havoc with the sustainable and environmentally fit production of food. Crammed into tight confines, animals are reduced from natural beings to manufactured products. Often thousands of animals fill a single building that lacks any natural sunlight, fresh air, or effective system for the removal of animal excrement, which means that disease constantly threatens to run rampant through the farms. To combat this, animals are routinely loaded up on antibiotics. Additionally, farmers have found that the daily administration of low doses of antibiotics causes the animals to grow faster. But it isn't the antibiotics alone that are cause for concern. In the beef industry the use of growth hormones has become routine. Of the thirty-six million U.S. beef cattle, two-thirds (or about twenty-four million) are given hormones to force faster growth.

Jacked up on antibiotics and hormones, stuffed with specialized feed, and with no room to move, these animals drop revolting amounts of waste on the cramped floors of their storage buildings. For the imagination's sake a relatively small factory farm with 1,000 hogs (*relatively* being the key word here) will produce more than six million pounds of waste each year. Whereas traditional, sustainable agriculture used animal waste to fertilize fields, the volume of feces and urine at a factory farm is too overwhelming to be dealt with efficiently. Thus factory farms utilize "lagoons"—sometimes dug immediately beneath the animals' building—to collect the

> ## tip
>
> More energy is now used to produce synthetic fertilizers than to till, cultivate, and harvest all the crops in the United States.

manure, which is flushed out with streaming water. Factory farms have been known to use millions of gallons of water a day, some running a constant stream through the storage buildings to flush out fresh manure. On these farms hogs and cows spend their entire lives standing in soiled water on concrete floors.

While the liquefied manure sits stagnant in lagoons, it emits gases such as nitrogen, hydrogen sulfide, and methane, which then fall back to the earth as acid rain. Many lagoons are themselves shoddily constructed— a North Carolina State University study estimated that half of America's lagoons leak badly enough to contaminate groundwater. This poisons the rivers, streams, lakes, and drinking water supplies in the area with nitrogen, phosphorous, bacteria, pathogens, and heavy metals. The liquid manure that doesn't leak from within the lagoons often overflows during heavy rain, running into local streams; any that remains is pumped out to fertilize the crop fields. There have been a number of recorded instances of factory farms so severely polluting local water sources that the surviving fish populations were unfit for human consumption and the groundwater needed to be treated before human consumption. The heavy metals, such as mercury and arsenic, that are abundant in manure find their way into the soil when the lagoons' swarthy brew is eventually sprayed onto fields. This heavy metal pollution of soil is essentially irreversible, and is notorious for stunting crop growth.

All of this hasn't yet touched on the wider-reaching environmental impact of industrialized crop growth and factory-farmed meat. Fossil fuels are burned throughout the food production process to fuel heavy farm equipment, process foods, refrigerate and transport foods, produce packaging

> **tip**
>
> The Department of Economics at Great Britain's University of Essex found that factory farms in the United States cost the country $34.7 billion annually in environmental damages.

FOCUS ON

## What Is a Factory Farm?

The evolution of the meat production industry has hinged, more than anything else, on the shift from family to factory farms. These highly industrialized sites couldn't be farther removed from the idyllic barns and pastures that most of us picture when we think of farms. But factory farming has become the norm, so it's important to know what exactly it is. While there's no formal definition of a factory farm—also known as a Concentrated Animal Feeding Operation (CAFO) and an Industrial Livestock Operation (ILO)—certain characteristics are commonplace, and the folks at Sustainable Table (www.sustainabletable.org) have assembled a comprehensive list, which I've paraphrased here.

- Hundreds to thousands of animals (cows, pigs, chickens, or turkeys, for the most part) confined together indoors, usually on concrete floors, using as little space as possible, with little or no access to sunlight, fresh air, or natural movement.
- The use of antibiotics, chemicals, and/or hormones to promote faster growth and ward off disease that would otherwise run rampant.
- The use of lagoons to store massive amounts of raw manure.
- The use of cages to restrict the natural behavior of animals.
- The routine mutilation of animals such as the debeaking of chickens and turkeys, clipping pigs' tails and teeth, and amputating cows' tails (docking).
- Farm owners that also own the feed company, slaughterhouse, and meat-processing plants (also known as vertical integration).
- Separation of farm ownership, management, and labor.
- An emphasis on high volume and profit with little or no regard for environmental quality, human health, safe food, humane treatment of animals, and the rural economy.

Source: Sustainable Table: www.sustainabletable.org/factoryfarming.

materials, and manufacture and transport pesticides and fertilizers. After the food is all gussied up and ready to ship, the average American meal travels more than 1,500 miles before it lands on your plate. We New Yorkers are proud to think of ourselves as the center of the world, but we're nowhere near the major regions of food production in this country, and our meals likely make a much longer trek than that national average. From California's fields—where much of the produce that lines the supermarkets' racks and adorns our restaurants' plates is grown—to the New York market, a typical vegetable rides 3,000 miles and ages four or five days. The vegetable varieties that are able to endure this journey are grown not for taste, but rather for survival. Of course, most of this food rides in the back of petroleum-guzzling trucks chugging across the country's interstates. When the stickers on your melons and oranges read CALIFORNIA and FLORIDA, consider diesel fumes to be the side dish to your healthy fruit salad.

Don't yet despair. There *are* ways to eat outside this system, and I'll tell you all about them in the next chapter.

## Your Health, Your Food

The vast distances that food travels from farm to shelf wouldn't be possible without additives. The average U.S. citizen consumes approximately 140 to 150 pounds of food additives annually. While the majority don't threaten human health at all, many may not have been adequately tested. Indeed, a number of additives that were initially approved by the Food and Drug Administration (FDA) were later proven harmful and then—in some cases after years of use—eventually banned. Furthermore, some approved additives are safe for some people but have harmful effects on others. Such is the case with sulfites, aspartame, and MSG, all of which

> **tip**
>
> The typical American meal contains, on average, ingredients from at least five foreign countries.

have brought about severe reactions—ranging from asthma to nausea to brain damage—in some individuals while allegedly safe for the masses. One common additive has proven unhealthy for all—trans-fatty acid. Trans fats are regularly linked to obesity and heart disease, yet they needn't be identified on package labels.

A potentially greater threat to a wider range of consumers, including New Yorkers with little knowledge of where their food comes from, is pesticides. With ever-increasing amounts of chemicals being sprayed on crops, it stands to reason that some of them find their way into humans. Indeed, after you've washed, peeled, and even cooked most produce, some pesticide residues remain. Of the most commonly used pesticides today, more than 80 percent have been registered as potentially cancer causing by the National Academy of Sciences. Nor do these dangerous chemicals go away easily. They remain in soil and water for literal ages. The pesticide DDT—described memorably in Rachel Carson's landmark book *Silent Spring*—was banned in 1972, yet thirty years later it was found in the breast milk of 99 percent of *all* mothers in America.

Crops grown to feed farm animals generally contain even higher levels of pesticides than those grown for human consumption. Pesticide residues, however, accumulate in the fat and tissue of the animals and are passed on to the consumer. In fact, in 2002 the U.S. Department of Agriculture (USDA) analyzed farm

## FOCUS ON

### Foreign-Born Food

The average American meal travels 1,500 miles from where it's produced to its point of purchase. Quite a hike, yet this statistic doesn't even factor foreign foods into the equation. It should. Americans are eating increasing amounts of food produced in other countries. In 2001 an estimated 34 percent of all fresh fruits, 12 percent of vegetables, over 10 percent of beef, 5 percent of pork, 51 percent of fish and shellfish, and better than 99.9 percent of coffee was imported. The environmental repercussions of such transport distances are enormous.

market beef and found that 47 percent contained pesticide residue.

It was once thought that pesticide risk was limited to the possibility of severe acute poisoning (coming into direct contact with the chemicals) and the long-term threat for development of cancer. Now, however, we know that these substances can also affect the nervous, endocrine, immune, and reproductive systems. They've been linked in studies to Parkinson's disease, learning disabilities, hyperactivity, emotional disorders, weakened immune systems, birth defects, and low sperm counts in men. These threats are increased in infants, the unborn, and young children, who of course can't choose which foods they eat.

Similarly troubling is the recent proliferation in genetically engineered (GE) crops. Unlike pesticides, regulated for decades by the EPA, crop varieties are overseen by the USDA and Food and Drug Administration, and they haven't been subject to much scientific scrutiny. We do know that the introduction of foreign DNA into any organism has the potential to trigger other DNA in the plant or animal to mutate or change. The cumulative effects of these changes, and their potential effects on human health, remain understudied. In addition, once GMOs have been introduced to the environment, they can't be simply recalled. Many fear that the agriculture and meat industries, in their endless quest for profit, are subjecting Americans to a test of GE food safety.

If this sounds alarmist, consider that 70 percent of processed foods in American supermarkets contains genetically modified ingredients. More than 75 percent of U.S. soybeans are genetically modified crops. This is a big business indeed, but one that the vast majority of the world is hesitant to dive into: 99 percent of GE acreage is confined to four countries—

> **tip**
>
> The Environmental Working Group recently found that the nation's twenty million children aged five and under eat an average of eight different pesticides every day.

## 🍎 FOCUS ON

# Specific Concerns over Genetic Engineering

✳ **Allergic reactions:** When genes from one species are implanted in another, allergens from the former may well end up emerging in the latter. For example, when a gene from a type of Brazil nut was inserted into soybeans, people with nut allergies—plentiful these days—who ate the altered soybeans were stunned by severe reactions. Thus, there is great concern that people with known allergies might not realize they are consuming food they're allergic to. There are no requirements for labeling GE foods at this time. Furthermore, new combinations of genes and traits may cause allergies yet unknown and undocumented.

✳ **Gene mutation:** The forced insertion of one gene into another gene has the potential to destabilize the entire organism, promoting mutations and abnormalities. The health effects of consuming mutated food have never been conclusively studied.

✳ **Loss of nutrition:** The genetic engineering of food doubtlessly changes its nutritional value. While there have been attempts to give foods more calories and nutritional value, evidence has shown that most GE foods that hit today's market have suffered an ultimate loss of natural nutrition.

✳ **Increased chemical use:** Since the majority of GE crops today are bred to be resistant to pesticides, the weeds around the crops develop over time a resistance to the chemicals, forcing the farmer to spray ever-increasing amounts. A recent study has shown that farmers growing GE soybeans use two to five times more pesticides than those raising natural varieties.

- ✳ **Superweeds:** GE crops can cross-pollinate (as is common in nature) with local weeds, creating "superweeds" that could be potentially devastating to ecological balance.

- ✳ **Frankenfood:** Some GE crops are actually classified as pesticides. One example is the New Leaf Potato manufactured by Monsanto and grown in Idaho since 1995. This "potato" is bred to produce the *Bacillus thuringiensis* (Bt) toxin, which will kill pests that attempt to eat it. Such crops are regulated by the EPA, not the FDA, and so are subject to less strict safety testing, despite the fact that they are regularly eaten.

- ✳ **Proliferation:** To date, thirteen crops that have been genetically engineered are in regular production around the county: beets, chicory, corn, cotton, flax, papayas, potatoes, rapeseed (or canola), rice, soybeans, squash, tomatoes, and tobacco.

Source: Sustainable Table, "Issues: Genetic Engineering," www.sustainabletable.org/issues/ge.

the United States, Canada, Argentina, and China—with the U.S. claiming the lion's share, 68 percent.

A similar predicament is arising with regard to hormone use in meat and dairy production. Expert scientists appointed by the European Union have found that the use of growth hormones in food animals does pose a potential risk for consumers' health. They reported that hormone residues in meat can disturb human hormone balance, causing developmental problems, interfering with reproductive systems, and even leading to cancer. These maladies are particularly threatening to pregnant women and children, and the report goes so far as to warn that hormone residues may cause the early onset of puberty in young girls, putting them at greater risk of breast cancer.

So alarming was this report that the EU has completely banned the use of growth hormones in cattle and has prohibited the import of hormone-treated beef since 1988.

Then there is the widespread use of recombinant bovine growth hormone (rBGH). Dairy cows injected with rBGH produce 8 to 15 percent more milk than untreated cows, but this milk has elevated levels of a chemical called insulin-like growth factor I (IGF-I). One study by the University of Illinois in Chicago suggested that the elevated level of IGF-I in milk of rBGH-treated cows may well promote breast and colon cancer in those who ingest it. In 2003, 33 percent of the nine million American dairy cows were treated with rBGH. The Illinois study took the liberty of offering some scathing commentary on rBGH: "In short, with the active complicity of the FDA, the entire nation is currently being subjected to an experiment involving large-scale adulteration of an age-old dietary staple by a poorly characterized and unlabeled biotechnology product." This last bit is important. Serious lobby efforts by the chemical

> **tip**
>
> A full 17 percent of all fossil fuel burned in the U.S. is consumed by industrialized agriculture.

giants that produce the hormone have ensured that dairy products hailing from rBGH-treated cows needn't be labeled as such.

Also of health concern in the realm of Big Meat is the sustained abuse of antibiotics. Every year at least twenty-five million pounds of antibiotics are administered to animals for the specific purpose of increasing growth rates and preventing disease. For comparison, this is more than eight times the amount used to treat disease in humans.

Such overuse breeds superstrands of resistant disease bacteria and germs: Any bacteria that survive the antibiotic treatment pass on their resistance so eventually all bacteria will be resistant to the medication. Antibiotic-resistant pathogens such as *Salmonella* and *E. coli* have gained notoriety of late because they've so frequently been found contaminating meat from factory farms. Bacteria adapt and evolve so quickly that human science and technology can't keep up. Patients once effectively treated for pneumonia, tuberculosis, or ear infections may now work through three or more antibiotics before they find one that works. We've already seen a $4-billion-per-year increase in health care costs due to resistant bacteria infections here in the United States. And as more and more bacterial strains develop resistance, more and more lives are at stake. With every animal routinely fed antibiotics, we move closer to a global pandemic. Living in a city as densely populated as New York, where disease-causing bacteria can spread with relative ease, such a threat hits close to home.

But don't give up hope. You *can* make a difference. It should be clear enough by now that the food you eat is enormously important to ensuring the greater ecological health of our city, country, and even world. The old maxim proves true: You *should* watch what you eat. As mentioned earlier, New York City is as good a place as anywhere in the world to do just that. The following chapter should help you navigate the many food options here in the Big Apple.

CHAPTER EIGHT

# You Are What You Eat

A lot of things are making it harder these days
to bond with one's broccoli.
—**KIRK JOHNSON,** *New York Times,* October 27, 2003

I t certainly is tough these days "to bond" with the food that
graces our plates. Tough, that is, but not impossible. Reaction
against the industrialization of food is bringing about a growing
diversity of options, many of which promote a healthier, more ecologically sound future by harking back to more traditional means and patterns of food production and consumption. And in a town as progressive as New York City, these options are abundant. Indeed, it often
seems you can't swing your canvas grocery bag on the streets without
hitting a farmers market, organic grocer, or green restaurant of some
sort. As green New Yorkers it is our desire and duty to search these
options out, to separate the truth from the hype, to learn how to pro-
cure the most sustainable fare, and to integrate these options into our
gastronomic lives.

# The Green Diet Basics

Nobody has done a better job of putting together a set of guidelines for shopping, cooking, and eating green than the folks at Sustainable Table (www.sustainabletable.org) and *The Green Guide* (www.thegreen guide.com). Consider what follows a basic list of suggestions for achieving a more sustainable diet, derived from these two sources. Both have on their websites a bevy of links and pages upon pages of information about these issues in a more general context, not specific to New York, either of which you could (and should!) easily spend a full afternoon browsing.

It's important to keep in mind that this is a list of ideals. Not all of the suggestions are practical for everyone, nor are they all categorical truths. Canning fall produce to eat in winter is a wonderful idea, but most New Yorkers don't have the time, the know-how, or—most important—the storage space to make it a reality. And while packaged foods have many drawbacks, they are certainly convenient and occasionally necessary—and natural food stores have canned and frozen food options that are good and green. Sure, in a perfect city, all New Yorkers would be fixing lavish meals with a grand variety of fresh, organic fruits and veggies from a bunch of local gardens, whole-grain breads from New Jersey oats, nuts and beans from Long Island, and all of it could be bought fresh with no packaging or preservatives. But New York City isn't perfect, nor are all these suggestions viable all the time. Think of them as guidelines adaptable to your life.

## Eat Local When Possible

Not only is local food fresher, but it's also much less likely to have been treated with post-harvest pesticides and preservatives, and uses much less energy to transport. Local food is also less likely to have been genetically

> **tip**
>
> Corn, rice, and wheat alone—in their various processed forms—account for nearly 60 percent of the calories Americans consume.

engineered; a lot of the genetic tweaking done to foods is intended to improve its transportability. New York City's best venues for locally produced food are the various farmers markets (Greenmarkets and community-run markets) and community-supported agriculture programs (CSAs). Natural food grocers, certain restaurants, and even some supermarkets also offer locally produced foods, but it's often less clearly labeled and you may need to pry the managers for information.

## Go Organic

True organic food has been grown, handled, and processed without the use of synthetic pesticides, hormones, antibiotics, artificial ingredients, preservatives, and irradiation. Avoid ingesting unnecessary chemicals and toxins, and reduce demand for chemical-dependent crops, meat, and dairy, by sticking to USDA-certified organic products in restaurants and stores. CSAs offer only organic foods, and farmers markets are generally loaded with organic options.

## Buy Produce in Season

When you find fruits and vegetables on store shelves that are out of their natural, regional growing seasons, you can be sure that plenty of fossil fuels were burned to deliver them. Assume the same for frozen and packaged foods. Furthermore, such foods are much more likely to have been genetically engineered and chemically preserved. In many cases these foods have been imported from foreign countries with pesticide regulations far less rigid than those of the United States To liven up winter meals, consider canning or freezing late-summer produce for consumption throughout the less agriculturally productive months. (Check the "Seasonal Produce Calendar" sidebar on page 94 to see when various fruits and vegetables are harvested around New York City.)

## Cut Out That (Factory-Farmed) Meat

While this certainly isn't the venue for the debate over whether vegetarianism is the only truly green diet, it is indisputable that the higher up on the food chain you eat, the more resources were used in the food's production. It takes almost five pounds of grain, for example, to produce one pound of beef. Steer clear of factory-farmed meats and dairy products, which require much more energy, water, and synthetic chemicals and hormones to produce. When you find a good source for organic, free-roaming, grass-fed, or locally raised meat, poultry, and dairy products, spread the word. Many farmers markets feature at least one local meat producer, and natural food grocers around the city tend to have plenty of options.

## Diversify Your Meals

By eating a wide variety of foods, you not only consume the most healthy, balanced diet, but also reinforce diversity of food production—a movement against the homogenation of crop species and the reduction of biodiversity in the agricultural world. By diversifying your diet, you can help strengthen the market for nonindustrialized foods.

## Eat Whole Foods

Whole foods such as fruits, vegetables, grains, beans, nuts, and seeds are void of the preservatives and additives—such as trans-fatty acid—that are playing a large part in the nation's health issues and obesity epidemic. A typical highly packaged, highly processed product found in a supermarket is likely to contain few natural food ingredients; rather, it's replete with genetically engineered soy- and corn-based additives and is disproportionately high in fats, salts, and sugars. The GMO crops and chemicals that make up these additives are the backbone of industrialized agriculture, given how thoroughly preserved and packaged foods dominate the country's shelves. Try to avoid packaged breads, snacks, ready-to-eat meals, and the like, and do your best to base your diet on natural, whole foods. Natural food stores and farmers markets are the best sources for whole grains here in the city, and most of the groceries and some supermarkets also do offer some healthy, eco-friendly, and convenient frozen and packaged foods that contain whole-food or even organic ingredients, and use modest amounts of preservatives, if any.

### Hold the Packaging

Most take-out restaurants serve their meals with an exorbitant amount of excess packaging—boxes, bags, disposable utensils, and so on. Ask for the minimum amount of packaging necessary. Similarly, most of what you find in a supermarket is so thoroughly sheathed in plastic and cardboard that the packaging can outweigh the food! Search out products that use minimal packaging, or recycled and recyclable material, and buy in bulk if your storage space allows. Many natural food grocers and farmers markets allow you to furnish and fill your own containers for whole grains, seeds, beans, or whatever strikes your fancy.

### Cook for Yourself

Aside from the pleasant reward of eating a home-cooked meal, when you cook for yourself, you control all of the ingredients and can use organic, fresh, and whole foods. If you, like myself, need thorough instruction in the kitchen, consider picking up one of the many green or natural food cookbooks on the market. Helen Nearing's *Simple Food for the Good Life* is a great collection of easy-to-prepare snacks and meals that were the favorites of the famous homesteader and self-described "anti-cook." *Taste Life: Organic Recipes* by Leslie Cerier offers a wider variety of meals from a wider variety of ingredients; it's not as "simple," but it's a good resource nonetheless. Also, the prominent Whole Foods Market institution has responded to the calls of hundreds of thousands of customers who asked, "How do I prepare this?" *The Whole Foods Market Cookbook* is packed with answers, and includes a great selection of recipes from the quick and easy to the intricate and impressive. With the help of one of these resources, or with your own resourcefulness, go ahead and be the master of your own meal; create your own green plate special!

## Natural Food Grocers

Perhaps one of the most visible developments on the city's commercial landscape has been the recent proliferation of natural foods and holistic grocers. It seems as if small markets with names like *Garden of Eden,*

*Natural Frontier, Wholesome Market,* and *Nature's All* have set up shop on streets and avenues the city over. These markets and grocers tend to be a great resource for finding organic—if not always local—produce, sustainably raised meats and dairy products, and good whole foods, typically in bulk, self-serve bins where you can fill up on grains, rice, beans, and countless other goodies. When grazing their shelves, you'll still want to pay close attention to labels (see "On Labeling," page 101), and don't hesitate to ask about the source of foods that are unmarked. Most of these stores have helpful, knowledgeable staff that are eager to help you find the food that you are most comfortable consuming. I've found that many of these grocers offer self-serve buffets with freshly prepared food, and deli counters that feature some of the choicest meats in the city. You owe it to yourself and your greening cupboards to find a local natural food grocery and take advantage of its offerings. My personal favorite feature at these stores is the peanut grinder that churns out pure, unadulterated peanut butter, the freshest, tastiest, *and* healthiest you can buy.

If you're not sure where your closest natural food grocer may be, there's a wonderful online resource called the Eat Well Guide (www.eatwellguide.org)—a free directory of stores and restaurants that offer sustainably raised meats, poultry, dairy, and eggs. Boasting "wholesome food from wholesome animals," the Eat Well Guide lets you search by zip code to summon up green-friendly establishments in your neighborhood.

In a different league from the typically modest-size natural food grocer is the now legendary Whole Foods establishment, which seems to be taking the city by storm. Indeed, generating as much popular buzz as a supermarket's arrival possibly could, in March 2005 a new Whole Foods supermarket opened its doors, to the delight of many Villagers, on 14th Street at Union Square. New York City's third Whole Foods—Chelsea has hosted one on West 24th Street and Seventh Avenue for a few years now, and a Columbus Circle branch has been serving Upper West Siders since fall 2004—this place can be called a "grocery" only with considerable understatement. All three stores spread over 30,000 square feet—

#  FOCUS ON

# Seasonal Produce Calendar

Want to know when the area's fruits and veggies are fresh?
Here's the Greenmarket harvest calendar for local produce.

| FRUITS | JAN | FEB | MAR | APR | MAY | JUN | JUL | AUG | SEP | OCT | NOV | DEC |
|---|---|---|---|---|---|---|---|---|---|---|---|---|
| APPLES | A | A | A | A | A | A | H | H | H | H | A | A |
| BLACKBERRIES | | | | | | | | H | | | | |
| BLUEBERRIES | | | | | | | H | H | H | | | |
| CANTALOUPES | | | | | | | | H | H | | | |
| CHERRIES | | | | | | | H | | | | | |
| CRANBERRIES | | | | | | | | | | H | A | A |
| CURRANTS | | | | | | | | H | | | | |
| GRAPES | | | | | | | | | H | H | | |
| NECTARINES | | | | | | | | H | | | | |
| PEACHES | | | | | | | H | H | H | | | |
| PEARS | A | A | | | | | | | H | H | A | A |
| PLUMS | | | | | | | H | H | H | | | |
| PRUNES | | | | | | | | H | H | | | |
| STRAWBERRIES | | | | | | H | H | | | | | |
| RASPBERRIES | | | | | | | H | | | H | H | |
| WATERMELON | | | | | | | | | H | H | | |

**A:** Locally grown product is available from storage during this month.

**H:** Product is harvested during this month and found fresh at farmers markets
and select grocers.

Source: Council of the Environment of New York City
(www.cenyc.org/htmlgm/harvestcalendar.html).

| VEGETABLES | JAN | FEB | MAR | APR | MAY | JUN | JUL | AUG | SEP | OCT | NOV | DEC |
|---|---|---|---|---|---|---|---|---|---|---|---|---|
| ASPARAGUS | | | | | H | H | | | | | | |
| BEANS, SNAP | | | | | | | H | H | H | H | | |
| BEANS, DRY | A | A | A | A | A | A | A | A | H | H | H | H |
| BEETS | A | A | | | | | H | H | H | H | H | A |
| BEET GREENS | | | | | H | H | H | H | H | | | |
| BROCCOLI | | | | | | | H | H | H | H | H | |
| BRUSSELS SPROUTS | | | | | | | | | H | H | H | |
| CABBAGE | A | A | A | | | | H | H | H | H | H | A |
| CARROTS | A | A | A | | | | H | H | H | H | A | A |
| CAULIFLOWER | | | | | | | | H | H | H | H | |
| CELERY | | | | | | | | H | H | H | | |
| COLLARD GREENS | | | | | | | H | H | H | H | H | H |
| CORN | | | | | | | H | H | H | H | | |
| CUCUMBERS | | | | | | | H | H | H | | | |
| EGGPLANT | | | | | | | | H | H | H | | |
| FENNEL | | | | | | | | | | H | H | |
| HERBS | | | | | | H | H | H | H | H | | |
| KALE | | | | | | | | | | H | | |
| LETTUCE | | | | | H | H | H | H | H | | | |
| LEEKS | | | | | | | | H | H | H | A | A |
| LIMA BEANS | | | | | | | | | H | H | | |
| MESCLUN | | | | H | H | H | H | H | H | H | H | |
| ONIONS | A | A | A | A | A | A | A | H | H | H | A | A |
| PARSNIPS | A | A | A | H | H | | | | | H | H | H |
| PEAS | | | | | | H | H | | H | H | | |
| PEPPERS | | | | | | | H | H | H | H | | |
| POTATOES | A | A | A | A | A | A | H | H | H | H | A | A |
| PUMPKINS | | | | | | | | | H | H | H | A |
| RADISHES | | | | | H | H | H | H | H | | | |
| RHUBARB | | | | | H | H | H | | | | | |
| SCALLIONS | | | | | H | H | H | H | H | | | |
| SPINACH | | | | | H | H | H | H | H | H | | |
| SUMMER SQUASH | | | | | H | H | H | H | H | | | |
| WINTER SQUASH | A | A | | | | | | H | H | H | A | A |
| SWISS CHARD | | | | | | H | H | H | H | H | | |
| TOMATOES | | | | | | | H | H | H | H | | |
| TURNIPS | A | A | | | | | | H | H | H | H | A |
| TURNIP GREENS | | | | | H | H | H | H | | | | |

the Columbus Circle facility is actually the largest supermarket in the five boroughs—and the literal acres of options are astounding. Produce, meats, and dairy are all well labeled, and it's easy to trace to their roots; vegetarian, organic, and whole-food options abound; and a friendly and incredibly knowledgeable staff make Whole Foods a very rewarding shopping experience.

All Whole Foods stores are further equipped with Take Action Centers that offer a wide variety of information on local, regional, national, and even international issues of environmental concern. Customers not only are invited to learn about issues such as genetic engineering, organic foods, pesticide use, factory farms, and sustainable agriculture, but are also offered the means to effect change with practical suggestions and updates on new legislation.

## Seafood

As Caroline Bates wrote in *On Earth* magazine, "These days, it's not easy to be piscatorially correct." Indeed, in today's global market it's increasingly difficult to wade through the litany of options to make ecologically sound choices. For starters, there's no real uniformity of nomenclature among fish found in markets or at restaurants. The current darling of the culinary world, the Chilean sea bass—regularly shunned by environmentalists as an endangered species culled from depleted fisheries—is also known as the Patagonia toothfish. A rockfish from California could be called a "snapper" and have no relation whatsoever to a Chesapeake Bay "rockfish," which is actually a striped bass. Equally tricky is the distinction between "wild" versus "farm raised." When some species, usually freshwater, are raised in a closed system and fed a vegetarian diet, the environmental impact is reportedly negligible. Among others, such as shrimp and salmon, the story is quite different. Often, farmed seafood is treated with antibiotics, and the waste pollutes the surrounding waters.

With so much variety and so many choices, it seems as if you'd need a graduate degree in marine biology to make truly informed and responsible choices. And if you think it's easy enough to simply ask your local fishmonger about where and how certain fish were caught, well, think again. A few degrees removed from the fishermen trolling the seas, the staff at these markets likely know as little as you about the history behind the fish. Fortunately, there are a few resources that help. One is the Audubon Society, which offers a comprehensive *Seafood Lover's Almanac* that evaluates the state of global fisheries on a species-by-species basis. Perhaps more practical (and portable!) is the Seafood Wallet Card (downloadable at http://seafood.audubon.org), which separates seventy popular seafood species into colored zones of green (abundant, well managed), yellow (some concern about fishing methods and management), and red (significant problems, best avoided). *The Green Guide* also has a downloadable pocket guide (http://www.thegreen guide.com/gg/pdf/fishchartissue97.pdf) for site members that includes more species and even recommends how frequently you can eat them. Another book, *One Fish, Two Fish, Crawfish, Bluefish: The Smithsonian Sustainable Seafood Cookbook,* focuses on the variety of species that are well managed and features about

# FOCUS ON

## Natural Food Co-ops

An interesting and potentially rewarding evolution of the natural food grocer is the co-op, of which New York City has three—in Flatbush, the East Village, and the granddaddy of them all in Park Slope (in fact, the largest such co-op in the country). What makes these venues unique is that they are fully owned and operated by their members, who are committed to working the store for a certain amount of time per month in exchange for significantly reduced prices. Members collectively decide what food to purchase and from whom—visits to farms and other food producers aren't uncommon. Aside from offering some of the greenest food in town, co-ops often feature cooking classes and many other services to their members.

If you're serious about natural foods, and you like the idea of being a true part of an organization that brings it to market, consider joining. See the appendix for exact locations and contact information for New York's three food co-ops.

150 recipes. The consensus among fisheries experts seems to be that the discerning consumer should focus on less popular (thus less prone to overfishing) species that can be a great alternative to tired staples such as farmed salmon and shrimp. With the oceans offering such vast natural variety, there is an array of choices for the ambitious consumer that can hold their own for any fish in the sea.

## Supermarkets and Bodegas

You may not always have the luxury of avoiding a large chain supermarket. This isn't the end of the world, or even the end of your quest for the greenest meal. Plenty of supermarkets, including some of the city's most prolific chains, have reacted to the recent market demand for natural, organic foods, and are doing a better job bringing them to market and labeling them appropriately. If you are diligent about searching out whole grains, organic produce, and more sustainable meat and dairy, you'll likely find some options. D'Agostino, Fairway Uptown, Gourmet Garage, and the Food Emporium all claim a commitment to providing natural, environmentally friendly foods, and they all do carry wholesome, local brands with a sustainable ethic. Even some Gristedes and Pathmarks have been improving their offerings of late. Again, the valuable resource at www.eatwellguide.com has a search function that'll let you find even large chain supermarkets in any area with greener offerings.

Regardless of where you are, don't hesitate to ask the butcher or manager of the meat department if any of the meats are antibiotic-free, organic, free range or pastured, or

> ## tip
>
> In 2004 the journal *Science* found that compared with wild fish, farmed fish contain ten times more PCBs (polychlorinated biphenyls, which can cause memory loss and stunt learning processes in humans), dioxins, and even banned pesticides.

from local farms. There are plenty of brands that labels themselves (see "On Labeling," page 101). Reliable products on New York City shelves include:

## EGGS
- Wise Kosher
- Giving Nature
- Egg Innovations
- Eggland Best
- Country Hen

## DAIRY
- Organic Valley
- Farmland
- Horizon Organic
- Organic Cow of Vermont
- Amish Country Farms Organics

## MEAT
- Wise Kosher
- Shady Brook
- Plainville Farms
- Empire Kosher
- Applegate Farms

For produce in particular, keep your eye out for the PRIDE OF NEW YORK label, a certification given by the state Department of Agriculture and Markets that indicates the food was grown in New York. Often markets also have signs marking fruit and vegetable products as organic or local. If signs aren't posted, ask the manager to start labeling foods. With such intense competition and slim profit margins, managers tend to listen to what customers want. If your requests for better labeling still seem to be falling upon deaf ears, take your business elsewhere.

# Audubon's Seafood Guide

## Green Light—Enjoy

Anchovies

Catfish (farmed)

Crawfish

Dungeness crab

Halibut (Pacific)

Mussels and clams (farmed)

Oysters (Pacific farmed)

Sablefish (Alaska, British
   Columbia)

Salmon (wild Alaskan)

Sardines

Striped bass (farmed)

Tilapia (U.S. farmed)

Tuna: ahi, yellowfin, bigeye,
   albacore (pole or troll caught)

## Yellow Light—Eat in Moderation

Cod (Pacific)

Lobster (American)

Mahimahi

Oysters (wild caught)

Rainbow trout (farmed)

Scallops (bay and sea)

Shrimp (U.S. farmed or trawl
   caught)

Squid (calamari)

Swordfish (Atlantic)

Tuna (canned)

Tuna: ahi, yellowfin, bigeye,
   albacore (longline caught)

## Red Light—Best Avoided

Caviar (imported or wild caught)

Cod (Atlantic)

Chilean sea bass (toothfish)

Flounder and sole (Atlantic)

Grouper

Halibut (Atlantic)

Monkfish

Orange roughy

Red snapper

Salmon (farmed, including
   Atlantic)

Sharks

Shrimp (imported)

Tuna: bluefin

Source: Audubon (http://seafood.audubon.org).

# On Labeling

As the natural food trend picks up steam, it's becoming increasingly tricky for the consumer to sort through the variety of labels often slapped onto allegedly "natural" food products. So how can you sort through the hype and find what's truly ecologically sound and healthy fare? Knowing what to look for in the labels is a great start. It's also not uncommon to find more than one of these claims on any given label, so a little research goes a long way.

With input from Sustainable Table (www.sustainabletable.org) and *The Green Guide* (www.thegreenguide.net), here's a comprehensive breakdown of food labeling—what to be wary of, and what to trust.

## PRODUCE LABELS

**USDA Certified Organic:** Representing the only true standardized national system of organic food labeling, the U.S. Department of Agriculture offers certification to any product that contains at least 95 percent organic ingredients. Raw produce with no supplemental ingredients, of course, is entirely organic if it bears the label. To be considered "organic," agricultural goods have been grown, packaged, and shipped without the use of synthetic pesticides or fertilizers, and were not genetically engineered crops (or GMOs). The USDA also offers a 100% CERTIFIED ORGANIC label for completely organic goods. Processed agricultural products that contain a minimum of 70 percent organic ingredients are designated as MADE WITH ORGANIC INGREDIENTS by the USDA.

**Beyond Organic:** Many small farms have dropped the official USDA organic certification because of the increased and expensive paperwork it requires, and the sense that the term has lost its meaning as it has been co-opted by big business—some larger-scale farm companies have started producing lines of organic foods, but don't share an overall commitment to sustainability. Many of these farmers grow their crops using sustainable methods even stricter than the USDA organic standards, and have created the label BEYOND ORGANIC. While you must trust the self-certification process, this is generally a very reliable label, and the goods that bear it were likely very carefully produced with a strong regard for environmental and human well-being.

**Biodynamic:** This holistic method of agriculture is based on the philosophy that all aspects of the farm should be treated as an interrelated whole, never using synthetic chemicals and relying on ecologically sound farming practices. Biodynamic agriculture is certified by a third-party agency, and is thus a reliable label.

**GMO-Free/Non-GMO:** This label indicates that the product was not genetically engineered, or that no genetically modified organisms were used in the course of its production. It is illegal to falsely label a food product as GMO-free, so it's a very trustworthy label.

**IPM:** This label indicates that the food was grown using integrated pest management, or natural pest control methods, only relying on pesticides in the smallest possible amounts to save a crop when other techniques prove futile. IPM is generally a trustworthy label, but is not quite as ecologically ambitious as BEYOND ORGANIC, the USDA's ORGANIC, or BIODYNAMIC.

**Sustainable:** A sustainable product is one that can be created repeatedly without generating negative environmental effects, without causing waste products to accumulate, and without compromising the well-being of workers or communities. There is no official regulation of the term, however, so it's most trustworthy when it appears on a label in conjunction with other known features—organic, pesticide-free, what have you—of the farm that produced the food.

**Natural:** There are no official standards for this term on food labels. They are *not* necessarily sustainable, organic, or free of pesticide residues. The term *natural* is virtually meaningless in the current produce industry, and should be regarded with at least some skepticism.

## MEAT, POULTRY, DAIRY, AND EGG LABELS

**USDA Certified Organic:** For meats, poultry, and dairy products, the USDA organic certification ensures that the animal was given only organic, vegetarian feed and was not administered antibiotics or hormones. Again, this is a nationally recognized certification and guarantees a product raised in a relatively ecologically sound manner.

**Certified Humane Raised and Handled:** This label—verified by third-party inspectors from the Animal Welfare Institute—ensures that the animals were raised with sufficient space and shelter, had access to fresh water at all times, and were never fed antibiotics or hormones. They have further been treated and handled according to the Humane Farm Animal Care (HFAC) standards.

**Grass Fed/Pastured:** This label ensures that the animals have grazed on pastures and eaten grasses for their whole lives, that their diets have never been supplemented by grains, animal by-products, or hormones, and that they've never received antibiotics to promote growth or prevent disease (although they may have been given antibiotics to treat disease).

**Free Range/Free Roaming:** These animals had some access to the outdoors every day, but this doesn't guarantee that the animal spent any time outside. Taking advantage of a loophole, some farms have received free-range status simply because an outside door was left open for some period of time every day. The USDA has only approved this label for chickens raised for consumption, not for egg-laying chickens or other animals, although the term is frequently used on all meats. Thus, FREE RANGE is a somewhat deceptive term with regard to beef and pig products, and doesn't live up to the standards of GRASS FED or PASTURED.

**No Antibiotics Administered/Raised without Antibiotics:** This label ensures that the animal was never fed antibiotics as a growth supplement, or for disease prevention or treatment.

**Hormone-Free/No Hormones Administered/No Hormones Added:** The animals were raised without the use of growth hormones. Legally, hogs and poultry cannot be administered hormones, so the term is specific to beef and dairy products.

**rBGH-Free:** A common label in dairy products, this guarantees that the cows have not been administered the genetically engineered recombinant bovine growth hormone (rBGH) that artificially increases milk production. Any milk or dairy you buy at a market should be rBGH-free if you hope to avoid the understudied and potentially dangerous hormone residues.

**Grain Finished:** Cattle that are raised on pasture but are then fed grain for a short time before slaughter (to be fattened for market).

**Grass Fed/Grain Supplemented:** Animals are raised on pasture but have grains introduced to their diet in a controlled amount, to supplement the grass feed.

**100% Vegetarian Diet:** This only indicates that the animal was not fed any animal by-products, thereby reducing the risk of mad cow and similar diseases. This label doesn't guarantee that the animal wasn't fed growth supplements or food additives, and says nothing of antibiotic or hormone use in the animals.

**Cruelty-Free:** While sounding rather pleasant, this term has no official definition or certifying agency. You should look for other indications of the meat's production.

**Cage-Free/Free Walkers:** Generally applied to poultry, this label only guarantees that the bird wasn't raised in a cage, but says nothing of whether it was indoors, outdoors, or in overcrowded conditions, or of what it was fed. Again, for poultry and eggs, a PASTURED label is your best bet.

Grain Fed: A delicate and deceptive term generally used by factory farms to indicate that the animal was raised on a diet of grain (standard for factory-farmed animals anyway), though the grain could have been supplemented with animal by-products or antibiotics. The GRAIN FED label is not a reliable indication of the sustainable status of the meat.

## SEAFOOD LABELS

Marine Stewardship Council Approved: A rare label that certifies that the fish has come from a well-managed fishery with a healthy population and was captured without damaging the ocean ecosystem. If you can find seafood bearing this label, you can be sure it was harvested in a sustainable manner.

Organic: Many farmed fish will come with an ORGANIC label ensuring that the fish's diet was exclusively organic feed. This is generally a reliable designation, and has only recently begun appearing at the market.

## GENERAL LABELS

Third-Party Certified: The food was inspected by a company or organization operating independently of the producer or distributor. Aside from knowing your farmer personally, this certification tends to be the most reliable way to ensure that the food you're eating is ecologically sound.

Self-Certified: With the exception of the USDA's organic and a handful of third-party certifications, most of the labels mentioned here are self-bestowed. It's always best to find third-party certification, but as a wary consumer, you often must trust the word of the producer.

Heritage: Heritage foods are derived from rare and endangered breeds of livestock and crops. Animals tend to be purebred species near extinction; this method of production saves the breeds and preserves genetic diversity. There is no legal standard, but the farmers and orchards aware of the heritage food movement are typically reliable and trustworthy.

# The Greenest Bean (Coffee, That Is)

They're an integral part of New York City's aesthetic—Greek-motif take-out coffee cups. An indigo blue cylinder bordered by a white geometric pattern, imprinted with three orange coffee cups steaming the pleasantry: WE ARE HAPPY TO SERVE YOU. To this popular deli and pushcart staple add the endless supplies of Starbucks, Dunkin' Donuts, and office- or home-brewed batches, and you start to get an idea of where this frenetic city gets its endless energy.

It is unfortunate, then, to realize that the majority of the coffee consumed in New York comes from sources that are significantly less than sustainable. The reality of where your average cup of coffee was born is as disheartening as the letdown from its powerful buzz. New Yorkers rely almost exclusively on imported coffee, mainly from Africa, Latin America, and Asia. Up until the 1970s almost all coffee was grown under the protective shade of (typically rain) forest canopies. But today more than half of the world's coffee bean crops are grown in the "full-sun" fields resulting from clear-cutting rain forests and dependent on heavy doses of chemicals and fertilizer to maximize crop yield. Furthermore, the working conditions for employees (often under the age of eighteen) of these coffee plantations have been famously publicized as being unsanitary and dangerous.

Fortunately, there are wholesome and just cups o' Joe to be found, so long as you pay attention to some key details. There are four labels to look out for, whether buying whole beans or grounds or an already brewed cup from a store or deli.

Certified Organic: This coffee is grown without the use of synthetic pesticides and fertilizers. Choosing organic coffee, you support growers who protect their workers, local wildlife, and local ecosystems from the often dangerous chemicals found in pesticides, and you avoid consuming any of the pesticide residues yourself.

Fair Trade: The term *Fair Trade* is increasingly popular in the coffee world, and you've likely come across it in your quest for caffeine. The organization TransFair offers Fair Trade Certification for coffee purchased directly from growers or cooperatives, at the premium rate of $1.26 per pound, which is more than double the market rate. This premium is reflected to some degree in your purchase, but your support ensures the just appropriation of money to smaller farms that provide health care for their workers and are able to afford more ecologically sensitive practices.

**Shade Grown:** Also gaining much popularity is shade-grown coffee, which indicates that the beans were grown and harvested under the rain forest canopy, and not on a clear-cut plantation. Two organizations offer shade-grown certifications—the Smithsonian Migratory Bird Center's BIRD FRIENDLY label is given to coffee that is grown organically under tree cover, and RAINFOREST ALLIANCE CERTIFIED coffee is shade grown by family farmers.

**Triple Certified:** Recently, some producers have begun offering a triple-certified coffee, which is organic, shade grown, and Fair Trade. Triple certified is tough to find in already brewed form, but packaged beans and grounds are available, particularly in natural food stores.

## Farmers Markets

It wasn't always easy to find fresh a fresh, juicy, local nectarine in New York City. In fact, until the mid-1970s it was virtually impossible. Fortunately, that was the time when the foresighted urban planner Barry Benepe—father of current parks commissioner Adrian Benepe—brought his dream to fruition. His dream: to establish open-air markets around the city, where family farmers from the local region could sell urbanites fresh, healthy, seasonal, and local produce. The idea—which started as one market in a parking lot on 59th Street and Second Avenue—was a raging success, and quickly grew into the extensive network of Greenmarkets that are scattered around the city today, complemented by a number of community-run markets independent of the official Greenmarket system. Farmers markets in whatever form offer New Yorkers one of the best opportunities to get their hands on nutritious and delicious fruits and vegetables (not to mention dairy products, eggs, meat, and various other treats), while immediately supporting local family farms with their purchases.

## GREENMARKETS

Greenmarkets are farmers markets that are run by the Council on the Environment of New York City (CENYC), which invites regional growers to cart their seasonal harvests into the city. Since the first market landed on New York's streets in 1976, the Greenmarket system has grown to forty-seven markets in thirty-three locations, and is represented in all five boroughs. Sixteen locations operate year-round, and in peak summer months more than 250,000 customers patronize Greenmarkets every week.

Only the growers themselves are allowed to sell at Greenmarkets, and they can only sell their own locally grown goods, with no middlemen or brokers allowed. Thus, the farmers receive the full market value of their crops, and the savings are passed on to the consumer. The Greenmarket system is itself supported by modest fees (relative to market location and stand size) that the farmers pay to participate. There are currently about 175 farmers and other food producers (such as bakers and makers of maple syrup, jam, or even wine!) that set up shop at the various markets, and by most accounts it's a wonderfully symbiotic relationship between the farmers and the New York consumers so eager for healthy, fresh, local foods. As one grower-seller once told me at the Union Square Greenmarket on a warm September afternoon, responding to my suggestion that he'd probably rather be in the country on such a lovely fall day: "I like bringing the country to you folks."

Greenmarket farmers markets are held in a variety of open-air venues, such as parks, playgrounds, plazas, parking lots, sidewalks, and closed streets. Most run one day a week, some twice; the largest—the Union Square market—runs four days a week.

In the appendix you can find a listing of Greenmarket locations and dates for 2005, but this list is constantly growing and evolving, so feel free to check out the updated list at the CENYC website (www.cenyc.org) or call (212) 788–7900 for current details.

## CITY FARMS AND COMMUNITY GARDENS

In certain parts of town where Greenmarket hasn't yet reached, community groups have begun to organize their own farmers markets, usually selling produce grown right in the neighborhood at a nearby community garden. Community gardens themselves will be discussed in greater detail in section 4, but the handful that are producing food and have established markets should be mentioned here. Just Food, the esteemed organization largely responsible for most of the city's CSA sites, has also helped local networks of community gardens in their quest to bring more nutritious food options to underserved, typically lower-income neighborhoods.

One group that has benefited from Just Food's assistance is La Familia Verde (Spanish for "the green family"), a coalition of four community gardens in the Bronx. As one of La Familia Verde's founders, Karen Washington, explained, the need for such healthier food options is important in many less

# FOCUS ON

## Greenmarket Farmer Facts

Throughout the Greenmarket system, the following assortment of farmers and other food producers sell their goods:

- Seventy-nine vegetable and fruit farms or orchards (including seventeen certified-organic farmers).
- Twenty-one producers of meat, dairy, poultry, fish, and wool.
- Thirteen producers of honey, maple syrup, jam, and wine.
- Twenty-six growers of plants, flowers, and even evergreen trees.
- Seventeen bakers.
- The total regional farmland represented by the various farmers is 15,898 acres.
- Amid a vast array of other foods, Greenmarket farmers grow: 47 varieties of peas and beans, 120 varieties of apples, 120 varieties of tomatoes, and 350 varieties of peppers.

Source: Council on the Environment of New York City (www.cenyc.org/htmlgm/maingm.htm).

# A Day in the Life of the Union Square Greenmarket

**C**limbing the steps from the steamy subway at Union Square on an August Saturday can bring perhaps the most sudden shift of atmosphere possible in New York City. For every Saturday (and Monday, Wednesday, and Friday as well), the Union Square Greenmarket—the granddaddy of them all—is in full swing. The sights, sounds, and especially the smells are enough to bring even the weariest subway rider a swell of energy. It's a lively scene, sure, but not like the frenzied claustrophobia of Grand Central at rush hour or Times Square whenever. Hundreds, maybe thousands of people mill about, ambling from cider stand (*the first apples are in!*) to the green veggie cart to the pure organic merino yarns to the dairy truck. Treat yourself to the freshest ice cream in the city, or cleanse the body with a shot of wheatgrass. As you make your way through the crowd, the air is lined alternately with the scents of fresh herbs and spices, open cans of jam for sampling, luscious flowers in bloom, homemade breads and pies. Even the local fisheries' fresh catch smells somehow sweet.

The vast array of options can leave you overwhelmed. But the farmers and sellers are more than happy to help you devise a meal. Steve from Hawthorne Valley may send you over to Windfall Farm's stand for the red mustard and hot peppers that'll perfectly complement his roast beef (organic, pastured, and antibiotic- and hormone-free, of course). The line at the Cato Corner Farm's stand is well worth the wait for the divine artisan farmstead cheeses. If you need more ideas, the Council on the Environment of New York City's own table has recipes printed, the ingredients for all of which can be found throughout the market. You could easily spend the afternoon browsing stand after stand, but eventually you'll have to settle on something. Don't worry, there will be more pears and focaccia and mesclun and "Berry Hot Garlic Jam" next weekend. Or Monday, if your palate simply can't wait.

affluent parts of the city: "It's an issue of food security and justice." She went on to describe the health problems plaguing poorer neighborhoods—higher rates of heart disease, childhood obesity, and diabetes—and attributed them to the lack of healthy food options. "We don't have supermarkets stacked with produce up in the Bronx, and the nearest Greenmarket is nowhere near. The options are limited, and we've suffered the consequences of a fast-food diet." As Washington alluded, most of these neighborhoods don't have supermarkets, and the only local sources for food are bodegas lined with highly processed foods, fast-food chains, and delis. (It's no secret to developers that a supermarket is the first sign of a neighborhood's gentrification.) Slighted of the basic ingredients of a good diet, the collective health of the community suffers.

When La Familia Verde, in the summer of 2004, tested the market with a modest farm stand, the results were impressive. "Everybody wanted fresh vegetables," Washington said. "People think the poor won't pay for fresh food, but they will." The group quickly expanded the program, coordinating with other community gardens as well as some regional farmers outside the city, and now the La Familia Verde farmers market, which operates from late June through October in the Bronx's Tremont Park, is a busy success, featuring a variety of produce—from Jamaican carambola to Mexican cilantro to collard greens—that reflects the geographic diversity of the neighborhoods, but is all grown right there in the Bronx. Washington added: "People are getting excited about trying new foods. We're teaching each other our recipes and our cultures. Food is a unifier; it brings our whole community together." To further enrich the local quality of life, leftover produce from the market is then donated to the Thorpe Family Residence, a nearby woman's shelter.

Similar community-run markets are present elsewhere in the city (see the appendix for a full listing). The Bissell and TAQWA markets, also in the Bronx, and the East New York Gardeners' Association in Brooklyn provide similar resources to their local communities. Another Brooklyn group, Added Value, has developed a very extensive program including a seasonal farmers market to provide for the long-underserved Red Hook neighborhood.

Added Value's stated mission is to "promote the sustainable development of Red Hook by nurturing a new generation of young leaders." This is accomplished, in large part, by developing a vacant lot and nurturing its growth into a productive garden. Co-founder Ian Marvy spoke excitedly of the potential in a neighborhood like Red Hook: "The energy for positive growth is there. You just need a platform for the growth. Plants will do it." And they've done it. Using organic methods, Added Value participants—kids between thirteen and eighteen years old generally, although many stick around in leadership positions after they outgrow the youth programs—grow more than forty different varieties of produce, which are then sold at the Red Hook Farmers Market. The market is open twice a week (Wednesdays at Wolcott and Dwight Streets and Saturdays at Columbia and Beard), and over 200 pounds of food are sold weekly. More is donated to shelters. (The owner of one local restaurant, 360, jokingly complained that they won't sell him enough veggies, even at a premium rate, because they give so much away.) Added Value's initiatives don't end with the gardening. Engaging the community through education, on top of activity, helps create opportunities for those often neglected. Added Value participants have attended conferences around the country, even presenting workshops on various community-based development solutions.

What's more, Added Value has in the works a plan to develop the nearby Todd Memorial Ballpark—a run-down, fenced concrete playing field that's long since been made obsolete by the opening of the vast, modern, well-kept fields at Red Hook Park—into a massive urban farm. The nearly three acres will be divided for direct use by the community and for Added Value's youth service programs to flourish, bringing even more produce to market and to local shelters for those in need. Marvy noted that the organization merely provides the platform for the community's potential energy: "This farmland can be that catalytic space. It can help people re-envision what is possible. It can turn kids into educators and a vacant lot into a farm." Facilitating such growth, ushering such potential into worth—knowledge, leadership, food, community pride—Added Value lives up to its name.

## Community-Supported Agriculture

One of the most direct routes produce can take from farm to fridge is through community-supported agriculture (CSA). In a CSA arrangement New Yorkers can prepay farmers directly for a season's worth of weekly produce deliveries. Urban consumers thus receive fresh, nutritious, organic food, while helping to sustain the livelihoods and stewardship of regional farmers they get to know personally.

It's no news to most folks that small farms throughout the Northeast are struggling just to survive. CSA programs create an arrangement in which the farmers themselves are rewarded fully for their hard labor and sound ecological ethic.

A CSA works like this: A farmer sells shares in his or her farm's harvest to individuals, families, or sometimes institutions. In most arrangements the farmer brings the produce to predetermined distribution sites—usually organized by community groups or local institutions—on a weekly basis. The cost of a share varies somewhat in the different CSAs, but typically lies in the $15 per week range. This amount generally translates to about a week's worth of produce for the average family of four. Of course, by investing in the harvest, members do share the risk of poor weather and crop damage, but they also share the full bounty of a plentiful harvest. While there is some variation among systems, the weekly cost of a share is almost always less than the cost of the same quantity of produce from a grocery store. And that's not to consider the inherent value of greater nutritional content and better taste of locally grown organic foods.

By participating, and particularly by paying for a full season's share in advance, shareholders help defray some of the farmers' upfront costs of growing produce.

One of the most progressive features of New York City's CSAs is that they're not restricted to the more affluent segment of the population that generally can afford loftier organic prices. Many CSAs were created with the explicit goal of bringing healthier foods to lower-income areas, where it's generally much harder to avoid standard pesticide- and preservative-laden produce. Many CSAs now accept food stamps, and others offer a sliding scale for share costs on the basis of household income. Food stamp customers typically pay as they go, and aren't required to make an upfront investment.

Each CSA is run by a partnership between the core farmer and the community organization or institution that helps set up the distribution site. Core farmers tend to provide all of the vegetables for the exchange, and they sometimes rely on associate farmers to add fruits, flowers, dairy, and eggs to the mix. Again, the specifics vary in each CSA, but the principle remains the same. A full listing of CSAs is provided in the appendix, with location, contact information, and the names of the farmers and farms that grow the food. If your neighborhood isn't yet served by a CSA, consider setting one up. Just Food, a local not-for-profit, works directly with community members to help establish and run CSAs all over the city. It has facilitated the creation of the forty such arrangements already scattered around the city, and is committed to promoting more.

## Restaurants

New Yorkers are spoiled by a restaurant scene that is for sheer volume and variety perhaps unparalleled anywhere. Boasting fare from around the world in all price ranges, the city is a food lover's dream, and even the greenest of New Yorkers would be remiss not to take advantage of it. Besides, an environmentally sound meal needn't always be made in your own kitchen.

For any true green New Yorker with a penchant for eating out, Patrick Martins and Ben Watson's *The Slow Food Guide to New York City* is a must-own resource. In this valuable guide the tenets of the Slow Food movement are applied to the immense array of restaurants, cafes, delis, and other food-serving establishments, resulting in a book jam-packed with listings and lucid descriptions of more than 600 of New York City's "slowest" food purveyors.

What exactly is "Slow Food," you may ask? For a more thorough definition, see the sidebar below, but simply put, the Slow Food movement is a reaction against the fast-food phenomenon that has swept the planet. Being such, it's also a reaction against the ecologically disastrous industrialized farming and food-production practices that tend to go hand in hand with fast food. Slow Foods are, generally and categorically, more sustainable foods. Patrick Martins explains this best in his preface to *The Slow Food Guide*: "Sustainable foods grown nearby simply taste better and likely come from independent family farms. They also represent a biodiversity in the food world that is at risk of disappearing in the flood of industrialized culture and big business. By supporting establishments that serve ecologically sound foods, you are supporting the vision of a landscape dotted with small, viable farms that today we are in danger of losing unless we understand that eating is a political act!"

Obviously, you won't always find yourself in restaurants with such a noble agenda. Regardless of where you eat out, though, the ideas and credo of slow and sustainable food should be close at hand when poring through the menu. Bring the same mind-set to a restaurant as you would to grocery stores—try to envision where the various options on the menu came from; consider what materials and processes brought the food to that kitchen. But don't fret too much over your decision. Eating out should be fun, and in New York particularly it should be an experience. Anyway, you'll likely find that the most delightful dishes are also the greenest.

In many places this is practically a guarantee. There are quite a few restaurants in this town that are committed to cooking and serving ecologically sensitive fare. How? Remarkably, they do on a larger scale what you try to do in your own kitchen. Many send buyers regularly to Greenmarkets. I alluded to one earlier, 360 in Brooklyn's Red Hook, that buys at the community-run farmers market. Another institution, Blue Hill in Greenwich Village, actually grows a great deal of its own food, most at a four-acre farm in Tarrytown, New York. Dan Barber, the founder and head chef, described to me a 20,000-square-foot greenhouse on the Tarrytown facilities, as well as an ample animal husbandry practice. Most

# Just Food

Just Food, a local not-for-profit organization formed in 1995, has been instrumental in the promotion of sustainably produced food here in New York City. The stated goal of the organization is to "link and pursue economic, environmental, and social justice through food systems." Its various initiatives "address regional farm and food issues by working to build a more just and sustainable food system [here] in New York City." It works to promote both the production, marketing, and distribution of fresh, nutritious food in local, urban settings, as well as closer ties between regional family farms and urban neighborhoods through community-supported agriculture.

The work Just Food has done in the development and promotion of CSAs throughout the city is unparalleled. There are now more than forty CSAs operating in neighborhoods all around the city, and Just Food has played an integral part in the start-up of almost all of them. Any community group, organization, or individual can contact Just Food and tap into the cumulative expertise developed over years of work with the system. In fact, Just Food offers a comprehensive tool kit—a thick, three-ring binder replete with information—that outlines the process of starting a CSA project in New York City. Structured chronologically by month, the kit covers every step of organizing and running a CSA, from recruiting members, to aligning with farms, to making food accessible to people of all income levels through the use of food stamps.

While the CSA programs help bring nutritious, natural food from rural to urban areas, Just Food's City Farms programs work to develop urban agricultural solutions to help feed New York's neighborhoods. Harking back to the Victory Gardens programs of World War II (which produced a full 40 percent of the nation's food during times of food shortages), City Farms programs work as an extension service to assist local communities in growing, marketing, and distributing produce from urban gardens. More than thirty urban farms and community gardens are now members of the City Farms, and to date four boast independent farmers markets run by the community, for the community.

In addition to these pioneering projects, Just Food offers a comprehensive education and outreach system that raises local awareness of the issues facing farmers and of regional farm economy, by providing educational materials and frequent workshops. In ten short years Just Food has literally changed the face of the local food economy, and it remains the most prominent and useful resource for New Yorkers who want a greener and more just diet.

of the ingredients that the farm doesn't supply come from the Union Square Greenmarket (where a buyer visits four times a week) or from other small farmers in the Hudson Valley. Because of Barber's commitment to freshness, the menu at Blue Hill changes weekly, sometimes daily. The staff also cart all of the restaurant's organic waste back up to the farm to be composted and resurrected as soil. Still, with all of these ecologically sustainable practices, Barber still doesn't promote Blue Hill as a "green" or "environmental" restaurant. "We're concerned with serving great food," he told me. "Fresh ingredients are the most important part of that."

I'd be negligent to talk about fresh ingredients and not briefly mention a certain East Village establishment, Counter Restaurant and Wine Bar, where co-owners Deborah Gavito and Donna Binder have gone so far as to put a garden on their roof! Adapting the green roof model described in chapter 2, Counter takes advantage of fifty-four rooftop planters that grow the herbs and produce that grace the menu. This rooftop garden fills plates with fruits and vegetables like chocolate and chile peppers, strawberries, lettuces, and fifteen different varieties of heirloom tomatoes, as well as orange verdana, lemongrass, chocolate mint, dill, rosemary, and chives. The organic, vegan menu follows the seasons, the coffee is Fair Trade, and the wine list runs long with more than ninety bottles of organic, biodynamic wines.

These are but three of the dozens of restaurants around the city that offer, in some way, a green plate special. In the appendix you can find a more comprehensive listing of establishments that prepare and serve eco-friendly fare. While it couldn't possibly be an entirely complete list—surely there's a new restaurant with green ambitions opening up every month—it should give you more than enough options to salivate over.

## Delis, Takeout, and Other Faster "Slow" Food

In a city like New York, and with a schedule like a New Yorker, it's often tough to find the time to prepare food for yourself or sit down for a more relaxed meal at a restaurant. In such rushed moments we city dwellers find ourselves queuing up at a deli, a pizza parlor, or any other "faster"-

food option. Still, if your schedule's tight and you need a quick bite, you don't necessarily have to disregard the environmental and health implications of the meal.

So whether you're craving a slice of pizza, a burger, a burrito, a salad, or a sandwich, and your time is tight, there are options aplenty. Again, the Eat Well Guide (www.eatwellguide.org) is a great resource for searching out healthier, sustainable culinary options, and its categorized listings include everything from fast-food chains to mom-and-pop delis and grocers that offer quality, environmentally friendly foods. You needn't settle for an overly processed, tasteless, and unhealthy sandwich ever again.

Regardless of where you queue up, here are a few tips for keeping a green tint in your faster food.

✴ **Patronize wise:** Some delis will have whole grains, some won't; some will feature in-season, fresh produce, many won't; some offer quality meats and, again, many don't. Likewise for take-out joints or pizza shops. Search out the finer establishments around your home and workplace and take advantage of their offerings. As mentioned previously, many natural food grocers offer a deli counter, a buffet, and even ready-to-eat warm and cold meals.

✴ **Stay in season:** Whether you're building a salad from a buffet or buying whole produce, if you choose fruits and veggies during their respective growing seasons, it's far more likely that they're grown in a more sustainable manner. (Of course, the only guarantee is in knowing exactly where the food is coming from.) Refer to the "Seasonal Produce Calendar" on pages 94–95.

✴ **Go whole:** A healthy, quick, and green meal can be thrown together in most places by simply sticking with whole foods such as grains, fruits, vegetables, beans, and nuts. Not only are these natural foods healthier, but they're also much more likely to have been sustainably produced. Quite a few take-out pasta eateries and pizza joints offer whole-wheat options.

✳ **Avoid meat when reasonable:** Not all, but most faster-food establishments serve meat that is significantly less than sustainable. If
your server doesn't know or won't bother telling you the source of
the meat, it's probably best to steer clear, or at least not to make
a habit out of it. If you're at all like me, there are times when you
need to chomp down some meat. In times like these try to stick
with places whose reputation you know and are comfortable with.
Again, the Eat Well Guide has plenty of suggestions.

While it's easy to write off most fast-food restaurant chains as unhealthy
and significantly far from green, some have actually made their mark by
offering natural, sustainably produced fare. One such franchise that
recently hit New York's streets is Chipotle, a Mexican grill renowned for its
burritos. Featuring organic vegetables and beans, and free-range, grass-
fed, hormone- and antibiotic-free meats, Chipotle has set the standard by
serving the best-tasting, greenest fast meal around, and does so at a very
reasonable price. A filling meal from Chipotle won't cost you more than
about $6.00. Another chain, Better Burger, prides itself on serving all-natu-
ral food. From the whole-grain buns to the organic, hormone- and antibiotic-free, vegetarian-fed meats, to organic, air-baked french fries and the
organic smoothies, it's virtually impossible to find a combination of ingredients that'll color your plate anything but green.

## Mail-Order and Internet Options

When you don't feel like going out, there are a number of reliable sources
for ordering sustainable foods directly to your home. In fact, it's a rather
burgeoning industry with some exciting and diverse options, represented
by both New York City–based businesses that personally deliver throughout the city and regional food producers that ship you the goods. The Eat
Well Guide mentioned above (www.eatwellguide.com) has a number of
great suggestions, and you can find a list of some local options in the
appendix. There is one business, however, that operates as an organic produce membership program of sorts, and deserves further explanation here.

# Slow Food

To help the green-conscious consumer navigate the seemingly endless options of food vendors throughout the five boroughs, Patrick Martins and Ben Watson's *The Slow Food Guide to New York City* is an indispensable resource. The Slow Food International Manifesto says: "In the name of productivity, Fast Life has changed our way of being and threatens our environment and our landscapes. So Slow Food is now the only truly progressive answer."

Slow Food puts the emphasis on the diversity of food in its production and preparation, on food's artisanship, conviviality, and freshness. To this note of freshness, Slow Food is best when made of local ingredients, grown by sustainable means, without chemicals or artificial preservatives to taint the natural state of the food. Slow Food puts the emphasis on the long-lasting enjoyment of delicious food.

New York City is a haven for the Slow Food maven. The artisan food options here are as diverse as the people—every culture has brought with it a rich culinary tradition. When these elements—diversity, tradition, artisanship—meet good ingredients from sustainable sources, there is no denying the merit of Slow Foods. Patrick Martins, one of the guide's authors and the executive director of Slow Food U.S.A., summarized perfectly: "Slow Food is about doing good and eating well—what could be better?"

Urban Organic offers weekly home delivery of fresh organic produce—all certified organic by the USDA and produced with absolutely no chemicals. While it has a few different sizes for smaller or larger households, the standard Value Box costs $33 and contains enough fruits and vegetables to feed a couple or small family for a week. The contents vary from week to week, but a typical box may contain carrots, tomatoes, arugula, green peppers, romaine lettuce, tangerines, Anjou pears, grapefruit, red chard, zucchini, broccoli, red potatoes, bananas, Gala apples, Valencia oranges, and mangoes.

As you can see, Urban Organic doesn't offer specifically local produce, but it is strictly organic. If the local farm economy and local ecology are of paramount concern, you'd probably be better served by joining a CSA or by buying direct from local growers at any of the city's many Greenmarkets. But if the convenience of regular home delivery is too great to pass up, you can rest assured that through Urban Organic you're getting produce that is significantly more ecologically sound than what you'd find in a typical supermarket, and significantly cheaper than any other traditional store's prices for organic food. Through its website (www.urbanorganic.com), you can see what products are to be delivered every week, and you can call or e-mail substitutions or omissions for anything that doesn't suit your fancy. The service is flexible, affordable, and environmentally beneficial, if a bit less personal and more fossil fuel–dependent than CSAs or farmers markets.

Hopefully somewhere among all these suggestions and resources you've found a way to fill up on the green plate special. It won't take long for your taste buds to agree with your conscience—all-natural foods produced locally really do taste better. I hope you'll find the process of searching out these foods as exciting as the act of eating them.

transportation

# Gettin' Around Green

The current American way of life is founded not just on
motor transportation but on the religion of the motorcar,
and the sacrifices that people are prepared to make for this
religion stand outside the realm of rational criticism.

—**LEWIS MUMFORD**, *The Highway and the City*, 1963

It's a little unfair to begin this section with Lewis Mumford's quote—
talking to New Yorkers about reducing automobile use is like preach-
ing to the choir. Indeed, for all its ecological ills, and for its drastic
sense of removal from the natural world, New York is an incredibly
efficient city when it comes to transportation-induced energy consumption. This is in large part due to its extreme density and compact land area; in many ways New York City represents the antithesis of the increasingly prevalent sprawling American city. As David
Owen noted in an October 2004 article for the *New Yorker*, "the average Manhattanite consumes gasoline at a rate that the country as a
whole hasn't matched since the mid-nineteen-twenties, when the
most widely owned car in the United States was the Ford Model T."

Specifically, each resident of the Big Apple consumes an average of 146 gallons annually, which is well under half the amount
used by those in Los Angeles and Chicago (392 and 376 gallons per

capita, respectively), and less than one-third of the 463 gallons consumed every year by the average American. There are other impressive figures you could flaunt at skeptical "green" friends around the
country: 64 percent of New Yorkers forgo cars and travel to work by
public transit, by bicycle, or by foot. This number jumps to 82 percent
when looking at Manhattan alone. Contrast these figures with the
meager 8 percent nationwide who hang up their car keys for alternative forms of transportation. The only major American cities that
even approach New York's car-free rates are Boston (34 percent) and
San Francisco (32 percent). A testament to the efficiency of such a
densely arranged city, Owens boasted, "New York City is more populous than all but eleven states; if it were granted statehood, it would
rank fifty-first in per-capita energy use."

This doesn't mean that New York City's transportation situation
is, from an environmental standpoint, a closed case. True, a small
percentage of New Yorkers rely on cars, but keep in mind how many
New Yorkers there are. The 36 percent of residents who drive regularly total more than 2.75 million. This is greater than the entire population of Houston and almost twice that of Phoenix, both of which
cover nearly twice the amount of land as New York City. In other
words, for its population, New York has relatively few drivers, but for
its physical area, it's comparatively packed with automobiles.

Anyone who has braved a Midtown intersection at rush hour (or,
for that matter, Queens Boulevard, Flatbush Avenue, Staten Island's
Victory Boulevard, or the Grand Concourse in the Bronx) knows this
clutter of automobiles all too well. And if you were to clean an air filter screen and take a look at the black stuff you've been breathing,
you would know full well that the filth that these vehicles spew is
certainly a concern. In fact, New Yorkers suffer regularly from levels
of ground-level ozone and fine particular matter (aka soot) that have
been deemed dangerous by the EPA. A recent study by the Environmental Defense Organization found New York City's air quality to be

the third worst in the nation, trailing only Los Angeles and San Bernadino, California. While it is true that some of this smog blows in from factories in the Midwest and central Canada, the majority is generated by local automobiles. As a result, many New Yorkers are literally struggling to breathe. According to the city Department of Health, a full million city residents are suffering from asthma—30 percent of whom are children. A particularly disturbing recent study found that in Harlem, more than 25 percent of children have asthma, the highest rate in the nation.

When considering greenhouse gases and other wide-scale environmental concerns, New York City residents don't have as high an impact *per capita* on air quality and global warming as do drivers in severely auto-dependent cities like Los Angeles, Phoenix, Detroit, or Houston. Still, because we're such an enormously populous city, the collective impact is even more severe. So even though 64 percent of New Yorkers choose not to drive to work, New York City is still responsible for over 2 percent of the entire nation's greenhouse gas emissions (and it's worth remembering that the United States is far and away the world's largest emitter of such global warming–causing agents).

As I discussed in chapter 2, global warming is a particular concern to us New Yorkers because the city sits at an extremely low elevation and is a true urban heat island. Climate change experts have painted a frightening picture of how it could affect this city and its residents, beginning with predictions that heat wave deaths could double with an average temperature increase of 1 degree Fahrenheit, which is expected to occur within the next ten years. Sea levels are expected to rise, putting low-lying areas of the city such as Lower Manhattan, Rockaway, and the JFK Airport at serious risk of increased flooding. Droughts are also expected to strike with greater frequency, increasing costs of importing fresh water to the city and further upping New York City's already staggering cost of living.

Without even considering the global implications of climate change, certainly these local threats should be incentive enough to reduce your own automobile use around town, and to work toward a less auto-dependent city in general.

Even if you don't own a car (and kudos to you!), there are ways you can help encourage this evolution. And if you do rely on a car in the city, look through this section for practical alternatives. Living in a city as compact and well serviced by mass transit as New York, and considering the perpetual stress associated with owning a car in the city—parking, traffic, tickets, and tolls are but a few of the harsh and inevitable truths—it's hard to justify driving as part of your regular routine. So while New York City as a whole represents a positive model of transportation efficiency, there is more that can be done to help clean New York City's air and reduce our collective contribution to global warming and fossil fuel dependency. The Big Apple can become an even cleaner and greener traveled town.

## CHAPTER NINE

# Getting the Most Out of Mass Transit

There's so much pollution in the air
now that if it weren't for our lungs there'd be
no place to put it all.—**ROBERT ORBEN**

New Yorkers love to complain about the Metropolitan Transportation Authority (MTA) and its subway and bus systems: of service changes and delays, of dirty stations and crowded cars, and of proposed fare hikes and annoying construction closures. But there really can be no argument against the fact that New York City is blessed with one of the best mass transit systems in the world—featuring around-the-clock service on twenty-seven different subway and 219 bus routes. It is largely due to this elaborate MTA system that New Yorkers are less likely to use, or even own, automobiles.

The environmental benefits of such an effective and highly utilized system are impressive. For starters, an estimated 700,000 cars daily are kept out of Manhattan's central business district alone (roughly everything below 60th Street) because of public transit use. Expanding the scope to the entire five boroughs, without the elaborate mass transit system, the city's air would be fouled each year by:

* Twenty-two million pounds of hydrocarbons (cause coughing and chest pains).

* More than a million pounds of soot and particulate matter (damage lung tissue and factor in breathing disorders).

* Fifteen million pounds of nitrogen oxide (cause breathing disorders and contribute to acid rain and ozone damage).

* 376 million pounds of carbon monoxide (reduce oxygen levels in blood, resulting in headaches, impaired coordination, and sometimes death).

* Over ten billion pounds of carbon dioxide (one of the world's most troublesome greenhouse gases).

Beyond these inherent emissions savings, the MTA has begun to implement a number of "sustainable development" programs that aim to reduce the whole system's impact on the local and global environment. For example, the entire fleet of new-technology subway cars use a regenerative braking feature, which feeds into the third rail energy that would otherwise have been lost as heat when a train grinds to a stop. In addition, the acceleration rate of all subway cars has been adjusted to maximize energy efficiency. As a result, 240 million kWhs of electricity are saved each year, an equivalent to nearly 5,500 typical New York City homes turning off all power for a whole year.

The bus system is also undergoing an environmentally minded transition. In 2000 the MTA's NYC Transit

tip

On any given weekday about seven million passengers swipe their Metro cards and pack into MTA subways and buses to get where they're going.

# FOCUS **ON**

# NYC Transit Facts

## Subway

✴ NYC Transit's Metro subways carry 4.5 million riders daily.

✴ Over the course of a year, this adds up to 1.4 billion riders, making NYC Transit's Metro the fifth most ridden subway system in the world (behind Moscow, Tokyo, Seoul, and Mexico City).

✴ The Metro's trains travel a total of 347,188,000 miles annually.

✴ The system's tracks total 840 miles, which if laid end to end would stretch from New York to Chicago.

✴ The longest continuous subway ride with no transfers is the A train from 207th Street in Manhattan to Far Rockaway in Queens. The total trip is more than 31 miles.

✴ With 468 subway stations, New York City is only 35 stations short of equaling the combined total of subway stations throughout the rest of the country.

## Buses

✴ New York's buses carry 2.5 million passengers every day.

✴ This totals 740 million riders annually, giving city buses more than twice the ridership of the nation's second most utilized system, Los Angeles.

✴ The fleet comprises 4,566 buses.

✴ These buses travel along 181 local and 38 express routes, combining to traverse 2,109 miles of NYC streets.

✴ Passengers get on board at 12,355 bus stops.

Source: Metropolitan Transportation Authority (www.mta.info).

became the first public transportation system in the country to switch its entire diesel fleet to ultralow-sulfur fuel, which contains 90 percent less sulfur than traditional bus fuels and reduces emissions significantly. On top of that, all 4,500-plus buses in the system have been retrofitted with catalyzed exhaust filters, a technology that reduces diesel emission by an additional 95 percent. Further supplementing these fleetwide enhancements, trials are being conducted with other advanced technologies: more than 600 buses are using newly engineered diesel engines that are up to 94 percent cleaner burning; almost 500 buses are running on cleaner-burning natural gas; perhaps most progressively, by the end of 2005, over 300 hybrid-electric buses will be running in regular service. Finally, all MTA building and construction projects are now reviewed and designed to meet sustainable green building standards that include energy efficiency, indoor environmental quality, water conservation, and pollution prevention. One such project is the Stillwell Avenue terminal in Brooklyn, which will include 60,000 square feet of integrated photovoltaic paneled roofing that will produce 200 kilowatts of solar power.

These developments and more on the horizon show how a system as inherently eco-friendly as the MTA is managing to make itself even greener.

## Using Mass Transit

Whether you grew up in the city or are a transplant, one of the first rites of passage in establishing yourself as a true New Yorker is to decipher the alphanumeric soup that is the NYC Metro subway system. With twenty-seven interconnected subway routes, it can take awhile to comfortably talk the talk. Beyond the ubiquitous Metro maps, there are other resources available to help navigate the dynamic system. The MTA's website (www.mta.info) is updated weekly with important route diversion information—including disruptions to regular bus and train schedules, which are also listed on the site.

For all its incredible efficiency, endless timetables, and elaborate layout around the city, the NYC Transit system still has its faults. The

# Mass Transit Advocacy: The Straphangers

A handful of organizations devote themselves to improving New York City's mass transit options, the most visible and influential of which should be recognized: The Straphangers Campaign—organized by the NYPIRG—has been a long-standing proponent for public rights and services with regard to mass transit.

When Straphangers was founded in 1979, it was a bad time for public transit in New York City. In the subways, track fires and derailments hit record levels; stations were dirty and, as crime increased, dangerous. Predictably, ridership dropped to the lowest levels in eighty years. As Straphangers explains on its website, "The system had become a symbol of the decline of the city itself." Businesses leaving New York cited "poor transit" as the leading reason for packing up and setting up shop elsewhere.

What a difference a quarter century makes! Straphangers has effectively lobbied—through rider organization, coalition building, research and reports, and media savvy—for more than $30 billion in new investments for desperately needed repairs and improvements. It has also campaigned for—and won—free transfers between buses and subways, initiated in 1997, and the introduction in 1998 of the unlimited-ride pass, which creates a great decrease in total cost of transit for the average working New Yorker. In the three years following the introduction of the unlimited-ride pass, ridership increased by better than 1.2 million passengers daily. Transit crime, fires, and derailments have also all seen steady decline. Today trains are ten times more reliable than they were in the late 1970s.

The Straphangers website (www.straphangers.org) provides a wealth of information about the various transit systems—from the practical to the political. Perhaps the most useful feature is a "subway diversions" e-mail notice. This service lets you select any Metro lines you frequent, then sends you weekly e-mail updates about any changes to typical service on those lines. The site also offers ongoing petitions to city and state officials for various transit battles, a comprehensive set of links to appropriate MTA sites for schedules and maps, its legendary and often cited reports on the quality of transit systems, and even a detailed ratings system for all of New York's subway lines. Whether you're a regular on MTA's NYC Transit or merely someone who benefits from the traffic and pollution it helps divert, the noble work of the folks at Straphangers is important to recognize.

most formidable—and most publicly bemoaned—is the seemingly con-stant threat of fare hikes. If the MTA wants to continue providing a practical alternative to cars, further fare hikes are a major threat. The $2.00 single-ride fare is already one of the most expensive in the country (in its defense, NYC Metro is easily the largest and most expensive system in the country to operate), and further increases would dissuade would-be riders from taking the train. Some may even opt to grab their keys.

Fortunately, there are incentives available. One very effective way to lower your fare is to get your employer to sign on to the TransitChek program. Basically, TransitChek offers you the opportunity to ride subways and buses for an average of 80 cents per ride. The program is hugely beneficial, if a bit tricky to first comprehend, so it's worth a thorough description. It works like this: By law, up to $65 a month of your salary or wages can be exempt from all income taxes if the money is going toward the cost of commuting to and from work by mass transit. After you sign up for the TransitChek program, the money is automatically set aside for redeemable vouchers, and never appears on your W-2 form as tax-able income. In other words, Uncle Sam never sees this $780 a year as part of your income. So if you're already planning on spending $65 monthly (almost the $70 cost of an unlimited ride Metro pass) on transit to get to and from work, it makes perfect sense to sign on to this pro-gram and avoid being taxed on it. Funneling the full amount allowed into TransitCheks effectively lowers your taxable income by $780 a year,

> **tip**
>
> While most of the country has seen public transit rider-ship stagnate or decline for the past couple of decades, the MTA's NYC Transit system accounts for nearly one-third of all the transit passenger miles traveled in the United States.

which translates to a tax savings of anywhere between $200 and $300, depending on your income bracket. And it should be easy enough to sell your employer on the idea—the company saves a similar amount on employer taxes. Show your boss the info on TransitChek's website (www.transitcenter.com) or call (800) 311-CHEK to get an information packet. The more businesses and organizations offer TransitCheks (and a great deal already do), the more apt people will be to keep patronizing the mass transit system.

With programs like TransitChek and advocates such as the Straphangers, New York's public transit continues to give residents a convenient and affordable alternative to the personal automobile. New Yorkers are blessed with an impressive system, and by using it you're contributing to the well-being of all New Yorkers—and of the greater global environment.

## CHAPTER TEN

# Bike and
# Pedestrian Options

Every time I see an adult on a bicycle, I no longer despair for the future of the human race.—H. G. WELLS

Many New Yorkers prefer a more personal approach to alternative transportation—hopping on bicycles or lacing up walking shoes. Indeed, cycling and walking around town benefits both your physical *and* your mental health while reducing dependency on automobiles and their inherent environmental damage. New York City's uniquely high density and relatively flat topography create a great environment for cycling and walking. In fact, New York was named by *Prevention* magazine along with the American Podiatric Medical Association (which should know!) as the top-rated city for walking in the United States. Cyclists account for about 110,000 commuters every day in the city, and that's not to count the scores of others who ride recreationally or to non-work-related destinations. While numbers are impossible to come by, it isn't hard to imagine the hundreds of thousands or even millions who daily depend on their feet alone for the majority of shorter distance travel.

That said, bicycling and walking aren't always reasonable. Distances can be daunting, particularly in the outer boroughs, and the weather isn't always accommodating (although there are plenty of devout cyclists who ride straight through the winter months, claiming that "there's no such thing as bad weather, just bad clothes"). The information and resources in the following sections should help you figure out how to conveniently incorporate these rewarding modes of transportation into your life.

## Transportation Alternatives: A Friend on the Streets

It would be impossible to talk about bicycling and pedestrianism in New York City without relying heavily on Transportation Alternatives (TA). Founded in 1973 and wielding remarkable influence on the city's transportation landscape ever since, TA's mission, as stated on their website (www.transalt.org), is simple: "Encourage bicycling, walking, and public transit as alternatives to automobile use, and reduce automobile use and its attendant environmental and social harms." TA "encourages" through political advocacy and the practical provision of resources for the public.

On the advocacy side, according to its mission, TA "seeks to change New York City's transportation priorities to encourage and increase non-polluting, quiet, city-friendly travel and decrease—not ban—private car use." It shapes its political goals around a "Green Transportation Hierarchy" (see the sidebar on page 140) that prefers modes of travel based on their benefits and costs to society. Its advocacy campaigns are

tip

On any given weekday about seven million passengers swipe their Metro cards and pack into MTA subways and buses to get where they're going.

divided into five fields: bicycling, walking and traffic calming, car-free parks, safe streets, and sensible transportation (basically, mass transit). Of course, many of these campaigns overlap—safe streets initiatives make riding and walking safer and often correspond with traffic-calming measures, for example. Also, since the field of sensible transportation is being pretty well addressed by the Straphangers Campaign described earlier, TA is able to focus more energy on its other work. These campaigns have accomplished an impressive amount over the years, and the effectiveness of the group's advocacy can be witnessed all over the city. Here's a short list of its most influential victories:

* Pedestrian and bike paths on all of the East River bridges, allowing unlimited access on all for the first time in fifty years.

* A complete Hudson River Greenway with 10 miles of uninterrupted car-free walking and cycling along Manhattan's Hudson River waterfront.

* A Manhattan Waterfront Greenway that circles the perimeter of the island in a complete 32-mile loop. As of spring 2005, 85 percent of this greenway was auto-free, and TA continues to apply pressure for the conversion of the remaining bits.

* Legal bike access on New York City subways and commuter railroads, including 24/7 access to the NYC Metro.

* Year-round increase in car-free hours in Central Park and Prospect Park.

* Full-time pedestrian and bicycle access on the George Washington Bridge.

* Numerous new bike lanes and bike parking facilities throughout the city.

* TA also helped create the landmark "New York City Traffic Calming law." Under a previous law, city speed limits could be no lower

than 30 miles per hour. Now planners at the Department of Transportation are allowed to reduce speed limits to 15 mph in potentially dangerous areas.

In addition, TA is currently working toward many more progressive transportation goals, such as a citywide ban on car alarms, a completely car-free Central Park and Prospect Park, better and safer connections between bridges and on-street cycling routes, secure bicycle parking at all ferry terminals and subway stations, better bus service, including express bus services with exclusive bus lanes, tougher law enforcement against dangerous drivers, safer streets with fewer road hazards such as potholes and grates, and more pedestrian-friendly sidewalks.

If you enjoy the benefits of TA's work (and pretty much anyone who sets foot on a New York City street does), consider becoming a TA member. For $20 a year you can help support its ongoing advocacy and reap the benefits of membership, which include discounts at many city bike shops and a subscription to the group's quarterly magazine, chock-full of useful information for the car-free New Yorker.

As important as their advocacy has been, TA also provides an array of resources for the car-free citizen. Be sure to check out its website (www.transalt.org) for heaps of information: maps of bike lanes and detailed bridge crossings, a directory of bike retail and repair shops, a list of group walks and rides, warnings about streets and intersections that are dangerous for cyclists and pedestrians, and much more. It also features information about the various events that TA organizes, such as its annual NYC Century bike tour and Bike Month May. You'll also find reports, essays, and articles about transportation issues. Comprehensive and readable, the TA website should be your first

> **tip**
>
> New York has seen a 50 percent reduction in automobile-caused pedestrian fatalities since 1990 throughout the city.

# 🍎 FOCUS **ON**

# The Green Transportation Hierarchy

Transportation Alternatives relies on the Green Transportation Hierarchy (below), which puts pedestrians and cyclists first, rewarding their low cost, space efficiency, and negligible environmental impact. Service vehicles and trucks are given an important position, because they perform vital commercial and municipal functions throughout the city. Importantly, these trucks are given priority over personal automobiles for the limited amounts of curbside parking, which helps to eliminate double-parking problems that plague so many of the city's streets. TA emphasizes, "In an ideal NYC, transportation decision-making, allocation of road space, and project funding and resources would reflect the green transportation hierarchy."

**PEDESTRIANS**
**BICYCLES**
**PUBLIC TRANSIT**
**COMMERCIAL VEHICLES/TRUCKS**
TAXIS
HIGH OCCUPANCY VEHICLES
SINGLE OCCUPANCY VEHICLES

Source: Transportation Alternatives (www.transalt.org).

stop in figuring out your alternative transportation options.

## Bikes in the City

In my many years of bicycling around the city, I've learned my share of lessons, good and bad. In a moment, a basic assortment of tips—gleaned from both TA's useful resources and my own personal experiences—for how to best approach biking around New York City. But first, it's worth mentioning that the most thorough and comprehensive resource for someone first tackling the New York City streets on two wheels is an essay called "Guide to Streetwise Cycling in NYC," written by TA member and avid cyclist Tom Hart back in 1992 for *TA Magazine.* It is available on the group's website (www.transalt.org; search for "streetwise cycling") and is a funny and practical collection of tips and stories about life on two wheels.

### TWO-WHEELER RULES OF THE ROAD

✳ **Bike = vehicle:** Legally, bicycles are vehicles and must obey *all* traffic laws. Ride with traffic, not against it, including one-way streets. Obey red lights and other traffic rules.

# FOCUS ON

## Time and Money:
### The Hidden Benefits of Biking

The health and environmental benefits of cycling are well documented, but what about the other perks? Biking has, in fact, proven to be the most efficient form of transportation in two other arenas where people are *always* looking for savings—time and money. While many people are convinced that they don't have time to bike to work, a typical bike commuter riding at the average speed of 12 miles per hour has never lost a commuter race to a car or train for a distance under 10 miles. Cycling also offers the most reliable trip times—you never get stuck in stop-and-go traffic or arrive at a subway platform only to see the doors of your train closing.

What's more, only walking is cheaper. Studies have found driving in the city to cost between $0.70 and $2.00 per mile. Subways and buses cost $2.00 no matter how far you travel, even a 3-mile jaunt from Midtown to Downtown. Taxis cost $2.00 per mile, and more at rush hour. Including routine maintenance and occasional repairs, bicycling averages about 11 cents per mile.

Source: Bicycle Habitat spring 2003 newsletter.

★ **Reliable routes:** Every year cyclists are rewarded with more and more bike lanes on city streets and auto-free bike paths in various parks, along waterfronts, and over bridges. Following these routes is definitely the safest and most relaxed way to negotiate the city. The Department of Transportation releases annually a New York City cycling map outlining recommended on-street routes and existing and planned off-street greenways. It also locates bike shops, parks, and schools, and shows how and where to access the subways, commuter rails, ferries, and bridges in detailed graphical information panels. The map is available for free at most bike shops or by calling 311. An online version is also available (http://home.nyc.gov/html/dot/html/trans_maps/bikeroute.html).

★ **Show respect:** Always yield to pedestrians and stay off of sidewalks. Pedestrians always have the right-of-way, so be respectful of their vulnerability. It's not only unsafe and disrespectful but also illegal to ride on the sidewalk, and tickets are common.

★ **Don't get doored!:** Avoiding car doors sounds basic enough, right? Wrong. Getting "doored" is *the* most common cause of bike crashes in New York City. On one-way streets and avenues, stay on the left side of the street where it's less likely that someone will be opening a door (not all cars have passengers, but all have drivers) and you are more visible from the road.

★ **Protect your head:** Always wear a helmet. Always. Buy a decent helmet that fits properly. It should fit snugly on your head without wiggling around.

★ **Dress smart:** Wear easily visible clothing—especially brighter colors at night. For colder weather, wear gloves, but don't overdress. Your body will warm up considerably as you bike, but sweating will actually reduce your body temp.

* **Illuminate:** Use front *and* rear lights on your bike, or the kind that attach to your helmet and clothing, during darker hours. Even at twilight and dusk, visibility from behind a windshield is drastically reduced.

* **Give 'em a brake:** Always check your brakes before you start a ride to make sure they're functioning properly.

* **Get pumped:** Pump up your tires to the recommended pressure (usually located on the side of the tire, and listed in pounds per inch, or ppi), or until they feel hard to the touch. This significantly reduces your chances of a flat tire on the ride.

* **Saddle up:** Adjust the seat of your bike so that your knee is just slightly flexed when the pedal is at its lowest point. This minimizes wear and tear on your knees and allows for the maximum transfer of your body's energy when riding.

* **Lock it up:** While the best solution is locking your bike inside your apartment, office, or building, it's not always possible. If you park outside, you simply must invest in a good lock. New York City is the bike theft capital of the world (truly!), and few are the regular cyclists around town who don't have a story of a stolen

## FOCUS ON

### TA's "Good Karma" Biking Tips

Beyond the standard safety and practicality rules provided, TA has a fun list of courteous cycling tips best heeded for optimum spiritual benefit.

1. **Stay off the sidewalk** (no ifs, ands, or buts). It bugs the hell out of walkers and frightens seniors.

2. **Yield to pedestrians and be courteous** (even if they are wrong and oblivious).

3. **Always cross pedestrians' path behind them** and not in front of them.

4. **Don't ride the wrong way.**

5. **Use a bell** to warn pedestrians of your approach.

Source: Transportation Alternatives' *Member Guide.*

# ☺ FOCUS ON

# CityRacks: Free Bike Racks from the City

A little-known but very constructive program run by New York's Department of Transportation is known as the CityRacks initiative. Through this program the DOT provides and installs free bike racks to any resident or business that requests one, as long as the proposed site fits the following criteria:

✳ City-owned property.

✳ Wide sidewalks (a minimum width of 12 feet).

✳ Removed from the natural flow of pedestrians, usually at the curb and never adjacent to a crosswalk.

✳ A minimum of 6 feet from other street furniture (street signs, mail-boxes, benches, and public telephones).

✳ More than 15 feet from other street features such as fire hydrants, bus stop shelters, and newsstands.

To request a CityRack, print out the application at this DOT website (http://home.nyc.gov/html/dot/pdf/cityrackapp.pdf), or fill out the online form at http://home.nyc.gov/html/dot/html/bikeped/rack frm1.html. You can also call (212) 442–7687 for more information.

Locations that meet the siting criteria will receive a rack, installed free of charge, from the DOT on a first-come, first-served basis.

ride. Use a heavy-duty chain and padlock or a Kryptonite-brand "NYC U-Lock." Talk to a local bike shop for details. When you do lock your bike, make sure you lock at least one wheel and your frame to a solid fixture. (Cagey bike veterans will often use two locks: one U-lock through the front wheel and frame to a post, and another cable lock to secure the back wheel to the frame. They'll also chain down their seat or remove it and take it with them.) Aside from traditional bike racks, any street sign, parking meter, or city-owned post is fair game for locking; be careful on private property.

Don't let all of this seemingly intimidating advice discourage you (especially the elaborate locking instructions). It's all fairly simple to incorporate into your routine, and the upfront costs of all the equipment—bike, lock, helmet, lights, attire—are quickly paid off by the savings in MetroCards, taxis, gasoline, and the like. Remember, as soon as you're outfitted with city-wise bike equipment, transportation is always free!

To help get you rolling, bike shops are almost infallibly kind and generous with their advice and expertise. Check TA's website or your local yellow pages to find a shop near you. And keep reading to learn about one organization that operates beyond the realm of a typical bike shop.

## Recycle-A-Bicycle: The Greenest Bike Shop

Launched in 1994 as part of a partnership among Transportation Alternatives, the Children's Aid Society, NYC Intermediate School 218, and Manhattan borough president Ruth Messinger, Recycle-A-Bicycle began as an after-school program that gave students practical experience refurbishing bicycles. The program has now taken that concept and expanded its scope dramatically. Recycle-A-Bicycle has grown into an independently operated not-for-profit

> **tip**
>
> The bicycle is the fastest vehicle between two points in rush hour.

organization that runs five youth training centers and operates two retail and repair shops where everyday New Yorkers can go browse the quality selection of used bikes or wheel up one in need of repair. While providing youth between the ages of ten and eighteen valuable workforce skills, Recycle-A-Bicycle also ensures that hundreds of abandoned or neglected bikes don't wind up in the landfill. After being refurbished, about half of the bikes are either awarded to students who've fulfilled a specific volunteer commitment or are donated to community groups in the surrounding neighborhoods. The rest are sold at very affordable rates at the stores on Washington Street in Brooklyn's Dumbo neighborhood (718-858-2972) and on Avenue C (between 5th and 6th Streets) in the East Village (212-475-1655). The proceeds of these sales cover the costs of the materials that couldn't be salvaged from old bicycles and help keep the stores in operation. The group's website (www.recycleabicycle .org) features listings of all bikes for public sale at the two stores, and includes basic descriptions, sizes, and prices.

By supporting Recycle-A-Bicycle, whether through the purchase of a nicely refurbished bike or through a repair or enhancement to your own ride, you're supporting a holistic program that provides valuable experience while redefining the concept of "recycling." Best of all, the kids are enormously talented and deliver a first-rate product.

A friend once told me that after relying on subways and taxis for five years, she discovered more of New York City in her first month of regular bicycle commuting than she had in her entire commuting life prior. Certainly this sentiment is familiar to all of us who bike! So go ahead and join the hundreds of thousands of cyclists and millions of pedestrians and hit the streets. Let your body, your mind, and the environment share the benefits.

## CHAPTER ELEVEN

# Automobiles and Traffic Calming

The automobile has not merely taken over the street, it has dissolved the living tissue of the city.... Gas-filled, noisy and hazardous, our streets have become the most inhumane landscape in the world.—**JAMES FITCH**

There are times when you just have to use an automobile. Even the greenest of city dwellers run across occasions—from picking up a new sofa across town to cruising up to the Catskills for a hike—when a car or truck is a necessity. So let's look at the basics of driving a little greener.

When you do find yourself behind the wheel, consider yourself a traffic-calming agent—one who creates a more positive space for those making the noble decision to go it on foot or by pedal. The easiest way to do this is to simply drive at a slower, more constant speed. Not only does this reduce acceleration and deceleration (which reduces gas consumption and emissions), but studies in San Francisco and Seattle have shown that even one car traveling at a steady rate effectively reduces traffic and creates a safer street for up to a mile behind it, depending on speed and local conditions. Outside the car, on a physical and structural level, traffic calming can be employed on a larger scale—block by block and neighborhood by neighborhood.

What exactly is *traffic calming*? Transportation Alternatives has said: "Traffic calming is a system that designs streets as a shared space—shared between people walking, bicycling, and driving." In practical terms it's a means of designing streets so that drivers are forced to drive safely. Already used in many European cities, traffic calming creates a streetscape in which drivers are naturally less inclined to speed through recklessly unaware of their surroundings. It's no big secret that New York City's roadways are dangerous for those on foot—in fact, pedestrian fatalities here are twice the national average. In communities where citizens have rallied for and won traffic-calming measures, however, these rates are drastically reduced.

Traffic calming has benefits beyond safety. From a municipal budget standpoint, traffic calming is a cheap, self-enforcing solution that, once implemented, doesn't require police officers on the clock to ensure safe streets. Creating an environment that compels drivers to travel at a slower, steadier rate has proven to actually reduce traffic. Less traffic results in less accelerating, braking, and horn honking, making a quieter neighborhood. It's also good for businesses. Finally, traffic calming is better for the environment, since automobiles traveling at slower, constant speeds accelerate and decelerate less and emit up to 50 percent less from their tailpipes.

And the best thing about traffic calming is that it can be employed in just about any neighborhood. Traffic

> **tip**
>
> Studies have shown that people are more likely to shop in a walking-friendly environment rather than along congested and polluted streets.

calming typically uses minor alterations to traffic signals or street lay-outs to create a safer, less auto-centric area. This might mean something as simple and cheap as a bike lane painted on the street, effectively narrowing the driving lane; studies have shown that this slows down traffic. Equally simple and cheap is altering the signal timing on cross-walks, making an intersection safer for pedestrians by either lengthening the walk signals for slower or handicapped citizens or employing "leading pedestrian intervals," which give people on foot a three- to eight-second head start before the light turns green for drivers. This allows folks on foot to get halfway out into the intersection before drivers start turning, making the pedestrians more visible from the cars. Simply lowering speed limits is perhaps the most basic traffic-calming measure. More involved is creating a pinch point—a section of street that is narrowed by the installation of curb extensions, islands, bollards, or even planting boxes. The narrowed road acts like a narrow bridge in slowing traffic. Other basic construction enhancements include speed tables or raised crosswalks, which act as speed bumps but are less rough on cars and are easier to install.

So how can you work toward calming traffic in your neighborhood? TA provides a six-step plan of action.

1.  **Identify the problem:** Gather a solid understanding of what the problems specifically are in your area. Are cars speeding down your streets? Is there too much traffic using your residential road as a shortcut? Is it unsafe to cross the street because the walk signal is too short? If you frame your arguments to the Department of Transportation as specific problems, the DOT is responsible for coming up with a solution.

2.  **Write letters to city council members:** Let your council member know what the specific problem is in your neighborhood. It's more effective to write a letter than to call or e-mail, since council members personally read all letters they receive.

3.  **Identify interested parties:** Figure out what other parties would be concerned about this issue and contact them. Consider contacting local residents or tenant associations, local businesses, the chamber of commerce, the Transit Authority (if buses are involved), the DOT borough commissioner, the community board, elected officials, and other civic groups.

4.  **Arrange for a site visit:** After contacting these interested parties, set up a time for a site visit for everyone to witness the problems firsthand.

5.  **Develop a solution:** Work with your neighbors and the interested parties to come up with a list of traffic-calming solutions that would help create safer streets. Figure out specifically how each traffic-calming measure would help solve the specific problem you've identified.

6.  **Develop support and apply it to the solution:** Mobilize the interested parties! With a larger base of support, the DOT will have a harder time ignoring your problem. Ask elected officials and the community board to help by calling and writing to the DOT. Keep a file of all of your correspondences to the DOT and send a copy of all letters to your council member, assemblyperson, senator, and community board. Keep at it until you hear back from the DOT, hopefully with good news.

For more tips and advice, don't hesitate to contact TA's Neighborhood Streets Network at (212) 629-8080 or visit its online resource page for more ideas (www.transalt.org/campaigns/nsn).

Since 1994 the Neighborhood Streets Network (NSN) has united more than a hundred block associations and civic and business groups into a citywide coalition of people who share tips, information, and advice, as well as collaborating to facilitate wider-scaled policy changes. As has become evident from the success stories of groups throughout the NSN, reclaiming your streets from automotive dominance represents perhaps the greatest overall influence you can have on the city's transportation infrastructure. Safe streets invite more use of alternative forms of transportation. Walking and biking become safer and more practical, businesses prosper from increased foot traffic, pollution—filthy emissions and loud engines, brakes, and horns—disappears, and ultimately your neighborhood becomes a nicer, greener place.

The benefits of traffic-calmed streets can even reach you behind the steering wheel. Rates of accidents and crashes are drastically reduced in calmed streets, and the frenetic aggression typical of New York driving grows impossible. Cruising down a reclaimed street is likely the most relaxed you'll ever feel behind the wheel in the Big Apple.

## Zipcar: The Greenest Driving Machine

It's not my place to advise for or against owning a car in the city. For many the headaches that come with car ownership are reasons enough not to bother, especially with such fine alternatives available. For others, though, cars are a positive benefit, even a necessity.

For the handful of readers in the market for a new vehicle, fuel efficiency is the obvious and most important consideration. Surely you're plenty familiar with the ecological ills perpetuated by SUVs and similar gas-guzzling behemoths, and you're just as likely to be aware of the environmentally redeeming values of the new hybrid-electric vehicles on the market. Chances are that a new Expedition or Hummer isn't on your shopping list, and that the Prius and its cousin hybrids are.

But there's another way to incorporate an automobile into your life, and one that proves more eco- and user-friendly—not to mention cost-effective—than any form of car ownership. The Zipcar is a sort of communal automobile system. Vehicles (marked with a circular green logo) are parked all around the city available for members to "rent" by the hour or day for a very reasonable price.

Are Zipcars really any greener than any other car in the city? It's true that anytime you drive, you're responsible for emitting greenhouse gases and pollutants into the air. Still, everyone, including the greenest New Yorker, needs a car every now and again, and the Zipcar system has proven quite eco-friendly. In Europe, where they've had comparable programs for a decade now, studies have shown that the car usage of individual members of the program is reduced by 50 percent. Since members pay as they go, they are more likely to think twice about driving. Indeed, the Zipcar company has found that each Zipcar introduced to a city replaces seven to ten privately owned vehicles. On joining Zipcar, many people sell their old car or rethink buying a new one. Fewer cars clutter up the city, and demand for parking is reduced—which, in many cases, leads to the preservation of some open space. Fewer cars, moving and parked, also opens up the roads for cyclists, public transportation, and safer walking.

If all this piques your interest, you'll be pleased to hear how user-friendly and affordable the deal is. For a onetime $20 enrollment fee, you can choose from a variety of membership levels. The standard membership allows you to pay only for the times you use a vehicle, as long as you use one a certain amount per month (roughly the equivalent of a one-day rental). In New York City hourly costs start at $8.50 and daily rates start at $65.00 (all vary by vehicle). Gas, insurance, and parking are always included in this cost (yes, parking!), as are 125 miles for any given day. More than twenty models are available—including trucks, hybrids, station wagons, even Mini Coopers—and the entire system is run on wireless technology that conveniently lets you reserve a car on the phone or online and simply show up and drive it away. Your Zipcar membership card will open the door and unlock the ignition, and you'll never have to wait in a line or pay a receptionist. To check out all the membership options and to see what types of Zipcars are parked in your neighborhood, check out www.zipcar.com or call (866) 4–ZIPCAR.

work/play

# section four

# Work Green, Play Green

Today, man and his environment, the condition
of his environment and its effect on man,
are not only of deep interest to all but of vital necessity
to our well being. Our environment is part
of us. How we care for our environment and live
with it, utilize and enjoy it, determines the kind
of people we are and will be.
**—LAURENCE S. ROCKEFELLER**

Most of us New Yorkers work—too much, it often seems—and all of us find ways to enjoy the endless opportunities this world-class city provides. So in this last section, you'll learn how to bring your environmental consciousness into your work and your play.

You'll find ways in "The Green Office Scene" to create a more eco-friendly workplace, without getting on your co-workers' nerves. While rampant consumerism is generally frowned upon by environmentalists, few are the folks who don't get excited about finding a special something—shopping remains one of New York's favorite hobbies. Thus "Green Eye for the City Guy and Gal" is devoted to approaching the city's vast retail landscape greenly.

Greenest of all, of course, is the outdoors itself, and New York City is the proud home of the most extensive urban park system in the country. "Recreation and Delight" takes a look at the history of the city's parks and open space, runs through a litany of outdoor activities, and suggests some less obvious ideas for eco-friendly outdoor fun. In "Green Goings-On" you'll find a calendar of landmark green events, as well as descriptions of organizations responsible for such proceedings.

I hope that by the end of this section, you'll be fully ready to work green, play green.

## CHAPTER TWELVE

# The Green
# Office Scene

If civilization has risen from the Stone Age,
it can rise again from the Wastepaper Age.
—**JACQUES BARZUN**, *The House of Intellect*, 1959

D espite the stereotype aired on sitcoms and Sunday comic
strips, no two offices are quite the same. Nor do all New
Yorkers work in typical offices. Considering the wide variety of settings—from public schools to retail stores to Midtown high-rise
hotels to Wall Street—it's tough to envision a "standard" workplace. Still,
New York City is a national and even global hub for a great number of
business sectors, including finance, media, publishing, fashion, theater,
insurance, international banking, real estate, law, advertising, account-
ing . . . the list goes on. According to the state Department of Labor,
more than 1.4 million New Yorkers work in office-based businesses. On
top of that, hundreds of thousands more provide administrative and
managerial functions throughout the manufacturing fields, in all levels of

government, and in the hospitality, retail, and health care industries. Clearly, the New York workplace defies categorizing. Still, most places of employment have enough in common that the following tips and guidelines for greening your workplace should have something to offer for everyone.

## Cutting Out Paper Waste

Paper is far and away the largest source of office waste: a full 72 percent. And no matter where you work, there's probably a fair amount of paper being shuffled around for various purposes, eventually to be tossed out. Put simply, most workplaces use more paper than necessary. Throughout New York City, veritable forests' worth of paper are needlessly wasted on a daily basis. Here are a few easy suggestions for reducing such waste.

✳ Set your printers to automatically print on both sides. Since most printed material is in draft form or for personal reference, having this setting as a default probably shouldn't be a problem. For official documents simply toggle to a one-sided setting.

✳ Likewise, photocopy on both sides of a sheet of paper.

✳ E-mail, circulate, or post memos rather than photocopying them for everyone at work. Or use routing slips to circulate paper memos, magazines, and other documents so that only one copy is necessary.

✳ Use Post-it fax notes rather than a full cover sheet.

✳ Create a newspaper and magazine share or exchange program with co-workers.

✳ Use presentation software (such as PowerPoint) or dry-erase boards rather than paper flip-charts for presentations.

✳ Use undated, erasable wall calendars.

✳ Keep a scrap-paper collection box near copy machines and printers to reuse sheets that have only been printed on one side.

✳ Don't print out each memo or e-mail that you receive. Read and delete the messages you don't need, and electronically file those you might need to reference but don't yet need a hard copy of.

✳ Update your mailing lists regularly and prevent wasteful mailings to obsolete business contacts.

✳ Read newspapers online. The *New York Times*, *Wall Street Journal*, *Financial Times*, *Village Voice*, *New York Observer*, *Daily News*, *New York Newsday,* and *New York Post* are all now available on the web. If your eyes grow weary of reading on the screen, print out only those articles that you're interested in (on the blank side of a sheet of scrap paper, of course).

✳ Replace printed internal phone directories with electronic ones. Hard-copy volumes must be updated and reprinted regularly, whereas electronic versions are easily updated with no waste.

So what of that paper waste that wasn't even generated in your office but arrived in the mail? Almost all businesses and institutions receive a great deal of unsolicited mail such as catalogs and advertisements. It's not uncommon for a workplace to receive mail for staff members long since departed, or identical mailings to multiple people in the office (or even to the same person!), or mailings that are altogether wrongly targeted to the needs of your business. Not only is all of this a waste of paper, but dealing with it is also a waste of time. A few easy steps, however, can help cut down on the waste.

✳ Call or e-mail businesses that send you unwanted catalogs or advertisements and ask them to remove you from their lists.

✳ Control your exposure to these lists in the first place by being wary of how you share your business's information. Mail lists are usually generated from purchases, conference registrations, websites, and even business cards. (Include a statement about preventing waste and protecting institutional privacy on purchase orders, registrations, conferences, and subscriptions.)

✳ If your organization maintains databases or mail lists, be very selective about how you use this data. Never distribute this information without the consent of the parties listed.

✳ Keep your mail lists up to date. You certainly don't want to be responsible for filling anyone else's office with unwanted mail.

✳ Spread the word to co-workers. Make sure the staff are equally wary about whom they give out the organization's information to.

✳ Reduce the number of telephone books sent to your workplace. The phone company sends one set of books (your borough's white and yellow pages) for each phone line, unless your business requests fewer. Figure out how many you really need and give them a call.

✳ Join the EcoLogical Mail Coalition (www.ecologicalmail.org), a free service that works to cease all mailings to former employees of your business. It takes just minutes to sign up, and is reportedly extremely effective in reducing these wasteful and annoying mailings.

✳ Subscribe electronically to newsletters and trade magazines when available.

✳ Print business cards and place advertisements with only your name, company, phone number, and e-mail address or website, unless your store or business depends on clients and con-

**tip**

Seventy-two percent of office-based waste is paper. The other 28 percent is made up of plastic (6 percent), glass (4 percent), metal (3 percent), other garbage (5 percent), and food scraps (10 percent).

sumers finding your location. Clients can still easily contact you, but mass marketers won't be able to add you to their lists.

## Cutting Down Other Waste

Further waste savings can be accomplished by using more reusable materials. Here are some ideas:

✳ Use refillable toner and printer cartridges. Most suppliers offer refillable cartridges and, upon request, packaging to send them back.

✳ Buy refillable office supplies—mechanical pencils, refillable pens, tape dispensers, and so on.

✳ Reuse packaging supplies such as large envelopes, boxes, and packing material (or shred unrecyclable paper for packing material).

✳ If coffee is brewed at work, buy reusable coffee filters.

✳ Also, for coffee, snacks, lunches, or "catered" meetings, supply your workplace with durable plates, silverware, coffee mugs, and glasses so that you don't have to rely on disposable ones.

✳ If you bring a lunch to work, do so in a reusable container—a durable bag or a sophisticated lunch box of sorts.

✳ Buy communal food and beverage supplies in bulk amounts proportionate to the number of workers. Why should everyone bring their own cream and sugar packets for coffee? Take up an informal collection and furnish your workplace with communal goods.

✳ Use rechargeable batteries, or use solar-powered small electronics like calculators.

## Recycling

Despite all our best efforts, we can't get rid of all waste. Fortunately, much of this is still recyclable. Recycling represents one of the most basic and elemental steps to take in greening a workplace—and it's not only good practice, but also the law. Under New York City's Local Law 87, enacted in

1992, all commercial businesses are required to recycle, often through their arrangements made with their private carter or recycler (since the Department of Sanitation doesn't service most commercial buildings). The NYC Wastele$$ website (www.nycwasteless.org) has a business section that includes the detailed handbook *Recycling: It's Not a Choice, It's the Law* (also available by calling 311), which gives a good breakdown of how to best incorporate recycling into your organization. By law, all businesses must recycle corrugated cardboard, office paper, magazines, catalogs, phone books, and newspapers. In addition, any business in the food or beverage service field must also recycle metal cans, glass bottles and jars, plastic bottles and jars, and aluminum foil products.

The same NYC Wastele$$ site will let you know exactly what your business's legal obligations are. And no matter the regulations, your workplace would benefit from a well-organized and well-labeled recycling center. Depending on the size of the workforce and the volume of recyclables produced, figure out how to best streamline the process, to make it even easier for someone to recycle than it would be to trash these recyclable materials.

## Conserving Energy and Water

We don't all have a whole lot of say in the institutional decisions of our workplace. Still, while you may not have any control over the heat or electricity source or type of toilet, you can accomplish quite a bit by working to individually combat inefficient systems. Here are some conservation tips that you can heed, and perhaps tactfully mention to others.

✳ Report leaking faucets immediately. If you work in a larger facility with a building maintenance department, notify it of any leaks right away, and also report them to the city DEP by calling 311.

✳ Turn off lights and computers when they're not in use. Try to get co-workers into the habit of turning off their monitors if they'll be away for fifteen minutes or more, or teach people how to program the computers' settings to do this automatically. Too many businesses leave computers and lights on 24/7, while it's typically better for the machines and for the environment to turn them off regularly.

❊ Suggest upgrading the lighting in your workplace to energy-efficient lamps and ballasts, and integrate a mix of lighting controls such as dimmers, timers, and motion sensors. When making these proposals, focus on the financial savings.

❊ Lobby for the installation of water-saving faucets or at least faucet aerators to reduce water flow. They're very cheap and easy to install, are practically unnoticeable in use, and can save volumes of water.

❊ For an extensive evaluation and collection of recommendations of the energy use of your workplace, visit the EnergyStar website (www.energystar.gov) and follow the "Business Improvement" link.

Of course, there's plenty more that can be done, particularly with regard to institutional purchasing practices, interior environmental health, and green building renovations and retrofits. If you happen to be responsible for these issues in your workplace, or if you're motivated to petition management for such changes, GreenBiz.com's very useful online resource (www.greenbiz.com) has answers to just about any question you could have. Another organization, Earth 911, also maintains a website (http://newyork.earth911.org) with a "Business Resource" section that offers suggestions and advice. As always, the appendix will provide more info on both of these resources and a bundle of other useful links and references for the eco-friendly workplace.

CHAPTER THIRTEEN

# Green Eye for the City Guy and Gal

I feel more confident than ever that
the power to save the planet rests with the
individual consumer.—**DENIS HAYES**

A recreational passion for some and a dreaded obligation for others, shopping is a huge part of a New Yorker's life and a powerful feature of the city's economic and cultural landscape. There are ways to shape your shopping habits around a greener and more socially just ethic. By using your powerful consumer dollars to support companies concerned with workers' rights, local community development, and environmental degradation, your purchases can positively contribute to a better global ecology.

Whether you're in the market for some new duds, cosmetics, a gift, or something for the home, it's important to look beyond the product itself. What is it made of and where was it produced? What went into its production and what life might it have after your need for it has been met? Throughout this chapter you'll find advice on all of the above, with sections focusing on two material goods that seem most regularly in demand around New York—clothing, and health and beauty products—as well as a look into an assortment of gift possibilities. Incorporate this info into your shopping trips and your consumerism can have a positive impact on the world's economy *and* ecology.

## Eco-fashion: The Green Wardrobe

An ecological glance into our wardrobes can certainly be a bit disturbing. Very few of us have a closet free from the fruits of sweatshop labor and environmentally destructive materials. So without indulging in too much doom and gloom, let's take a look at materials best avoided and some greener alternatives.

All too often the production of popular clothing is environmentally degrading and unsustainable. Here's how.

### COTTON

Cotton is the most popular fiber in the world—in fact, the millions of tons of cotton grown each year account for half the world's fiber needs. Unfortunately, its production is a far cry from the idyllic fields of puffy white crops that you see in the commercials. According to the Pesticide Action Network of North America (PANNA), conventionally grown cotton crops are sprayed with more insecticides than any other single crop in the world—more than 25 percent of the total insecticides used globally.

Worldwide, $2.6 billion is spent on pesticides each year by cotton producers alone, a full 11 percent of global pesticide use. The most commonly used pesticides in cotton production are also some of the world's

> **tip**
>
> Farmers use an average of a third of a pound of pesticide for every pound of cotton that they produce—roughly enough for one T-shirt.

most hazardous. Agricultural journals are filled with studies showing the drastic effects these pesticides have on farmworkers, on wildlife and domestic animals, and on ecological systems. The Organic Consumers Association (www.organicconsumers.org) has noted the dangers clearly: In Egypt in the 1990s, more than 50 percent of workers on cotton plantations suffered from symptoms of chronic pesticide poisoning, including neurological and vision disorders; in India cotton workers who are exposed to pesticides for at least eight hours per day have a 91 percent chance of experiencing some type of health disorder, including cellular death and abnormal chromosome behavior. According to PANNA, 10 percent of all fatal occupational injuries in developing countries are attributed to pesticides.

From an environmental standpoint it's no prettier. A 1995 study in Alabama found that 240,000 fish were killed from pesticide runoff from cotton fields, drastically altering the aquatic ecosystems. Birds suffer similar consequences, and livestock animals also regularly show pesticide contamination from nearby cotton fields. Furthermore, as pests grow tolerant of various pesticides, uncontrollable outbreaks are more common, resulting in crop catastrophes. Perhaps most alarming is the fact that in the United States alone, fourteen million people routinely drink water that is contaminated with carcinogenic pesticides, because 90 percent of municipal water treatment facilities are ill equipped to remove these chemicals. As if this all weren't enough, after harvest, cotton is generally dyed with chemicals that often contain toxic heavy metals, further polluting local waters and ecosystems.

## WOOL

While natural wool is generally considered a desirable and eco-friendly material, many wool producers these days include a great deal of hormones and antibiotics in the sheep's diets to augment the growth of their coats and to prevent sickness in often hazardous living conditions. Many industrialized sheep farms also regularly "dip" the sheep in parasiticides to keep their coats free of blemishes. After shorn from the sheep, wool is generally treated with toxic solvents and detergents. These chemicals, along with the parasiticides, often wind up polluting surrounding bodies of water and harming local ecosystems. For a reminder of the dangers of excessive hormone and antibiotic use in farm animals, look back to section 2, "The Green Plate Special."

## RAYON

Rayon is actually made out of wood pulp, which on first glance might seem pretty natural and eco-friendly—that is, until you find out that the pulp is treated and processed with a number of toxic chemicals. The process of turning a tree into fiber also requires an incredible volume of water, and only about a third of the pulp obtained from a tree will eventually form into rayon thread. Suddenly, wearing wood doesn't sound quite so natural! Rayon garments typically must be dry-cleaned as well, a process traditionally notorious for releasing cancer-causing fumes into the local air.

## SYNTHETICS

While a whole slew of synthetic materials have hit the clothing industry over the past half century or so, most are derivatives of the original and most popular—polyester and nylon. Both of these are born of petroleum-based chemicals. Turning these chemicals into clothing is very energy-intensive and involves hazardous emissions. Ground-level pollutants such as nitrogen oxide, particulate matter, and carbon monoxide are all released, as is a great deal of carbon dioxide, the global-warming beast.

Fortunately, there are some fine alternatives to these troublesome fabrics—in many cases the same material can be produced by more sustainable means. Clothes made with more eco-friendly materials (discussed below) are on the market, and New York City has its fair share of retailers that carry them. A thorough listing is provided in the appendix.

## ORGANIC COTTON

Sustainably produced organic cotton is increasingly available in the retail clothing world. It is now being grown in eighteen countries worldwide, with farms in Texas and California leading the way here in the

United States. When you choose a T-shirt with a USDA CERTIFIED 100% ORGANIC COTTON label rather than one made with regular cotton, you choose not to sponsor the release of one-third of a pound of pesticides into the environment.

## ORGANIC WOOL

Organic wool is also a growing industry. As with cotton, the USDA offers organic certification for homegrown wool, with standards equal to those required of certified organic foods. The sheep that grow "organic" wool are fed neither hormones nor antibiotics and are never dipped in parasiticides. This wool is free of the toxic solvents and detergent residues that much standard wool carries to market. Regionally, Vermont has stepped up as a significant producer of organic wool products. A particularly sustainable strain of wool comes from the alpaca, a close cousin of the llama that reside high in the Andes Mountains. Alpaca wool has been used for centuries by the Andean people, and is naturally softer, stronger, and more water-resistant than sheep's wool. It also lacks lanolin, the greasy, yellow oil embedded in sheep's hair that is generally removed in conventional wool production by harsh chemicals. What's more, it naturally grows in a range of different colors and shades, so it's much less likely to be dyed before coming to market.

## LINEN

Born of the flax plant, linen is a good, sturdy material that is commonly and easily produced without pesticides. Flax is not yet grown domestically for production into linen, but certified organic linen is imported regularly from Europe. Because it's all coming from abroad, don't bother to look for a USDA label, but keep your eye out for comparable labels given by the foreign counterparts.

## SILK

Remember how your eyes widened in astonishment when as a kid you first saw a silkworm in action? Well, all of the world's silk still comes from the fannies of these tiny insects—the vast majority of them in

# Eco-friendly Dry Cleaning

While typical dry-cleaning practices are dangerous for the environment as well as for workers and customers, there are eco-friendly alternatives. Dry cleaning itself requires detergents and a solvent—usually Perc, a known carcinogen—that prevent water from penetrating the threads but also release fumes that can escape a dry-cleaning facility and invade neighboring spaces. Perc and other dry-cleaning chemicals can also stay trapped in your clothes, polluting your home's interior when you take them out of the bag to hang in the closet.

One alternative to this is "wet" cleaning. Wet cleaning is a relatively new process that is water- rather than chemical-based and comparable to dry cleaning in results while costing about the same. Wet cleaning is available at a growing number of locations around the city; you can find a list in the appendix. Another cutting-edge alternative cleaning method uses liquid carbon dioxide, a mild detergent, and a highly pressurized tank. After the cleaning, the carbon dioxide is collected and reused. One New York City–based company offers pick-up and delivery $CO_2$ cleaning services. Check out www.greenapplecleaners.com for more information. Another company, Hangers Cleaners, is leading the charge in this growing industry. Its website (www.hangerscleaners.com) regularly updates its directory of franchises throughout the country, and it's very likely that they'll soon be represented here in New York.

China. Many animal rights activists are uncomfortable with recent developments in the silk-producing industry: Pupae wrapped in the silk cocoons are often killed before they can break through the fine threads. Also, environmentalists would prefer to stop the application of moderate quantities of pesticides on the silkworms to stunt their growth and extend the silk-producing period of their lives. Even so, silk is relatively benign for environmental and human health, and organic options are increasingly available that don't use any pesticides.

## RECYCLED SYNTHETICS

More and more fleece products are coming to market that have been created from post-consumer recycled materials such as plastic bottles and even old car parts. Most popular are the EcoSpun materials produced by Wellman Fabrics; these are used by Patagonia in its Synchilla line of fleece products and in Malden Mills' Polartec products. As winter approaches and you start to think *fleece,* be sure to seek out the kind that is giving new life to some old used plastics.

## HEMP

Largely because of its controversial association with the marijuana plant (they belong to the same species— *Cannabis sativa*), hemp isn't as popular or available a material as it, from an environmental standpoint, deserves to be. Even though the growth of hemp has been banned in this country by the U.S. Drug Enforcement Agency since the 1950s, it is widely produced in Europe, Asia, and Canada. Hemp clothing can be legally imported and can be found in various eco-friendly retail stores around the city.

tip

Hemp is one of the strongest and most durable natural fibers in the world—much stronger than cotton—and is naturally quite resistant to pests and weeds, rendering pesticides and herbicides largely unnecessary in its growth.

## CLOTHING PRODUCTION

Aside from the materials that make up the garment, the discerning green consumer will want to pay some attention to the conditions in which the item was produced. Not only do the sweatshops that have become synonymous with clothing manufacture force employees into hazardous working conditions for wages well below what they need for a decent, healthy life (an average of 85 cents an hour in Mexico, and 15 cents in Indonesia), but they're also notorious for their disregard for local community and environmental investment. Thus, clothing labeled MADE IN THE U.S.A. or in other first-world countries is much more likely to have been produced by well-treated workers and with significantly less environmental impact. Having a UNION MADE tag is also a good assurance that the clothes in question were produced by workers with fair compensation and decent, safe working conditions.

This isn't to say that all goods produced in developing parts of the world should categorically be avoided. In fact, the informed and conscientious consumer can find clothing and other goods from the third world produced while empowering the local communities and respecting the local environment. To purchase such goods—popularly referred to as Fair Trade—is to support locally and often cooperatively owned businesses that don't exploit sweatshop labor and focus on the quality and betterment of the local communities and environment. As I discussed in the coffee section of chapter 8, the TransFair Federation gives its Fair Trade certification to goods—including some clothing—that have been purchased from the producers at a fair price, ensuring livable wages for the workers, and also requiring that the producers show a serious commitment to environmentally sustainable practices, equal employment, poverty reduction, and sensitivity to native cultures. New York retailers that carry Fair Trade, organic, sustainably produced, or any sort of green apparel are listed in the appendix, as are the bevy of online sources for such goods.

Another practical and economical—not to mention hip—alternative to buying new clothes is to think *vintage*. New York City is replete with secondhand-clothing stores, from the extremely wallet-friendly Salvation

# Made in Mariana Islands

Unfortunately, the MADE IN THE U.S.A. label can sometimes be deceiving. Few Americans know that an archipelago of fourteen islands in the South Pacific has been home to a billion-dollar garment industry since the 1980s. Nor do they know that these islands are the U.S. commonwealth of the Northern Mariana Islands, and that truly deplorable sweatshop labor has been exploited around the clock and calendar to produce clothes marked MADE IN THE U.S.A. How bad is it? Well in the last five years alone, more than 1,000 citations have been issued by the U.S. Occupational Safety and Health Administration (OSHA) for safety standards violations. Over 90 percent of the workers in these sweatshops are foreigners who have, with the promise of good pay, signed contracts waiving basic human and workers' rights such as the right to form unions, attend religious services, quit, or even get married. In an appalling practice of indentured servitude, workers spend years working to pay off the "recruitment fees." On an up note, a recent labor rights court case with twenty-seven major American clothiers (including The Gap, Calvin Klein, Target, Tommy Hilfiger, JCPenney, Talbots, Polo Ralph Lauren, and Sears Roebuck, to name the most prominent) saw a settlement requiring the companies to oversee vast improvements in the working conditions in the Northern Mariana Islands. Still, not all have yet complied, and it will doubtlessly be an ongoing legal and political battle for years to come. If you find any indication on a label that the garment was produced in the Northern Mariana Islands, you might want to think twice about the purchase. A full list of companies with plants based there, as well as updates about the legal rulings and company compliance, is made available by the Sweatshop Watch organization (www.sweatshopwatch.org).

Armies and Goodwills to the more trendy vintage fashion boutiques that pepper the city. Between these two ends of the spectrum lie an abundance of secondhand stores that you can hardly miss when cruising around town; a listing of some popular and convenient favorites is available in the appendix. Buying secondhand clothing is recycling in its most efficient form—plus the Levi's you find at a thrift shop likely cost about a tenth of the price of a new pair that have been chemically dyed for the same "vintage" look.

## Green Kicks: Eco-friendly Footwear

Shoes and sneakers come with their own set of environmental ramifications. The main culprits are the main components of typical footwear—leather and plastic. Leather is a major export product in a lot of developing countries, and the shoe industry accounts for 70 percent of leather production in these areas. While Nike, Reebok, and Adidas represent the only true multinational corporations in the footwear business, a small shoe company in Italy likely assembles the product from a bunch of different parts—a sole, an instep, a heel, and so on—that were all produced in different countries. The global-warming agents emitted when so much fossil fuel is burned shipping all these parts around is but one factor in this environmentally troublesome business. More acutely, the local environment in developing countries is paying a serious price for their part in the business, and human health is threatened as a result.

While leather production once relied on tradition tanning processes using vegetable-based tans, modern tanning methods employ a veritable chemical soup that can include zinc, arsenic, cadmium, and, most of all, chromium. A tanning process that once, using natural fluids, could take up to two years, with chromium now takes only about two days. The price for this newfound efficiency is paid by both the local environment and tannery workers' and community health. Jonathan Harr's call-to-arms book (later turned into a big-budget Hollywood movie) *A Civil Action* famously depicted the legal fallout for a leather tannery in Woburn, Massachusetts, that leaked its toxic effluent into the local water table, causing abnormally high rates of leukemia in the town's residents. If this could happen in the suburbs of Boston as recently as 1980, imagine the potential conditions of communities in the relatively unregulated developing countries that now accommodate the majority of the world's leather tanneries. The chromium, of course, is not alone when flowing into local waters. The industrial runoff from tanneries regularly includes high concentrations of other pollutants such as lime, sulfides, and acids, all of which wreak havoc on aquatic ecosystems, and—as we saw in Woburn—can be highly dangerous to humans.

A lot of footwear also incorporates plastic parts, and frequently this plastic is PVC (polyvinyl chloride, or vinyl). PVC is another material that's potentially hazardous to both human health and the environment, the trouble coming at the beginning and end of its life span. During the production of PVC, and then again upon its disposal by incinerator (it is very rarely recycled), dioxins are generated. These are a class of chlorine-based carcinogens that are generally recognized as among the most toxic chemicals in production. Once released during PVC production, dioxins are easily spread around a region, riding both air and water currents, accumulating in soils and in vegetation, then working their way into fish, wildlife, and even domesticated animals that humans consume. Through the air humans breathe, the water they drink, and the food they eat, dioxins can enter the body, accumulating in tissue matter and potentially contaminating the bloodstream and mothers' breast milk. Immune

> ## tip
>
> Less than half a century ago, the United States and European countries accounted for more than 90 percent of the world's shoe production, but increasingly strict environmental standards have pushed the industry away, and now well over half of the world's shoes are produced in third-world countries that buy only 5 percent of them.

system damage and abnormal development in children are two of the biggest threats of chronic, long-term, low-grade dioxin poisoning.

Now the good news. On the PVC front this troubling plastic is being used a lot less now in footwear than it was even a decade ago. This is in large part due to an aggressive campaign by Greenpeace, an element of which was the publication of *Athletic Shoe Shopping Guide* in 2001. While somewhat outdated, the report—presented as a report card with letter grades from A to F—remains the authoritative resource for finding which major shoe manufacturers are phasing PVC out of their footwear. To see for yourself which brands are PVC-free, and for more information about the dangers of PVC and what other common products contain it, check out the "Go PVC-Free" page on the Greenpeace website (http://www .greenpeaceusa.org/campaigns/intro ?campaign_id=512832).

In lieu of PVC, shoe manufacturers can use recycled rubber or other synthetics. Or they can design shoes around the use of plastic altogether. Similarly, leather can be simulated without the use of actual animal skin, the resulting treads regularly referred to as vegan shoes. Vegan shoes are often made out of a high-tech synthetic microfiber material blended from polyamide fibers and polyurethane, which have considerably less impact on environmental and human health when produced than tanning leather does. The renaissance eco-friendly fiber hemp (see page 169) is also a popular alternative shoe material on the market. Hemp shoes are sturdy, durable, breathable, and can be waterproofed with a plant-based solvent. Vegan and hemp shoes can run the stylistic range from high fashion to business smart to street chic, and are available in a number of stores around the city.

A handful of more widely recognized companies are noted for their commitment to reducing the environmental impact of shoe production, but don't necessarily use hemp or vegan practices. Birkenstock shoes and sandals have been produced by the same family for centuries, and the factory in Germany uses a number of progressive environmental techniques throughout the production process. Advanced in-factory recycling practices, energy-efficient machinery, and many natural and salvaged materials are the norm at Birkenstock. All the cork found in Birkenstock footwear comes from oak trees in Spain and Portugal and is the ground-up by-product of the European bottling industry; many other ingredients in the shoes are similarly created or acquired. Another European company, Ecco, packages and ships its shoes in entirely recycled paper products. Even more impressive, each of their manufacturing plants is equipped with its own effluent treatment facility to ensure that no dioxins are released into the local environment. The Spanish company Camper is yet another European shoemaker with a proven commitment to the environment, as well as to its local Majorcan community and its workforce. Camper has made recent headlines with its sponsorship of an Amazonian rubber-manufacturing cooperative in Brazil, and with the release of a new line of shoes, Wabi, which are made of recycled materials. All of these companies are well represented in New York, and can be found in typical shoe retailers throughout the city.

Two Manhattan shops that deal exclusively in eco-friendly footwear are 99x in the East Village (212-460-8599) and MooShoes on the Lower East Side (212-254-6512; www.mooshoes.com). Some of the suggested clothing retailers listed in the appendix also carry footwear, and there are plenty of online resources for green shoes, which you can also check out in the appendix.

Unfortunately, vegan and hemp shoemakers have yet to tackle performance or athletic footwear. For your more active needs, some of the industry's top dogs are now trying sustainable shoes on for size. Despite a long-standing reputation as an environmental and social villain, Nike now seems to be making strides toward more sustainable production practices and is actually leading the charge among major shoe manufacturers with alternative green materials. In terms of high-tech eco-friendly innovations, Nike's ACG line of sneakers is perhaps the best example around of the positive green evolution of footwear. Sustainable materials and production practices employed by Nike and other progressively green shoe manufacturers include:

✳ **Reground soles:** Nike acquires recycled rubber from old athletic shoes through it's Reuse-A-Shoe program, which invites people to ship their old sneakers back to the Nike factory to be reground and reused in new sneakers.

✳ **Water-based, solvent-free adhesives:** Rather than chemical-based glues that pollute the environment during production, these water-based adhesives have little, if any, impact on local ecosystems.

✳ **PVC-free:** Nike and others are phasing PVC and its dangerous by-products out of their footwear.

✳ **Green rubber:** An independently certified green material, this reformulated rubber blend contains fewer toxins than regular rubber.

✳ **Waste-reducing design and assembly:** Smarter designs reduce the amounts of materials wasted during production, and what excess molding material remains is ground up and recycled into shoe linings.

✳ **Biodegradable soles:** It's not yet on the market, but Nike is developing a material for the soles of sneakers that would safely and harmlessly biodegrade in soil.

If you're concerned about sweatshop labor, the sneaker industry still has a way to go to appease concerned labor and human rights watchdogs. Nike and Reebok are both under close scrutiny and serious pressure from groups such as Co-op America (www.coopamerica.org) and Sweatshop Watch (www.sweatshopwatch.org). Legal battles are fought regularly, and promises are continuously made and broken by big shoe companies. I don't intend to decide for you whether Nike's new-found commitment to environmentally conscious production practices outweighs its questionable labor policies, and the formula for determining this for yourself is a dynamic and constantly changing one. For athletic and active footwear, the only company that seems to score high in both environmental and social commitment is Timberland (and even so, some of its shoes still contain PVC). So it's worthwhile to do a little research and get the most up-to-date info about the current state of shoe production. The Co-op America and Sweatshop Watch websites are a good place to start, and more resources are also provided in the appendix. Also, before taking the plunge and buying a new pair, reconsider those shoes already filling your closet or shoe rack. New York City is blessed with hundreds of shoe repair stores and cobblers, and for a small fraction of the cost of new footwear, these tradesmen and -women can work wonders in bringing new shiny life to old shoes.

## Natural Health and Beauty

Environmentalists and human health advocates alike have taken the cosmetic industry to task for its unabated dependence on toxic chemicals in personal care products. Without even mentioning the highly charged issue of the allegedly cruel practices of testing products on animals, the majority of health and beauty products on the market contain ingredients that have proven hazardous to human health. Most consumers would be surprised, even shocked, to hear that the government neither conducts nor requires safety testing of the chemicals that go into these products. With hundreds of such chemicals commonly used in cosmetics, it'd require an entire volume—one that would more closely resemble a chemistry text—to evaluate all of them. But it's still a good idea to take a quick look at some of the more commonly used ingredients that have been proven hazardous, especially when considering the fact that the average American adult uses nine personal care products a day. Here are some particularly troubling chemicals to look out for.

✳ **Coal tar:** Coal tar coloring is used in some shampoos, makeup, and hair dyes. It's also a known carcinogen that is only considered safe to use by the USDA when rinsed quickly from the body. You probably aren't likely to immediately rinse makeup from your face, and shampoo and hair coloring residues can often remain on the scalp even after rinsing.

✳ **Phthalates:** These industrial plasticizers are enormously controversial: They have repeatedly proven to have serious health implications but can be disguised on a label under the term "fragrance." Frequently used in deodorants, nail polishes, moisturizers, hair products, and other lotions, phthalates can have devastating effects on both female and male reproductive systems. To avoid phthalates it's best to choose products that are fragrance-free.

✳ **Formaldehyde:** You won't find this probably carcinogen and respiratory irritant on any labels, but you'll likely find some chemicals that release it in skin, body, and hair care products, as well as antiperspirants and nail polishes. DMDM hydantoin and urea are two common preservatives that release formaldehyde, and all can trigger heart palpitations, joint pain, headaches, chronic fatigue, and loss of sleep, as well as serving to weaken the immune system.

✳ **Lead acetate:** This heavy metal, renowned as a hormone disruptor, carcinogen, and toxin that targets the nervous system, is found in many hair dyes and makeup. Even trace amounts of lead acetate are dangerous; they remain in the body, accumulating for a lifetime. Researchers have found that residues can remain on the hair, forehead, and hands of hair dye users for days after application. Lead acetate is also particularly dangerous to babies and young children, whose developing brains can suffer.

☀ **Parabens:** Common in deodorants, skin care products, and make-up, alkyl hydroxyl parabens can mimic estrogen in the human body, and have been linked to the development of breast cancer in women. These cosmetic preservatives are very widely used, so it's best to look for paraben-free products.

☀ **DEA, MEA, TEA:** Die-, mono-, and triethanolamines are hormone-disrupting chemicals that often form cancer-causing nitrates and nitrosamines in the body. These chemicals are already restricted in Europe, but are commonly used to create "foam" in shampoos and shaving creams here in the United States.

☀ **Triclosan:** This synthetic antibacterial ingredient is actually registered as a pesticide—one with significant risks to human health and the environment—but is widely used in deodorants, toothpaste, and antibacterial cleansers. Its manufacturing process produces the dangerous chemical dioxin, a powerful hormone dis-ruptor also released in leather-tanning processes described earlier. For the user, triclosan increases the development of resistant bac-teria, making your body more susceptible to serious infection.

☀ **Sodium lauryl sulfate:** Another detergent used in foaming prod-ucts, SLS can separate skin layers, damage the immune system, and dissolve proteins in the eyes. In certain combinations SLS is transformed to nitrosamines, and it resiliently can stay in the body for five days, coursing into the heart, liver, lungs, and brain.

☀ **Glycols:** Polyethylene (PEG), propylene (PG), and butylene glycols are all petroleum-based chemicals that quickly penetrate the skin and can weaken protein and cellular structure. PG is so toxic that the EPA warns against any skin contact and requires workers to wear protective clothing when disposing any PG solutions. Unfortunately, there's no warning on the deodorant stick that has a higher concentration of the chemical than most industrial applications.

✳ **Toluene:** Toluene is a type of volatile organic compound (or VOC, which were already warned against in chapter 6, "The Green Clean") that can pollute indoor air when released by using a product that contains it. High levels of toluene exposure have been found to put pregnant women at risk of giving birth to babies with neurological and developmental problems. While chronic low levels of exposure—such as you would get from the perfumes, nail polish removers, and aerosol products that contain VOC—haven't been studied, it can hardly be considered worth the risk of being an experimental guinea pig when there are fine alternatives.

Besides keeping your eye out for these troublesome ingredients in your personal care products, here are a handful of basic tips for finding a greener, more natural alternative to healthy and beauty.

✳ First, visit the Environmental Working Group website (www.ewg.org/reports/skindeep). Use its searchable product guide and "Custom Report" feature for suggestions on products that have fewer potential health risks and those to avoid.

✳ Use fewer products. Decide what products are most important to you, and which you could probably live without. Reducing the number of chemicals coming into contact with your skin every day obviously reduces the health risks associated with them.

✳ Be careful with labels. While the FDA has tried to better regulate use of the terms *natural* and *hypoallergenic,* federal courts have yet to approve this sensible action. Thus, these labels essentially carry no guarantee. More reliable are *fragrance-free, paraben-free,* and *cruelty-free.*

✳  That said, look past the claims on the labels and into the ingredient list. Natural oils and herbs tend to be safer and more environmentally sound than chemicals. Organic oils and plant bases are best.

✳  Avoid the unknown. The more details are provided on the package about a product's ingredients, the more trustworthy the company tends to be.

Here in New York good green cosmetic products are generally found in the same local natural food grocers mentioned in chapter 8. Some reliable brands that can be found in stores right here in the city are listed (with websites for mail order, if that's your preference) in the appendix. In the appendix you can also find a handful of health and beauty salons and spas that employ only natural ingredients and toxic-free treatments.

## Mixed Greens: Made in New York City

Beyond the more obvious green goods—recycled glassware, cloth napkins, canvas shopping sacks, rechargeable batteries, and so on—there are a bundle of other eco-friendly products that could spruce up your home or make a great gift. A number of eco-friendly stores and retail outlets have opened up around New York City, carrying various home and lifestyle goods, and a more complete listing of these can be found in the appendix. Here, though, are a few companies that share a progressive vision of environmentally sensitive design and production, while bringing to market some very cool and stylish products.

### ECO-WRAP, STATIONERY, AND CARDS

Why use freshly manufactured paper to wrap gifts or send cards when you can use some salvaged stock that's recognizable, promotes alternative transportation, and is sure to draw a laugh and a bevy of questions? New York City–based Forest Saver Designs (www.forestsaver.com) has taken the initiative to rescue the thousands of MTA subway maps that regularly go out of date, turning them into a bunch of paper products including "MAPelopes," "Map Stationery," and "MapWrap"—perfect for wrapping up holiday or birthday gifts for that person on your list with a love of mass transit, waste prevention, and eccentric design! Similarly—although it's not based here in New York—New England Cartographics (www.necartographics.com) figured it was ridiculous to throw out its stock of obsolete and surplus USGS topographic maps, so the firm has started turning them into stationery and envelopes, or "Geolopes."

## GOOD GREEN WOOD

You don't have to look far to find the convergence of high design and ecological sensibility in the world of furniture. Two young companies in Brooklyn are turning an ethic of sustainability into a smart, chic, urban style for the home. Bart Bettencourt has forsaken hardwoods in his sleekly designed furniture. Instead, the clean lines and simple geometric proportions that define Bettencourt Woodworking's tables and chairs are accomplished with bamboo—a regenerating, sustainable raw material that grows from the base up, and is thus not killed when harvested. Bamboo is also one of the fastest-growing plants in the world; a plant can grow to harvest in less than a year. On top of the bamboo line of furniture, Bettencourt recently collaborated with nearby Brooklyn designers Carlos Salgado and Colleen Rae Smiley to reduce woodshop waste. Reshaping and conjoining scraps of wood collected from their own and others' woodshops, the Scrapile line was created. Pictures of both bamboo and Scrapile furniture can be found on Bettencourt Woodworking's website (www.bettencourtwood.com) and can be purchased at The Future Perfect in Williamsburg (718-599-6278) or IIKH in Chelsea (212-675-9400).

## GREEN GARMENT DISTRICT

Another Brooklynite, Sara Cross, has turned some heads in the fashion industry with her line of organic cotton, alpaca wool, and hemp clothes, coolnotcruel. Fashion-conscious and urban chic for the socially and environmentally responsible consumer, coolnotcruel's products contain zero traces of pesticides or sweatshops. All alpaca wool products are handmade in Bolivia by a group of indigenous Aymara women, who are well compensated and work in a respectful, healthy, and safe workshop. All organic cotton and hemp products are made right here in New York City in a garment district production studio owned by Chinese immigrant women and run with a familial and friendly atmosphere fitting the "skilled artisans who take pride in the high quality of their work." The company's website (www.coolnotcruel.com) is well equipped with pictures of the various garments available, modeled by nonprofessionals—or "realmodels"—as well as details about the materials used and production venues.

## CHAPTER FOURTEEN

# Recreation and Delight

The measure of any great civilization is its cities and a measure of a city's greatness is to be found in the quality of its public spaces, its parks and squares.—**JOHN RUSKIN**

New York City is the proud home of the most extensive urban park system in the country. This is all the more impressive when considering that the five boroughs cover a relatively small area of land compared with many modern American cities, particularly those newer towns in the South and West whose borders were drawn after the advent of the automobile. It's safe to say that New York would be a far less tolerable place without its hundreds of parks and its location among the rivers emptying into New York Harbor and Long Island Sound. These open spaces and coastlines provide the necessary balance to the vast expanses of concrete streets, tall buildings, growling automobiles, and often claustrophobic ambience they combine to generate. These areas also help balance the city's ecology while aiding the collective physical *and* emotional health of the population. And to any New Yorker with an appreciation for the outdoors, the city's park and waterfronts also provide places to play—the best venues for the greenest recreation.

These parks and waterfronts, however, shouldn't be taken for granted. The city's open-space infrastructure is the result of centuries of hard work, planning, and advocacy, and today there are hundreds of organizations—from ultralocal neighborhood advocates to citywide planners—beyond the municipal government that work tirelessly for the constant expansion and improvement of open space. The waterfront, too, is subject to an ongoing battle, with parks and human-use advocates constantly coming head-to-head with industrialists for use of the valuable space. It is an interesting and important story to see how New York City's parks and waterfront have arrived at where they are today, and to look at and applaud the parties that helped (and continue to help) get them there.

## New York City's Parks: A Brief History

In 1733 the first official park in New York City, which was Bowling Green in Lower Manhattan, was designated and ordained "for the Beauty and Ornament of the Said Street as well as for the Recreation and Delight of the Inhabitants of this City." These words still ring true, and created the philosophical foundation for the importance of parks in what would become one of the world's largest and most cosmopolitan metropolises. The conditions of Bowling Green's designation also predicted future trends in the evolution of city parks.

In all, New York City hosts 28,000 acres of parkland and a remarkable 578 total miles of waterfront—and, as is obvious to anyone venturing out to either on a nice summer day, a great many New Yorkers take full advantage of this space.

The land, after being established by a resolution of the Common Council of New York City as a public park, was leased at an annual rate of one peppercorn to three private investors, forming the theoretical model for the public–private partnerships that currently help enhance and maintain New York City parks.

And what a long way they've come! Soon after Bowling Green was established, the Battery at the southern prow of Manhattan was ordered to be kept clear of any "manner of Houses and Edifices whatever." Thus began a trend that continued through the turn of the nineteenth century. Small parcels of open space were kept clear of development throughout the Lower Manhattan area, and places such as Washington Square Park and City Hall Park were the result. Throughout the early 1800s, though, as the city's population swelled significantly, open space couldn't seem to keep up with the city's density. In 1811 a mere 470 acres of public land were planned for all of Manhattan, the space committed to small squares, markets, and parade grounds, a handful of which remain in the form of Union Square, Madison Square Park, and Tompkins Square Park. Meanwhile, the incorporated townships that now represent the outer boroughs, free of the extreme density issues that plagued Manhattan, drew up more progressive plans for the generation of open public space. Large landscaped "pleasure grounds" were thought to be important to the livelihood of the community, and famous advocates such as Walt Whitman of Brooklyn successfully pitched for a greater number of open spaces. Greenwood Cemetery and Washington Park in Brooklyn and Port Richmond (now Veterans) Park in Staten Island were born of this era.

The 1850s were a watershed decade in the history of New York's parkland. With increasing pressure from an increasingly cramped public, proponents, including William Cullen Bryant, editor of the *New York Evening Post,* led the charge for a large central park to help alleviate crowded conditions—Manhattan's population had exploded from 97,000 in 1811 to more than 500,000 in 1850. By 1858 the design of Frederick Law Olmsted and Calvert Vaux was chosen from a field of thirty-three competing entries for a truly impressive Central Park. By the time of its ultimate completion in 1871, the now revered team of Olmsted and Vaux was busy planning other spaces the city over, most notably Prospect Park in Brooklyn, which served the same function in that city—which had grown from 48,000 citizens in 1840 to 280,000 in 1859—that their previous project had for New York proper. The late 1800s saw a similar trend of massive park and open-space expansion, with the city purchasing nearly 3,500 acres from private landholders in the newly annexed Bronx—including what is now Pelham Bay, Crotona, and Van Cortlandt Parks—and Brooklyn seeing its parkland double in acreage. By the time Brooklyn, Queens, and Staten Island were incorporated to the city of New York in 1898, the newly unified five boroughs contained a total of 6,800 acres of public parkland. That year also saw the first modern example of a true public–private partnership: The privately funded "Outdoor Recreation League" subsidized slides, seesaws, and chaperones for the playgrounds that were increasing in popularity and prevalence around the city's public spaces.

The first half of the twentieth century is perhaps best defined by two major developments: the 1934 consolidation of the five independently governed borough park commissions, and the appointment of Robert Moses as commissioner of the newly unified Parks Department. Moses' legacy on the city's landscape is certainly a controversial one, and one lucidly described in Robert Caro's book *The Power Broker.* His position as head of the Parks Department for decades overlapped his spot atop a number of other city bureaucracies, including the Triborough Bridge Authority and various public works and transportation agencies. Moses, as was common at this time in American history, was a great friend of the automobile, and many of his plans for public space favored transportation's right-of-way over parkland. Many automotive parkways—usually wide, tree-lined avenues—were constructed under the Parks Department's jurisdiction (and budget), but it'd be unfair to label Moses as someone with complete disregard of open space for public use. Indeed, he helped usher the 1939 World's Fair into New York City, and the prominent expanse of Flushing Meadows in Queens was the fortunate result. Taking full advantage of Franklin Roosevelt's commitment to public works with the New Deal, Moses also opened up dozens of public pools, playgrounds, golf courses, and recreation centers, facilities that to this day provide exceptional physical options to New Yorkers. Starting with Jones Beach in 1929, Moses also helped give the shore to the city—sandy beaches were opened in all of the outer boroughs. While naysayers complain that he did little to bolster waterfront development on the rivers and favored roads over parks, telling statistics do indicate what a significant and ultimately positive impact Moses had on public open space throughout New York City. By the time he retired as parks commissioner in 1960, the entirety of the parks system had grown from 14,000 acres to 34,673 under his governance.

## tip

Hundreds of organizations representing tens of thousands of New Yorkers have formed public–private partnerships with the Parks Department, raising hundreds of millions of dollars in private investment and providing active support through volunteerism, event organization, and assorted assistance.

Since Moses' retirement, the evolution of the city's parks and waterfront has largely mimicked the municipal economy. In the 1960s the Parks Department focused much energy on the development of "vest pocket parks," acquiring and revitalizing small abandoned lots to bring some green community space to local neighborhoods. Then, with the severe budget crisis of the 1970s, public investment in parks took a serious blow. Capital projects were repeatedly put on hold or canceled altogether and many jobs were cut throughout the system, including basic maintenance positions. Parks throughout the city deteriorated; they became increasingly dirty and dangerous and very nearly fell out of the public consciousness.

Fortunately, with an economic upturn toward the end of the decade that continued through the 1980s, and ambitious new commissioner Henry Stern taking office in 1983, the Parks Department began to restore public land around the city to its former glory. Stern implemented a city "greening" policy, which invested heavily in the enhancement and expansion of open green spaces around the city and was dedicated to the planting of trees in parks, in plazas, and along public streets and walkways. The year 1984 saw the introduction of progressive and proactive ideas and programs into the Parks Department. The Natural Resource Group was formed to preserve and protect the 7,000 acres of undeveloped natural forests and wetlands within parkland, and the Neighborhood Park Restoration Program committed hundreds of parks workers to the highly trafficked neighborhood parks for routine maintenance in order to prevent the costly capital project resurrections that would be necessary after long periods of heavy use and neglect. Stern's administration also helped nurture the return of true public–private partnerships in parks. The Adopt-A-Monument program allowed private investment for the conservation and maintenance of various sculptures, fountains, and memorials throughout the parks system. The Central Park Conservancy (CPC), first formed in 1980, took full control over the management of Central Park through a contract with the Parks Department, and has since raised more than $300 million to help transform the revered space into a model for urban parks

> **tip**
>
> The Natural Resources Group manages more than 10,000 acres of true natural land in the form of forests, woodlands, wetlands, and salt marshes. With its team of biologists, natural resource managers, mapping scientists, and restoration ecologists, the NRG is involved in restoration, protection policy, and acquisition of more lands.

worldwide. In 1987 the Prospect Park Alliance was formed following the example of the CPC; its success has been comparable. Employing a similar idea on a wider scale, Commissioner Stern in 1989 created the City Parks Foundation, a not-for-profit organization that raises private money to support programs and renovations throughout all of the city's parks and playgrounds. Meanwhile, in keeping with his greening policy, Stern introduced GreenStreets in 1986, which to this day converts paved properties within or adjacent to streets into green spaces filled with plants, trees, and flowers.

In the 1990s capital projects, renovations, and new park developments boomed. With increased revenue from various programs around city parks and a healthier municipal budget, the late 1990s saw the addition of many playing fields around the city, giving thousands of New Yorkers better places to meet for sports and recreation. At the same time, major capital enhancements took place in some of the cities most renowned and frequented park spaces, including Prospect Park's Ravine, Blue Heron Park in Staten Island, and Van Cortlandt Park.

The turn of the millennium seems to have brought with it a renewed commitment throughout the Parks Department to the city's abundant waterfront. Starting in 1999 with the monumental restoration of the Bronx River—including the hoisting of twenty abandoned vehicles from the river's depths—the waterfront's potential as a place for public retreat and recreation seems to be at the forefront of Parks Department policy. Mayor Bloomberg and newly appointed parks commis-

tip

Throughout the year the Parks Department sponsors hundreds of events, all outdoors and open to the public, ranging from highly celebrated concerts in Central Park to beach volleyball tournaments, a Winter Festival, and pumpkin carving before Halloween.

sioner Adrian Benepe partnered with the state government to contribute the city's share to the massive Hudson River Valley Greenway that will someday stretch more than 150 miles from Battery Park to Waterford in Saratoga County. To this end, the team worked diligently to bring about the fast revitalization of Manhattan's West Side, connecting a handful of small public spaces below Riverside Park in the massive and publicly adored new Hudson River Park. The Brooklyn and Queens waterfronts are still works in progress, but it certainly seems that Benepe and Bloomberg are fully committed to reclaiming the shorelines from long-standing neglect and making them accessible to the public.

## Parks and Waterfront Today

Herewith, a handful of interesting statistics and facts about the city's public spaces today:

* More than 1,700 parks, covering over 28,000 acres, are under the Parks Department's governance. This space accounts for about 14 percent of New York City's total area.

* A total of 14 miles of beaches are open to the public and staffed by city lifeguards in all five boroughs.

* More than 2,000 GreenStreets now adorn the city's concrete throughways.

* Hundreds of Urban Park Rangers are employed by the city to interact with and educate the public, as well as protect the valuable public lands.

* Environmental, educational, and recreational programs are abundant throughout the parks system, from wildlife seminars to ice-skating lessons to horticultural training.

* Public outdoor athletic facilities in city parks include baseball and softball fields, basketball courts, pools, cycling tracks, bocce courts, cricket fields, football fields, golf courses, handball courts,

ice- and roller-skating rinks, running tracks, skate parks, soccer fields, tennis courts, and volleyball courts.

✳ Other facilities include thirty-one dog runs; two zoos, three wildlife centers, and an aquarium; eighty-four playgrounds; barbecuing facilities in twenty-eight different areas; twenty-six rec centers; and twenty-two preserved historical houses on parkland.

✳ The state of New York runs six state parks within city limits, in addition to its involvement with Hudson River Park. These are Riverbank, Clay Pit Ponds Preserve, Empire-Fulton Ferry, Valley Stream, Roberto Clemente, and Bayswater Point State Parks.

✳ Additionally, the National Park Service oversees more than 26,000 acres in New York City and on the neighboring New Jersey shoreline that together make up the Gateway National Recreation Area. This area includes beaches and wildlife refuges in Staten Island, Brooklyn, and Queens.

## Twenty-five Exceptional Green Activities

Beyond the many dog runs, playgrounds, barbecue spots, utility fields, and volleyball, tennis, and handball courts, there remain a number of treats for the New Yorker seeking an activity a little out of the ordinary. Here are twenty-five ways to take full advantage of the city's outdoor offerings. When available, some contact information has been provided. Get out there and enjoy!

1. **Ride around Manhattan** on the 32-mile-long Manhattan Waterfront Greenway bikepath that forms a complete loop around the perimeter of the island. Along the way you'll ride through a stunning variety of neighborhood cultures and unique urban waterfront environments. The path occasionally jaunts in from the riverside, and about 15 percent of the route requires road riding. But by following the green circular signs, you'll find plenty of

adventure and see all that the Manhattan waterfront has to offer. For maps and a virtual ride, check out the greenway section of the website maintained by the Department of City Planning at www.nyc.gov/html/mwg/mwghome.html.

2. **Toss bocce or 'shoes:** First played in Egypt around 5000 BC and brought to New York City in the 1800s by the city's Italian immigrants, the relaxed game of bocce can turn any afternoon into one of intense competition or frivolous fun. Likewise, a couple of stakes and four horseshoes can bring any barbecue to the next level. Claim some lawn space at any of the city's grassier parks, or find one of the Parks Department's forty official bocce courts throughout all five boroughs or horseshoe pits at Seward, Central, and Washington Square Parks.

3. **Cast away** into the East River, the Hudson River, or New York Harbor. Grab a fishing pole and reel for stripers at prime casting spots including the East River Promenades on the Upper East Side and below 21st Street, the West Side's Pier 25, and Historic Battery Park. Particularly abundant are the striped bass under the Verrazano Bridge, where thirty- to forty-pounders aren't unheard of.

4. **Pound the pavement** with the New York Road Runners. Sponsoring races practically every weekend of the milder months (and some in the colder ones!), NYRR gives anyone the opportunity to compete, or just to scamper off any lingering stress from the workweek. From friendly jaunts to heated competitions, everyone has something to run for. If you're feeling particularly ambitious, start training for the New York City Marathon. If you enter nine NYRR races, you earn a highly coveted marathon entry, which many runners slighted by the lottery in the past consider well worth the basic $35 membership fee.
*New York Road Runners: www.nyrr.org or (212) 860–4455.*

5. **Rollerblade en masse** with any number of organized in-line skating events. Every Wednesday from April to October, a wild band of Rollerbladers convenes at Union Square at 8:00 PM to take blades to the street in the largest weekly group street skate in the city. All are welcome so long as you're equipped with a helmet and wristguards and are comfortable skating in the street. The skate is free and open to anyone who wants to join in. Or join the Parks Department–sanctioned "Rock 'n' Rollerblade" disco jams on summer nights in various parks around town. Blades, music, and a disco ball are all provided for free!
   *Wednesday Night Skate: www.weskateny.org.*
   *Rock 'n' Rollerblade: www.nycgovparks.org or call 311.*

6. **Serve up Ping-Pong** at the free outdoor tables on Pier 25 in Hudson River Park. Slapping paddles on the waterfront offers the closest simulation to a cruise ship atmosphere that you'll find in the five boroughs (except, perhaps, the Maritime Hotel's lobby). Paddles and balls are supplied for free at the snack shack. Just make sure to adjust your serve for the wind.
   *Pier 25: www.hudsonriverpark.org or (212) 627–2020.*

7. **Cut the concrete** and dance the summer night away at an out-door dance event. Learn to swing, tango, or salsa dance at Pier 25's Moondance every Sunday night through July and August. Or head to the Lincoln Center for Midsummer Night Swing in June and July.
   *Pier 25: www.hudsonriverpark.org or (212) 627–2020.*
   *Midsummer Night Swing: www.lincolncenter.org/programs or (212) 875–5456.*

8. **Play roller hockey** in a pickup game at Central Park or practi-cally any other city park with an expanse of pavement. Official roller hockey rinks are located in the Bronx at Mullaly Park; Manhattan at Riverside Skate Park, Martin T. Tanahey Playground,

and Stanley Isaacs Park; and Queens at American Park, Baywater Park, Beach 109th Street Playground, Dutch Kills Park, George U. Harvey Park, and Mafera Park.

9. **Skate or die** at one of the Parks Department–run skate parks—Millennium Skate Park in Bay Ridge, Brooklyn; Riverside Skate Park on Manhattan's West Side; Mullaly Skate Park in the Bronx; or Forest Park and Rockaway Skate Parks in Queens. All allow skateboards, in-line skates, and bikes; be sure to bring your helmet and be ready to sign a waiver.

10. **Ski Central Park** or any sizable city park when the temperature drops and the snow falls. It's the best workout around, and the best way to keep warm in the blustery months. Cross-country skis can be rented at many of the city's sporting goods stores (check your phone book), but you should act fast—the snow doesn't stick for long.

11. **Fly through the air** with the greatest of ease at the Trapeze School in Hudson River Park in Tribeca. Take a two-hour lesson and swing 25 feet above the pavement. Don't worry, there are safety nets.
*New York Trapeze School: www.newyork.trapezeschool.com or (917) 797-1872.*

12. **Surf's up** at Rockaway. Take the A train to Far Rockaway for some of the most underappreciated swells on the East Coast.
*Rockaway Beach Surf Shop: (718) 474-9345.*

13. **Canoe the Gowanus,** Brooklyn's own little canal of adventure. Join the Gowanus Dredgers Canoe Club, which supplies canoes and life jackets for exploring this interesting stretch of water with its industrialized shoreline, unique bridges, and reborn estuary. If you have your own canoe, kayak, or rowboat, find a launch point and go it alone.
*Gowanus Dredgers: www.gowanuscanal.org or (718) 243-0949.*

14. **Rock climb** in Central Park. Unbeknownst to many, Central Park actually offers a nice assortment of bouldering and climbing routes. Join the online forum with Climb NYC to learn more about these and other climbing possibilities around the city and region. *Climb NYC: www.climbnyc.org.*

15. **Kayak the Hudson** from Pier 26 and Pier 64 with the free programs offered by the NYC Downtown Boathouse. Walk-up solo kayaking is allowed in protected embayments on the Hudson, and from Pier 26, three-hour river and harbor tours are available at no cost. *NYC Downtown Boathouse: www.downtownboathouse.org or (646) 613–0740.*

16. **Hit the beach:** Believe it or not, New York City offers some fine sandy beaches, so grab your sunscreen, boogieboard, and trashy paperback and head to one of the city's best tourist-free summer attractions. In Queens hit up Rockaway or Jacob Riis Beach; Brooklyn's coast boasts Brighton Beach (and the famous Coney Island Boardwalk) and Manhattan Beach. The best-kept secret in the Bronx is possibly Orchard Beach on the Long Island Sound in Pelham Bay Park. Staten Island is home to three sandy seasides: South and Midland Beaches on Lower New York Bay and Wolfe's Pond Beach on Raritan Bay.

17. **Manhattan, tip-to-toe:** Stroll down Broadway for all 13 or so miles from the Broadway Bridge down to the Battery. Take the A train to 225th Street, find Broadway, and head south. Wear a comfortable pair of shoes, because the walk is as long as it is rewarding. You'll stroll through dozens of distinct neighborhoods and unique parts of Manhattan—from historic Uptown enclaves to Times Square to Downtown's fascinating mix of modern business and antique architecture. If your legs triumph, reward yourself at the Battery with a seat on the lovely promenade benches among vibrant perennial gardens and an amazing view of New York Harbor and Lady Liberty.

18. **Saddle up** and enjoy New York's finest parks from the back of a horse. Horses can be rented by the hour, and lessons are available at Pelham Bay, Van Cortlandt Park, Prospect Park, Central Park, Forest Park, and on a wide variety of trails on Staten Island. *http://nycgovparks.org/sub_things_to_do/facilities/at_horse back_riding.html.*

19. **Take in the wildlife**—and that doesn't mean the East Village nightclub scene. You can scope out herons, egrets, and all sorts of other wildlife at the city's nature centers, including Pelham Bay, Crotona, Van Cortlandt, and Orchard Beach in the Bronx; Brooklyn's own Salt Marsh in Marine Park; Inwood Hill, Belvedere Castle, and Abbey Pond in Manhattan; and Blue Heron Park and Preserve in Staten Island. A particularly prime location for birding is the Clay Pit Ponds State Park Preserve, which offers 260 acres of wetlands and woodlands on Staten Island. Find a full listing of nature centers and wildlife preserves in the appendix.
*Parks Department nature centers: www.nycgovparks.org or call 311. Clay Pit Ponds State Park Preserve: www.nysparks.state.ny.us or call (718) 967–1976.*

20. **Or the plant life:** The Conservatory Garden in the northeastern corner of Central Park is a hidden six-acre escape right in Manhattan. Fountains spray among fruit trees and lush vegetation as you stroll on paths carving through nicely manicured hedges. Or make your way up to the New York Botanical Garden and its lavish 250-acre spread. Be sure to check out the Enid A. Haupt Conservatory where eleven unique plant habitats make up A World of Plants, letting you visit tropical rain forests, a cactus-filled desert, and a northern New England forest in full fall foliage. Or find botanical gardens in every borough in the appendix.
*Conservatory Garden: www.centralparknyc.org or (212) 310–6600. New York Botanical Garden: www.nybg.org or (718) 817–8700.*

21. **Tee off** in any of the city's eleven golf courses, all run by the Parks Department. Unbelievable as it may seem, somehow there's space enough in this town for some legitimate golf courses. Tee times can be reserved online or by calling the courses directly, and the fees are remarkably reasonable—starting at around $12 for nine holes.

    *Parks golf courses: www.nyc.e-golf.net.*

22. **Historic house tours:** Architecture and history buffs will love the opportunity to peek into New York City's past through the twenty-two historic house museums located on city parkland. What's more, they are found in some of the city's least public retreats amid wild forest settings. The houses are cared for by the Historic House Trust of New York City, which offers tours and even rentals for weddings and other special events.

    *Historic House Trust: www.historichousetrust.org or call (212) 360-8282.*

23. **Swim the Hudson:** Thanks to increased attention to the health of regional watersheds and the advocacy of groups such as the Riverkeepers, the Hudson River is now safe for swimming! The Manhattan Island Foundation organizes river swimming events and free clinics all around the city.

    *Manhattan Island Foundation: www.swimnyc.org or call (888) NYC-SWIM, (888) 692-7946.*

24. **Walk a bridge:** The beauty of this activity is its simplicity. For many Brooklyn residents who commute onto the island, the East River bridges are just a part of life, but for others, setting across one on foot awards the postcard-picture of Manhattan's downtown skyline, the emblematic perspective of the New York City that so many who live here forget to appreciate while caught up in the frenetic life. For the quintessential "New York moment," take to John Roebling's masterfully designed and much-revered Brooklyn Bridge

in the late afternoon and walk back toward Manhattan as the sun sets behind the city.

25. **Take me out** to the ball game. Of course, everyone knows about the Yankees and the Mets, but if you've grown tired of watching multimillionaires parading around the diamond in front of tens of thousands of fans, maybe you should check out one of New York City's two minor league ball clubs. Filling a void that opened in 1957 when the Dodgers departed town for sunnier climes, the summer of 2001 saw baseball return to Brooklyn. The Brooklyn Cyclones joined the Staten Island Yankees—the "Baby Bombers"— as New York City's proud representatives in the Class A New York Penn League. The Cyclones, affiliated with the Mets, play out on Coney Island, so leave yourself some time before or after the game to hit the boardwalk, take in the utterly unique scene, and brave a ride on the team's namesake roller coaster.
*Brooklyn Cyclones: www.brooklyncyclones.com or call (718) 449-8497; Staten Island Yankees: www.siyanks.com or (718) 720-9265.*

## CHAPTER FIFTEEN

# Green Goings-On

I have seen that in any great undertaking
it is not enough for a man to depend simply upon
himself.—**LONE MAN, Teton Sioux**

Y ou're not the only one taking steps toward a more environmentally conscious life. All around the city tens of thousands of New Yorkers shop the Greenmarkets, switch to
solar energy, forsake conventional cotton, or make any of a number of
other green choices. It is with this strength in numbers that an environmental consciousness can take firm hold in a city whose colossal built
environment has squeezed out the natural world, leaving it for those
who will make an effort to seek it out. The number of people willing to
embrace a greener life is growing, and so is the strength of the movement. The clear consequence is that organizations are being formed,
and citizens are banding together in their professions, in their recreation, and in their activism—with occasional and fortunate overlapping.

Organizations gather and create events, formulating schedules of
various happenings to further propagate the idea of a more sustainable

New York City. Many of these organizations have already been featured through the course of this book, and their accomplishments heralded. Still, there remain a bunch that haven't necessarily fit snugly into any of the categories discussed. This section will introduce a number of them, particularly those responsible for bringing events and activities to the Big Green Apple. Because so many will undoubtedly escape mention here, be sure to take full advantage of the appendix, which contains brief profiles of those organizations doing good and acting green for the benefit of New York City and for the greater ecological good.

The Big Apple plays host to a whole slew of events of deep interest to green New Yorkers. Concerts, conferences, conventions, group rides, festivals, speeches . . . . The sheer volume of events and activities in this town can make identifying those you might actually be interested in overwhelming. If you're at all like me, and you consistently lag a week or two behind in getting to the *Village Voice*, *New Yorker*, and your *Time Out* listings, then it's easy for interesting and fun events to pass you by before they even register on your radar. Unfortunately, many events with an environmental tilt don't get a great amount of publicity, and to find out about them, you really have to know where to look. Here's a collection of organizations that regularly schedule greener events. After these listings you'll find the "Green Events Calendar," made up of some larger-scale happenings that dependably go down on an annual basis.

### GREENHOMENYC

This community-oriented nonprofit organization promotes environmentally sustainable urban building practices. With a stated mission to "facilitate the adoption of sustainable building methods and materials by owners of small residential and commercial buildings in New York City," GreenHomeNYC organizes a monthly forum as well as a number of other events related to green building, sustainable development, and the urban environment, including an annual Green Building Open House tour. The free monthly forums run the third Wednesday of every month at 6:30 PM; past topics have included "Learning from Green

Universities," "Financing Green Buildings," and "Sustainable Wood and Wood Alternatives." Other sponsored events have included a talk with Nobel Peace Prize laureate and founder of the Green Belt movement Wangari Maathai, design conferences, and even practical workshops such as the three-day "Photovoltaic Installation Training Workshop." Visit the group's website (www.greenhomenyc.org) and check the events section to see what's planned.

## O2 NYC

o2 is a group of design professionals dedicated to fostering environmental sustainability through design. Meeting once a month in a variety of different studio and outdoor urban spaces, o2 NYC offers a good networking and learning opportunity for those in the design field. It also organizes the occasional conference or charette, all of which can be found on its website (http://o2nyc.org/).

## EARTH PLEDGE

You may remember the Earth Pledge Foundation from its Green Roofs Initiative, discussed earlier. It also organizes and runs seminars, conferences, lectures, and other events relating to its three initiatives—green roofs, organic waste as fuel, and Farm To Table agriculture. Current events can be found on its website (www.earthpledge.org)—and be sure to check out its weekend-long Verdopolis conference on the "Green Events Calendar."

## COMMUNITY ENVIRONMENTAL CENTER

The same not-for-profit organization that brought Solar 1—New York City's first stand-alone, solar-powered building, discussed in detail in chapter 1— uses that same space for a number of artistic and ecologically focused events including nature walks, readings from environmental writers and poets, concerts, and dance performances. A current schedule of events can be found alongside plenty of other information about the CEC's various programs on its website (www.cecenter.org/scschedule.php).

## RECYCLE THIS NYC

This not-for-profit group committed to sustainable waste management assembles monthly meetings to discuss the state of recycling in New York City, and also organizes events such as film screenings and discussions to educate New Yorkers on the importance of proper waste management. Recycle This NYC frequently organizes Recycling Collection Days to give New Yorkers a place to bring electronics and other waste that won't be recycled by the city DOS. A calendar can be found on the organization's official website (www.recyclethisnyc.org).

## EARTH INSTITUTE AT COLUMBIA UNIVERSITY

This academic institution consolidates expertise from throughout the university in order to address the complex issues facing the planet and its inhabitants, with particular focus on sustainable development and the needs of the world's poor. Aside from the multitude of research and academic projects facilitated by the Earth Institute, it also puts on frequent events—mostly seminars, lectures, workshops, and readings—for the community at large. With programs looking at third-world development issues and a locally focused New York City Sustainable Development Initiative, you're sure to find interesting events dealing with both local environmental problems and the global good. These events can all be found on the institute's website (www.earthinstitute.columbia.edu).

## AUDUBON

The world-famous advocate and protector of natural wildlife habitats is also committed to educating and informing the general public about environmental issues. For more than a quarter century now, the New York City Audubon chapter has brought city residents on nature walks and field trips; it also organizes exhibitions and events throughout the city that deal with local environmental and wildlife issues. Its calendar is available online (www.nycaudubon.org).

## THE WATERWIRE

The Metropolitan Waterfront Alliance not only is the leading advocate for sensible development of the New York City area's waterfront, but also helps program events and exhibitions that connect the public with this great natural resource. On its website (www.waterwire.net), you can find a calendar of such happenings, which just may include a Winter Waterfowl Walk on Staten Island or a gallery photo exhibition called "Changing Tides: The Landscape of the East River." The MWA also helps coordinate more "skilled" scientific seminars and even mobilizes citizens to assemble at important public legislative and policy meetings.

## EARTH DAY NEW YORK

"Every day is Earth Day" goes the maxim. And it is true that even New York City's own Earth Day–centric event organizer maintains events year-round. While you can read more about true Earth Day happenings on the "Green Events Calendar," the official website of Earth Day New York has a great events page (www.earthdayny.org/events) where you can find cool green events all year.

## CITY PARKS

The amount of organized activity going on regularly throughout the city's parks is astounding, and there are similarly diverse ways to find out about it all. A good place to start is the Parks Department's official website (www.nycgovparks.org), which includes a list right on the main page of events taking place within the next couple of weeks, and has a link to the entire calendar of events planned throughout the city parks. The Partnerships for Parks website (www.partnershipforparks.org) keeps listings of upcoming volunteer events, many of which are plantings and shoreline restoration projects that a lot of participants consider to be social events in their own right. It also lists some conferences of various environmental and park-related issued that aren't featured on the Parks Department's more activity-focused listings.

And what better place to look for events around the city's parks than the organization whose mission it is to create free arts, education, and sports programs there? The City Park Foundation program annually hosts thousands of events and activities of an artistic, educational, or athletic nature, from puppet shows in small neighborhood parks to headline events at the Central Park Summerstage; from corporate tennis leagues to free after-school track-and-field coaching; from an educational City Safari for students to a Greening Your Lessons institute for teachers. The website (www.cityparksfoundation.org) is also armed with an "Event Finder" that lets you search by event type, date, zip code, or even park name, so you can track down practically any activity you might be looking for.

Yet another effective parks advocacy group is New Yorkers for Parks, which also has event listings—including naturalist walks, outdoor yoga in city parks, and talks—on its website (www.ny4p.org/projects/calendar .php).

### "WILDMAN" STEVE BRILL

New York City's best-known naturalist brings groups on foraging tours in some of the city's larger parks. With a focus on wild food and ecology, Brill's famous tours introduce all participants to edible and medicinal plants and mushrooms that grow right here in the city. The Wildman offers tours in the five boroughs once or twice a week from May through November, and a full schedule can be found on his website (www.wild-manstevebrill.com/).

### TIME'S UP!

TIME'S UP! is a grassroots, direct-action environmental group that works hard to educate the public on the environmental impacts of everyday decisions such as food and transportation. Campaigns include Auto-Free Streets and Parks and Greenways Today, and to these ends the group organizes public demonstrations and educational seminars. To get yourself involved in a demonstration, a seminar, or just to join others for a nice group bike ride, TIME'S UP! has a full calendar on its website (www.times-up.org).

### TRANSPORTATION ALTERNATIVES

On top of tireless campaigning, advocacy, dissemination of information, and the Bike Month described later in the "Green Events Calendar," TA also organizes regular events. Partnering with other local groups, it helps stage public workshops and lectures on issues such as the "Brooklyn Waterfront Greenway" and "Freedom from Car Dependency." In case you missed it earlier, its website can be found at www.transalt.org or call (212) 629–8080.

### GREEN DRINKS NYC

One branch of an international networking and social green movement, Green Drinks NYC is a loosely organized monthly get-together with a diverse assortment of people who work in, or are simply interested in, environmental fields and issues. The second Tuesday of every month, a bunch of New York's greener citizens meet up, network, hang out, and learn more about what other green folks are doing around the city, all over a beer or two. The venue changes from month to month, but you can check out the website (www.greendrinks.org) for updated info and sign up for an e-mail reminder. A smaller Brooklyn Greendrinks has followed the mode, meeting the third Wednesday of every month.

## Green Events Calendar

Every year there are a handful of fixtures in the green calendar that can be counted on. Here's one for every month. (Disclaimer: Of course things change, and in a city as dynamic as New York, it'd be shortsighted to guarantee that these events will keep running from year to year. In other words, make sure you check the websites or call the organizations responsible for these events—which I hope will remain fixtures.)

### JANUARY

There aren't really any singular landmark green annual events in the month of January, but there are a couple of yearly traditions that are well worth a mention. For instance, near the end of the month, the Brooklyn

Botanic Garden hosts its annual **Plant-O-Rama**, a free trade show that features dozens of exhibitors (in 2005 there were forty-five, to be exact) that represent the best of the metro region's specialty nurseries and wholesale growers, as well as horticultural suppliers, other botanic gardens, various greening organizations, and garden book authors. Plant-O-Rama's agenda also includes a symposium with talks and presentations relating to hot horticultural topics. For info on the next Plant-O-Rama, check the BBG's website (www.bbg.org) or call (718) 623-7200.

Another January ritual is the Parks Department's **Mulch Fest**. Started in the mid-1990s and a yearly occurrence in early January ever since, Mulch Fest provides New Yorkers a convenient and environmentally friendly way to dispose of their Christmas trees. Recyclers are invited to dozens of city parks throughout the five boroughs where trees are stripped of their boughs and ground into wood chips, which are then used to line tree pits along city streets and in parks. Participants are also welcome to bring home wood chips and fir boughs for use in their private home or community gardens. Check the Parks Department's website (www.nycgovparks.org) or call 311 for more info.

### FEBRUARY

A new highlight on New York City's green calendar is the weekend-long **Verdopolis: The Future Green City** sustainability summit. Organized by Earth Pledge, Verdopolis brings together business, cultural, and political leaders to highlight issues and innovations in the sustainability of modern cities. The summit is kicked off by the FutureFashion runway show, coinciding appropriately with New York Fashion Week, where top designers show off eco-friendly fashions that employ renewable, reusable, and nonpolluting fabrics to create clothing not just for elegant occasions, but also for the street and for professional life. The three-day LeaderSummit conference then includes panels, workshops, and presentations from the fields of architecture, energy, technology, transportation, health care, design, food, and fashion. The FutureCity exhibition is an interactive and informative installation that uses exciting and entertaining media—such as animation and video architectural design—to make immediate the visions and realities of future sustainable urbanism. Additional information can be found, and tickets can be purchased, at www.verdopolis.com or by calling (212) 725–6611, ext. 232.

## MARCH

In March the annual **BioDiversity Expo** moves into the New York Marriott at the Brooklyn Bridge. A large-scale professional and consumer trade show focusing on natural health and the environment, the expo features exhibitors presenting a wide array of products and services ranging from organic foods to homeopathic health, from rain forest protection to environmental literature, from transportation alternatives to herbal teas. The only such trade show in the outer boroughs, and the best represented in New York City, the BioDiversity Expo is a great opportunity for businesses and individuals alike to go sift through the abundance of options for natural health and environmentally sustainable living available both here in the city and nationwide. The expo's website (www.biodiversityllc.com) includes a directory of all exhibitors and also free access to *BioDiversity* magazine, the periodical accompaniment to the exposition.

## APRIL

If every day were really **Earth Day,** then April 22 wouldn't be such a landmark event on the calendars of greens around the country. Since 1970 activists have used Earth Day to rally and call attention to the many important environmental issues of our time. Because April 22 only sporadically falls on a weekend, many groups now organize events on the following weekend. Here in the city Earth Day New York—the not-for-profit organization devoted to increasing awareness of Earth Day and its implicit lessons—has taken to establishing a full **Earth Week,** with its epicenter at Grand Central Station. The terminal's Main Concourse is transformed for seven days by the Giant Earth Images, a projection show that runs continuously on the room's famous pillars, creating inspiring visions through interplayed images of earth-related artwork, photographs, and quotations. Famous contributors to the installation over the decades have included Andy Warhol and Keith Haring. Earth Week culminates with the two-day EarthFair festival of music, performance art, education, and, above all, fun. In Vanderbilt Hall more than fifty environmental organizations invite sponsors and visitors to participate in hands-on activism and education. Eco-friendly products are sampled, petitions are signed, and eyes are opened to the variety of environmental issues worthy of attention and concern. On top of these Earth Day New York–sanctioned events, plenty of the city's other environmentally related organizations—from the Parks Department to bike and pedestrian groups, recycling activists, and sustainable food buffs—also coordinate events and activities of their own. A good comprehensive schedule of Earth Week events is updated frequently in the weeks leading up to Earth Day, and is readily available at the Earth Week New York website (www.earthdayny.org).

## MAY

What started in 1990 as a one-day celebration of biking to work soon became a weeklong collection of events, and since has grown to a full month. Henceforth, every May in New York City is officially **Bike Month**, as designated by the Department of Transportation and coordinated by Transportation Alternatives. The hundreds of individual events that together make up Bike Month are anchored by established traditions. The New York Mets host Bike to Shea Day, where anyone arriving on two wheels is treated to free bike parking and discounted tickets. The city's famous Velodromes—time-honored cycle tracks—host public races and free rides. Commuters are encouraged—or maybe baited—into giving bike transit a shot with Bike to Work Borough Breakfasts, literally food pit stops along popular and highly trafficked routes presided over by the borough presidents who themselves serve up pancakes, fruit, and energy food to anyone on a bicycle. Perhaps the most renowned event of Bike Month is the legendary Five Boro Bike Tour—a 42-mile ride that escorts the thousands of participants through New York City's historic neighborhoods, down beautiful boulevards, avenues, and parkways, around many flagship parks, and offers the exclusive, once-a-year opportunity to ride over the world's second longest suspension bridge, the Verrazano-Narrows. A hard copy of the complete schedule of bike month's events can be ordered in advance or can be viewed online at Transportation Alternative's website (www.transalt.org); more information is available by calling (212) 629–8080.

## JUNE

The arrival of summer comes with many rites and rituals throughout the world, and one of the best possible places to welcome it is at the **Clearwater Festival** in Croton Point Park. Technically in Croton-on-Hudson in Westchester County, the festival's inclusion on this list is warranted by its proximity and easy access from the city (about forty-five minutes by train from Grand Central) and its status as one of the preeminent environmentally conscious festivals in the country. The weekend-long celebration, alternately dubbed the Great Hudson River Revival, is fully powered by solar, wind, and biodiesel sustainable energy, including all audio, lighting, vehicles, and operational facilities. Expect an exceptional and eclectic mix of contemporary and traditional music and dance, from blues to bluegrass, rock to gospel, funk to folk, not to mention Cajun, contra, zydeco, and salsa. Beyond the music there's storytelling and dance performances, all set against a backdrop of environmental education and activism. For more information check out the Clearwater organization's website (www.clearwater.org) and then make plans to head for the banks of the Hudson to welcome summer with open arms and a green mind.

Another annual occurrence that you can take advantage of without leaving the city limits is **National Trails Day**, a nationwide celebration of trails, rural and urban, that takes place the first Saturday of every June. The city's parks fill with Urban Park Rangers and citizen volunteers who work to maintain and beautify the thousands of miles of trails—both rugged and well kept—that traverse the hidden reservoirs of natural beauty throughout all five boroughs. From the Greenbelt in Staten Island to Abbey Pond Park in Queens to the Bronx River, and on plenty of trails in between, participating in National Trails Day is a great opportunity to escape the city without ever leaving.

## JULY

The summer months tend to bring a sort of battered lethargy to the city's overheated population. What better way to overcome the heat than a powwow? That's right, every July brings the **Thunderbird American Indian Mid-Summer Pow Wow,** where the descendants from more than forty Indian nations convene for three days of intertribal dance competitions and artisanship. It's easy to forget that before this city was covered in concrete, its fields and forests were inhabited by American Indians, some sharing the bloodlines of the participants at the Thunderbird Pow Wow. The event is held in the apple orchard of the Queens County Farm, which is a spectacular venue in its own right—at forty-seven acres it's the largest remaining tract of undisturbed farmland in New York City and the only working historical farm in the city; it's also the longest continuously farmed site in all of New York State. For more information about the truly fascinating powwow, see the Queens County Farm's website (www.queensfarm.org).

## AUGUST

In my mind, August in the city means one thing—music. Whether by design or coincidence, this sweltering summer month always brings a seemingly ceaseless string of concerts, performances, and festivals. To single out one such event would be woefully inadequate, so here are some of the finest (and free!) annual aural treats of August.

The midweek nights are covered in Upper Manhattan for three weeks in August: **CityParks Concerts** bring Latin beats to Highbridge

Park on Tuesday evening, then heads over to Jackie Robinson Park on Wednesday for jazz; by the time Thursday rolls around, Marcus Garvey Park is set to host yet another night of Uptown tunes, here accompanied by narrative paintings and drawings. Then the following evening, every Friday throughout the summer, Marcus Garvey Park is traversed by the **Jazzmobile**, a rolling concert in the Pied Piper mode. On one August weekend the **Charlie Parker Jazz Festival** takes over the very well-programmed Marcus Garvey Park and then Tompkins Square Park down in the East Village, with some of the best jazz in the city (and that's saying something!) jamming throughout the afternoon.

Across the East River the **Queens Symphony Orchestra** fills Forest Park with strings, horns, woodwinds, and booming and rattling rhythm during a handful of public performances (call 718–326–4455 for specifics). Over in Brooklyn the **Martin Luther King Jr. Concert Series** fills Monday night in Wingate Field Park through July and August with classic soul, jazz, R&B, oldies, and contemporary music. Over at the shore Asser Levy Park hosts the **Seaside Concert Series**, a string of classic rock, pop, contemporary, and salsa shows on Thursday night through July and August

Grab a date and head back to Manhattan for the perfectly named **Basket and Blanket Concert Series** on the waterfront in Morningside Park. The series runs on Saturday night all summer long (until mid-August) and boasts a lineup of jazz, gospel, and R&B performances. Down at the Battery, in one of the city's most unusual outdoor venues, **Music at Castle Clinton** fills the historic landmark with a variety of musical styles from jazz to indie rock to bluegrass on Thursday evening through July and August. Finally, few musical experiences can really compare to a major act at **Central Park SummerStage**, the season-long arts festival that brings big names in pop and world music, as well as dance and spoken-word performances, to one of the world's most legendary venues.

Remember that while most of these series and programs are annual traditions, schedules can change from year to year, so the "Concerts, Performances, and Films" section of the Parks Department's website (www.nycgovparks.org) is an essential resource for sorting your way through the plentiful notes of summer.

## SEPTEMBER

As the streets start to show signs of cooling, the largest single environmental event on the East Coast takes over the outdoor courtyard at Lincoln Center. **ECOFEST** is a unique daylong cultural and environmental event, and is free to the public. The theme of ECOFEST is the conservation of natural resources and innovative alternative energy technologies, and the festival is shaped around the SEOTO (Sources of Energy Other than Oil) Exposition. Hundreds of exhibitors of various alternative energy innovations and products fill tables and give presentations to tens of thousands of green New Yorkers. Perhaps the most popular feature of SEOTO is the opportunity to test-drive solar car prototypes. Alongside that exposition an eco-friendly fashion show pleases the crowd, while others check out the lectures and panel discussions of the Environmental Education Conference. Other entertainment ranges from music to dance to celebrity speakers and Broadway singers. All in all ECOFEST is a great learning experience with plenty of fun and entertainment to balance the seriousness of the subject matter. More information is available on the event's website (www.ecofest.org) or by calling the hotline at (212) 496–2030.

## OCTOBER

Twice a year, the Parks Department and its associate nonprofit organization Partnerships for Parks invite New Yorkers to come together in caring for and celebrating the city's parks. On **It's My Park! Day** on a Saturday in October (and May), thousands of volunteers join in to help beautify this valuable New York City resource. Sometimes as many as 200 parks are tackled by citizens who understand the worth of the city's open space and recognize the difficulty of maintaining such a vast system. Projects are generally organized by local community groups, or Parks Department or Partnerships for Parks staff. Bulbs are planted for their emergence in spring, leaves are raked, and trees are cared for; benches are painted, beaches are swept, and mulch is laid on beds for protection through the winter. It's not all hard work, though. It's My Park! Day insists, above all else, that New Yorkers come out to their local parks, enjoy the outdoors, and mix with the community. Volunteers and visitors alike are treated to organized events such as nature walks, canoe rides, pickup games, and pumpkin carvings. Check out the organizational website (www.itsmypark.org) and see how you could help out your neighborhood park. Without the thousands of New Yorkers lending a couple of hands on It's My Park! Day, New York would truly be a lesser city.

## NOVEMBER

Perhaps the greatest gathering of New York City–centric organizations and individuals committed to the ecological redemption of this town, the **Eco-Metropolis Conference** endows the city with a weekend's worth of pointed talks, panel discussions, presentations, and performances, all of which concern New York City as an ecological specimen. The conference focuses on sharing knowledge and expertise from a variety of fields with a common cause—"toward a green, just, sustainable greater NYC," as the tagline reads. Sustainable building designers are introduced to environmental justice advocates from disadvantaged neighborhoods. A panel on "Communicating Sustainability" is created, featuring speakers from three widely diverse fields discussing how to best promote eco-sensibility. The only disappointing thing about this conference is that there's too much interesting stuff going on. With nearly twenty panels, each ninety minutes long, packed into a single day, it's tough to pick and choose which to attend: "Farmers Markets & Food Justice" might interfere with both "NYC Alt-media" and a panel on socially responsible entrepreneurship, featuring two New York City green business owners and one representative of a workers' cooperative. Obviously, the dilemma is of the best sort, and Eco-Metropolis is not to be missed by anyone at all interested in New York City–focused environmental issues. The conference is brought together by the Graduate Center of CUNY, the Bioneers Conference, and the New York Open Center, whose website (www.open center.org) contains all the relevant information.

## DECEMBER

For too many New Yorkers, the realities of the holiday season don't reflect the warmth and goodwill romantically identified with the twelfth month. At work projects and reports demand attention and finality before colleagues and associates disappear until the New Year. At schools and universities students cram for finals and type until dawn to finish up term papers, theses, and dissertations. Finding gifts for friends and relatives becomes a chore rather than an act of love. Travel plans are invariably inconvenient. Lost in all of this is the true magic of the holiday season. Which is why the **Holiday Train Show** at the New York Botanical Garden is such a treat. For inside the garden's Victorian-style glass conservatory stretches a truly wondrous New York City landscape, with replicas of more than a hundred New York landmarks such as the Statue of Liberty and the Brooklyn Bridge, the re-creations made entirely from parts of the garden's own plants—berries, twigs, mushrooms, and pinecones. The enchanting scene offers the romantic vision of a holiday season in New York City that can be so hard to find out on the crowded streets with a packed schedule. Around this idyllic Big Apple, trains and trolleys chug along, passing the Apollo Theatre, crossing a bridge high overhead, then bending 'round the Jewish Museum and zipping past Rockefeller Center. Somehow, within the glass walls, amid the landscapes of eleven distinct plant habitats, the harsher realities of this city life dissolve and you're left with the New York City of the movies and the black-and-white photographs, the New York City of wide-eyed childhood imagination, a New York City of true holiday warmth and goodwill. The exhibit runs from late November through early January, and more information, as well as photos of the exhibit and directions for how to get to the NYBG, are all available on the website (www.nybg.org).

So there you have it—a good, green event for every month, and a guarantee that you'll connect with others bearing similar minds and ethics. And be sure to take full advantage of those many other organizations that regularly put on events and assemble New York's greenest. There are, of course, more ways to get yourself involved, and I'll again ask that you check out the appendix, where you'll find categorized listings of the vast array of groups, businesses, and organizations that do their respective parts in driving the city's green evolution.

# Sustainability in the City

*There are two types of environmentalists: those who understand that the city is part of the environment and those who do not.*

—**PAUL SOGLIN,** Mayor of Madison, Wisconsin

I t's easy for people to write cities off the environmental agenda, conceding the inability of an urban system to function in a sustainable manner. They'll then focus energy and effort elsewhere—on, say, forest conservation or endangered species or toxic industrial pollution. In the media we see battles raging over the destruction of spotted owl habitat, or the construction of a new dam that will flood a river valley, or the spilling of hundreds of barrels of petroleum that will pollute the sea and damage wildlife. These are important issues, absolutely, but they are also acute, confined predicaments, whereas the world's overriding environmental concerns and crises have roots in the structural systems of societies—systems of energy use, of food production, of trade, of transportation, and so on.

It is unfortunate that a city's isolation from natural ecosystems fosters a sense of the urban system's removal from any impact on the environment and its various fragile components. The built environment is not conducive to natural production from the land; very little energy is generated within a city's limits, and waste tends to flow away from it; no tangible markings of the city's impact are visible to the general urbanite. But the perspective that cities are their own entity, apart from ecological systems, is a shortsighted one. In 2004 this planet ventured into the first true urban age: For the first time in history, more than half the global community lives in cities. By all indications the urban share of the world's population will keep growing. Any attempts to manage the foremost environmental challenges of our times must take a good hard look at the function of cities in the equation.

New York City is a particularly important factor in this equation. With more than eight million New Yorkers, the city is responsible for a full 2 percent of the entire country's production of carbon dioxide—that's one-half of one percent of the entire global $CO_2$ emissions, generated right here within the confines of the five boroughs. Yet from an energy-consumption standpoint, New York City represents one of the most efficient urban systems on the planet. These seemingly contradictory facts are revealing: There sure are a lot of New Yorkers with a substantial collective impact, and New York City is doing a lot of things right—whether by design or by happenstance—to moderate what could be a far more formidable, even calamitous, impact on environmental welfare. This isn't to say that New York is a model green city, we all know far better, but it is an indication of the unique physical and geographic elements of this town that create favorable conditions for more efficient, more resourceful, and ultimately more sustainable structural systems. The incredibly effective and enormously utilized mass transit system is the most obvious example.

Still, *sustainability* is a tricky concept. In terms of literal meaning, there are probably as many definitions as people trying to define it. A murky puddle in Central Park could contain a sustainable system with insects, algae, bacteria, and maybe the odd tadpole or two, all soaking up different nutrients, one discharging wastes that feed another, nutrients and energy cycling naturally through the system from one class of organism to another. So long as the raw input of sunlight and rainwater remain relatively constant, the system carries on, or sustains.

Would that it were so easy for cities! The sober truth is that New York will never be a truly sustainable city. (For that matter, none will.) Nevertheless, it is a place that caters well to a *more* sustainable life for its residents, particularly those New Yorkers who choose to actively seek out the variety of programs and services made available by the organizations, businesses, and government departments that work toward a more environmentally sensitive urban system.

Unfortunately, these aren't always easy to find. New York City is distracting, deceiving, and prone to causing sensory overload. Life here can be full of an overwhelming array of possibilities and choices; it can be fairly challenging to sift through all the information, all the stimuli, to find what you're looking for. Such was my experience when settling into the city and striving to establish an environmental ethic in my new urban lifestyle. It took me a few years to discover many of the environmentally progressive possibilities here, and to fully realize how best to take advantage of them—to search out the community-supported agriculture programs, to flip the switch to wind power, to win a bike lane on my street, or to find the deepest seclusion in a natural preserve. It took time to understand that despite the "unnatural" sense of the city—that is, it's a city where the natural world is at a remove—New York plays a critical role in the ecological well-being of systems both local and global.

Although everybody involved in any aspect of urban environmentalism wants their work to be known, it can be tough to connect with an audience in this town. A long and not always easy process of searching out and discovering all of New York City's positively green possibilities was my experience upon settling in here, and perhaps it has also been yours. I can only hope that in these pages you've learned things you didn't know, discovered services and programs and organizations you weren't familiar with, and found yourself motivated to get out there and go green. I trust that in edging your way to a more sustainable lifestyle, you'll find that a greener life is indeed a better life.

# notes and references

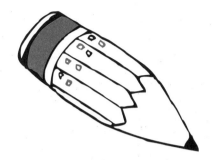

## section one

# A Greener Apple Begins at Home

### CHAPTER ONE
The Juice Is Loose: Conserving Electricity at Home

6–7: Sources of New York City's electricity: New York State Department of Public Service (NYS-DPS), "Fuel Sources and Air Emissions to Generate Your Electricity: Consolidated Edison" (www.dps.state.ny.us/envlabels/end_12_03/CONED.PDF).

7–8: Impacts of power plant pollution in New York: New York Public Interest Research Group (NYPIRG), "Impacts of Power Plant Pollutions" (www.nypirg.org/energy/env_impact.html).

7: More on global warming's effects on the New York area: Anthony DePalma, "Forecast for New York This Century: Hotter and Wetter," *New York Times*, June 27, 2004.

9: Lighting as a heat source and efficient lighting fixtures: Dianna Lopez Barnett with William D. Browning, *A Primer of Sustainable Building* (Snowmass, CO: Rocky Mountain Institute Press, 1998); Clark Public Utilities, "Lighting as Heat Source" (www.clarkpublicutilities.com/Residential/TheEnergyAdviser/Archives2001/6-01-1).

## CHAPTER TWO
Natural Comfort: Climate Control in the Green Home

24–25: More on energy-efficient climate control: ConEd Solutions, "Saving Energy for Residential Customers" (www.conedsolutions .com/Residential/Saving_Energy.htm);

Natural Resource Defense Council, "Easy Energy Saving Habits (Free!)" (www.nrdc.org/air/energy/genergy/easy.asp); Barnett and Browning, *A Primer of Sustainable Building.*

## CHAPTER THREE
Bringing Alternative Energy Home

28: Local Green Power options: Dan Harris, "Green Power in New York City," *GreenHome NYC*, March 2003 (www.greenhomenyc.org/ page/greenpower).

## CHAPTER FOUR
Water, Water Everywhere, Leaking from a Sink

39: New York City's drought and water use history: City of New York Department of Environmental Protection (NYC DEP), "History of Drought and Water Consumption," February 15, 2002 (www.ci.nyc.ny.us/html/dep/html/droughtlist.html).

39: On the global freshwater shortage and its implications, see Paul Hawken, Amory Lovins, and L. Hunter Lovins, *Natural Capitalism: Creating the Next Industrial Revolution* (New York: Little, Brown and Company, 1999), pp. 213–233.

40: Residential water use trends in New York City, and leaks: NYC DEP, "Residential Water Use," February 15, 2002 (www.ci.nyc.ny.us/ html/dep/html/wateruse.html); NYC DEP, "Leaks and Their Costs," February 15, 2002 (www.ci.nyc.ny.us/html/dep/html/waterleak .html).

## CHAPTER FIVE
The Space of Waste

46–48: History of recycling in New York City, including the recent resurrection of the collection program: Recycle This NYC, "What Happened to Recycling in NYC?" (www.recyclethisnyc.org/about.jsp); Ian Urbina, "Mayor Recommits to Ambitious Recycling Pact," *New York Times,* September 14, 2004.

## CHAPTER SIX
The Green Clean

62–66: For much more information on toxic household cleaners, see the Environmental Media Services website (www.ems.org), particularly "Eco-friendly Alternatives to Common Household Cleaners" (www.ems.org/household_cleaners/alternatives.html) and "Toxic Household Products" (www.ems.org/household_cleaners/household_toxics.html).

# section two
# The Green Plate Special

## CHAPTER SEVEN
What's Wrong with Our Food

72: For statistics on farm subsidies, see Environmental Working Group, "Farm Subsidy Database" (www.ewg.org/farm).

72–73: Economics of industrialized farming: Stewart Smith, "Farming Activities and Family Farms: Getting the Concepts Right," presented to the U.S. Congress Symposium, "Agricultural Industrialization and Family Farms: The Role of Federal Policy," October 21, 1992.

74–77: Monocultures in industrialized agriculture and pest proliferation: Hawkens et al., *Natural Capitalism*, pp. 194–195; Natural

Resource Defense Council, "Organic Foods 101" (www.nrdc.org/health/farming/forg101.asp); Janine M. Benyus, *Biomimicry: Innovations Inspired by Nature* (New York: William Morrow, 1997), pp. 17–19.

76–77: Genetically engineered crops and increased pesticide use: Charles M. Benbrook, "Impacts of Genetically Engineered Crops on Pesticide Use in the United States: The First Eight Years," *BioTech InfoNet,* November 2003.

77: Different types of pesticides: U.S. Environment Protection Agency (EPA), "Types of Pesticides" (www.epa.gov/pesticides/about/types.htm).

78: Growth hormone use in livestock: Janet Raloff, "Hormones: Here's the Beef: Environmental Concerns Reemerge Over Steroids Given to Livestock," *Science News,* January 5, 2002 (www.sciencenews.org/articles/20020105/bob13.asp).

78–81: Environmental ramifications of factory farms: Sustainable Table, "The Issues: Environment" (www.sustainabletable.org/issues/environment); Helena Norberg-Hodge, Todd Merrifield, and Steven Gorelick, *Bringing the Food Economy Home: Local Alternatives to Global Agribusiness* (Bloomfield, CT: Kumarian Press, 2002).

81: Long-distance transport of industrialized food and the environmental ramifications: Sustainable Table, "Environment"; Rich Pirog, "Checking the Food Odometer: Comparing Food Miles for Local Versus Conventional Produce Sales in Iowa Institutions," Leopold Center for Sustainable Agriculture, July 2003; Northeast Organic Farming Association of New York (NOFA-NY), "Why Should You Care About Organic Farming?" June 2002; Tim Lang, "Food Safety and Public Health: Will the Crisis Ever End?" Cardiff Law School Public Lecture Series: Thames Valley University, 2001.

81–82: For more on food additives, see Patricia Redlinger and Diane Nelson, "Food Additives: What Are They?" Iowa State University Extension Service, November 1993 (www.extension.iastate.edu/Publications/NCR438.pdf).

82–83: Pesticides and human health: Sustainable Table, "The Issues: Pesticides" (www.sustainabletable.org/issues/pesticides); NOFA-NY, "Pesticides in Food" (www.nofany.org/hottopics/pesticideinfood.html).

83–86: Genetically engineered crop statistics, U.S. and abroad: California Department of Food and Agriculture, "A Food Foresight Analysis of Agricultural Biotechnology," January 1, 2003 (www.cdfa.ca.gov/exec/pdfs/ag_biotech_report_03.pdf); Sustainable Table, "The Issues: Genetic Engineering" (www.sustainabletable.org/issues/ge).

86–87: Bovine growth hormones and human health: Bradford Duplisea, "The Real Dope on Beef Hormones," Canadian Health Coalition, 2001 (http://www.healthcoalition.ca/hormones.html); NOFA-NY, "Bovine Growth Hormone" (www.nofany.org/hottopics/bovinegrowthhormone.html); Sustainable Table, "The Issues: Hormones" (www.sustainabletable.org/issues/hormones).

87: Antibiotic use in livestock and effects on human health: Union of Concerned Scientists, "Food and Environment: Antibiotic Resistance," October 2003 (www.ucsusa.org/food_and_environment/antibiotic_resistance/index.cfm); Keep Antibiotics Working, "Antibiotic Resistance: A Growing Health Threat to You and Your Family," July 2003; Sustainable Table, "The Issues: Antibiotics" (www.sustainabletable.org/issues/antibiotics).

America (PANNA), "Problems with Conventional Cotton Production" (www.panna.org/resources/documents/conventionalCotton.dv.html).

166: Use of wood pulp in rayon fabric: Co-opAmerica, "Woodwise: Fashion from Forests" (www.woodwise.org/guide/clothing.html).

169–171: For more on the environmental and social ills of sweatshops, see Global Exchange, "Sweat Free: A Movement Towards Ending Sweatshops" (www.globalexchange.org/campaigns/sweatshops/background.html).

172–173: Leather production and tanneries: Fair Trade Federation, "'Made in Dignity' Campaign" (www.fairtradefederation.org/ws_leath.html).

177–180: For more on toxic chemicals in health and beauty products, see Environmental Working Group, "Skin Deep" (www.ewg.org/reports/skindeep).

## CHAPTER FOURTEEN
Recreation and Delight

185–191: For a more thorough description of the history of New York City's parks and the various agencies that have governed them, see New York City Department of Parks and Recreation, "Parks History" (www.nycgovparks.org/sub_about/parks_history/historic_tour/historic_tour.html).

the green pages

# The Green Pages

## New York City Environmental Directory

Please use these Green Pages to find organizations, businesses, websites, and various resources pertaining to all of your New York City–based environmental curiosities and needs. This directory is divided into sections of interest, listed alphabetically for your convenience.

## ⌂ Apparel

### General Info

**Clean Clothes Campaign** (www.cleanclothes.org): Up-to-date info about various companies' involvements with sweatshop labor around the globe. Features an "urgent appeals" section that decries the most immediate and troubling labor abuses in the garment industry.

**Co-op America** (www.coopamerica.org): Promising "practical steps for using your consumer and investor power for social change," the Co-op America website features a variety of resources for the conscientious consumer. Programs include:

- **The End Sweatshops Campaign** (www.sweatshops .org), with information on how to avoid products produced in sweatshops and how to urge companies to end sweatshop labor. Includes a useful "Retailer Scorecard" grading large retailers on their contribution to sweatshop demand.

- **The Green Pages Online** (www.greenpages.org), a directory of 170 product categories—including clothing and shoes—searchable by state, featuring only companies that have demonstrated a commitment to social and environmental responsibility.

- **A Responsible Shopper** (www.responsibleshopper.org), database that invites you to find company ratings on a range of issues including sweatshops, pollution, community investment, discrimination, and human rights, to help you figure out what your shopping could support.

*The Green Guide* (www.thegreenguide.com): This authoritative bimonthly eco-living newsletter is truly an invaluable resource for navigating your way through the many choices of modern life and consumerism with hopes of living a healthier, more sustainable life, including detailed reports on clothing and shoes The extensive research is boiled down to a raw, critical evaluation of products, trends, and practices. Consider it a *Consumer Reports* for human health and the environmental movement with a touch of DIY (do-it-yourself) sensibility. *The Green Guide* is *the* authoritative source for the environment- and health-conscious consumer.

**The Greenpeace 2001 Athletic Shoe Shopping Guide** (www.greenpeaceusa.org/ features/details?item_id=530133 &campaign_id=512832): A report card-style list grading shoe companies on their commitment to phasing PVC out of their footwear.

**Organic Consumers Association** (www.organicconsumers.org/ clothes): The Clothes for a Change campaign by the OCA contains substantial background information about pesticide use in the garment industry, and includes up-to-date headlines and direct-action campaigns.

**Sustainable Cotton Project**
(www.sustainablecotton.org):
Promotes the Fair Trade of organic
cotton clothes. Features facts,
case studies, and background
information on cotton production.

**Sweatshop Watch**
(www.sweatshopwatch.org):
Information and advocacy about
sweatshop labor issues. Monitors
companies' involvement with
sweatshop labor and organizes
labor-empowerment campaigns.

## Clothing: Local Retailers

These are some stores around
the city that deal eco-friendly
duds. Many such stores—but
not all—carry both clothing
and shoes, and some also sell
household goods and various
other green items. Distinctions
have been made when possible, but it's always best to
call first.

**Earth Speaks Organic Fashion**
33 Flatbush Avenue, Brooklyn
(718) 797-6898
www.earthspeaks.com
Wide assortment of women's
fashions, all from organic fibers.

**Gaelyn and Cianfarani**
155 East 2nd Street
(212) 614-6998
www.gaelyn.com
High-end women's fashion, using
sustainable materials including
recycled bicycle inner tubes.

**N. Asano**
24 East 35th Street
(212) 696-4003
Men's and women's clothing,
including many eco-friendly
options.

**NY Artificial**
223 West 10th Street
(212) 255-0825
Vegan and faux leather clothing
and accessories.

**Organic Avenue**
23 Ludlow Street, Loft #2
(212) 334-4593
www.organicavenue.com
Men's and women's clothing,
footwear, accessories, housewares, health and beauty, food,
and media.

## Clothing: Online Retailers

There are hundreds of quality
online retailers for environmentally responsible clothing

and footwear. Here are some that have earned my respect either through personal transactions, references, or repeated mention in reputable sources.

### Ecolution
www.ecolution.com
Clothing, shoes, accessories, and more.

### Eco-Wise
http://ecowise.com
Clothing, shoes, housewares, even biodiesel!

### Global Citizen
www.beaglobalcitizen.com
Women's clothing, organic fibers.

### Indigenous Designs
www.indigenousdesigns.com
Cooperatively produced organic fibers.

### Under The Canopy
www.underthecanopy.com
Women's, men's, bed and bath, footwear, and more.

### Vivavi
www.vivavi.com
Clothing, shoes, housewares, lifestyle products.

## Footwear: Local Retailers

### MooShoes
152 Allen Street
(212) 254–6512
www.mooshoes.com
The best assortment of vegan shoes in the city!

### 99x
84 East 10th Street
(212) 460–8599
A wide variety of vegan and hemp shoes, plus some eco-friendly clothing.

## Footwear: Online Retailers

### Birkenstock
www.birkenstock.com
Also available in many New York City stores.

### Camper
www.camper.com
Also available in many New York City stores.

### Earth Shoes
www.earth.us
Also available in many New York City stores. Use the "Store Locator" function.

### Ecosandals
www.ecosandals.com
Import recycled rubber sandals from a cooperative in Kenya.

### shoes with souls
www.shoeswithsouls.com
100 percent vegan shoes.

### Splaff
www.splaff.com
Sandals made from 100 percent recycled rubber.

### Vegan Essestials
www.veganessentials.com
Mostly shoes, some accessories, and T-shirts, too!

### Veganline
www.veganline.com
100 percent vegan shoes, boots, and accessories.

### Vegan Wares
www.veganwares.com
Shoes, boots, sandals, and accessories.

 Construction

## Green Building

### Build It Green! NYC
(www.bignyc.org; 718–777–0132): A program of the Community Environmental Center (see page 241 and the sidebar in chapter 1), BIG NYC is a not-for-profit retail outlet—housed in an Astoria, Queens, warehouse—where builders can buy and sell reusable, low-cost, environmentally friendly building materials, including much salvaged or reclaimed material.

### GreenHomeNYC
(www.greenhomenyc.org): A community-oriented, volunteer-run not-for-profit, GreenHomeNYC works to facilitate and further development of sustainable building practices in this urban setting. See the description in chapter 15.

### Greening Gotham
(www.greeninggotham.org): A project of the Earth Pledge Green Roofs Initiative, described in detail in chapter 2.

### NICHE Environmentally Smart Design Group
(www.design-niche.com; 203–253–2724): NICHE is an interior design firm focused on creating beautiful spaces with an emphasis on sustainability.

**U.S. Green Building Council—
New York Chapter**
(http://www.usgbc.org/
Chapters/newyork/): Brings
together experts from all facets of
the building industry to promote
environmentally responsible construction and design practices.

## i Consumer Info

**Co-op America**
(www.coopamerica.org):
See pages 230–231 for a detailed
description of Co-op America's
services.

**Eco-labels**
(www.eco-labels.org): A project of
the Consumers Union, the Eco-
labels website is a clearinghouse
of information about environmental labels on products. Search by
product category—food, household
cleaner, personal hygiene, and
wood/paper—or by specific label
claim; you'll receive analysis of the
claim's legitimacy and compare
the product in question with a
conventionally produced similar
item.

**Energy Star**
(www.energystar.gov): Provides
certification and information for
and about energy-efficient appliances, lighting fixtures, climate
control systems, even homes.
See the thorough description in
chapter 1.

**Fair Trade Federation**
(www.fairtradefederation.org):
The FTF is an association of producers, wholesalers, and retailers
who all support and operate
under certified Fair Trade conditions. The website has useful
information about Fair Trade and
directories of Fair Trade product
retailers and wholesalers, as well
as links to online catalogs that
deal the goods.

**Global Exchange**
(www.globalexchange.org): An
international human rights organization with a wide variety of information relating to environmental,
political, and social justice issues
with a focus on commerce and
Fair Trade. There is also an online
"Fair Trade Store."

*The Green Guide*
(www.thegreenguide.com):
See page 231.

**Green Seal**

(www.greenseal.org): Green Seal is an independent not-for-profit organization that identifies and certifies—with its "Green Seal"— products and services that "cause less toxic pollution and waste, conserve resources and habitats, and minimize global warming and ozone depletion." Most of the certified products tend to be household goods (paints, water-efficient fixtures, windows and doors), but the group also certifies wood and paper products, vehicles, and even lodging facilities.

**Scientific Certification Systems**

(www.scscertified.com): Formally the "Green Cross," SCS now offers its Single Claim Certification to Environmentally Preferable Products. The certifications are a confirmation of the product's label claims for any of three aspects—recycled content, biodegradability, and volatile organic compounds present. These certifications are available for many manufactured goods such as carpeting, paints, paper products, and many more.

## Educational Organizations

**Brooklyn Center for the Urban Environment** (www.bcue.org; 718-788-8500): An educational outlet engaging the city's youth and adult population with classes, tours, and various projects related to urban ecology and the city's built environment.

**Community Environmental Center** (www.cecenter.org; 718-784-1444): Aside from providing green building and energy services to the New York City community, the CEC operates two Learning Centers in Long Island City and Stuyvesant Cove. See the sidebar in chapter 1 for more info.

**Cornell Cooperative Extension** (http://www.cce.cornell.edu/ ~NewYorkCity): Dedicated to improving the quality of life of New Yorkers through community and economic development, family and youth development, urban environment, lifelong learning, nutrition and health, and urban food systems. CCE helps facilitate partnerships and community organizations to address urban ecological issues.

### Earth Institute at Columbia University

(www.earth.columbia.edu; 845-365-8565): A collective of university professors and resources that addresses the complex issues facing the planet and its inhabitants, with particular focus on sustainable development and the world's poor. Also addresses local New York City ecological issues.

### Lower East Side Ecology Center (212-477-4022): See page 276.

## Environmental Activism

### Audubon

(www.nycaudubon.org; 212-691-7483): Dedicated to the protection of grasslands, woodlands, wetlands, and wildlife throughout the five boroughs, with a focus on scientific research, educational and recreational programs, and conservation advocacy.

### Bronx Council for Environmental Quality

(www.bceq.org; 718-817-7700, ext. 537): BCEQ "seeks to establish a sound, forward looking environmental policy" for the New York City area using committees, education, and political force to promote intelligent land use and waste management.

### Council on the Environment of NYC (www.cenyc.org; 212-788-7900): The CENYC is a privately funded citizens organization run through the Office of the Mayor of New York City that promotes environmental awareness while creating programs to deal with urban environmental problems. CENYC is responsible for organizing the city's vast Greenmarket system, but also has programs in Open Space Greening, Waste Management and Recycling, Environmental Education, and other important eco-initiatives.

### Earth Day New York

(www.earthdayny.org): See page 243.

**Earth Pledge** (www.earth pledge.org; 212–725–6611): Earth Pledge is a not-for-profit organization that promotes innovative techniques and technologies to help restore the balance between human and natural systems, using demonstration, education, and research. It uses the New York City region as a "laboratory" for various initiatives— including the Greening Gotham project (see page 234) and Farm To Table (see page 250).

**Green Drinks** (www.greendrinks .org): A casually organized social and networking group that meets the second Tuesday of every month at a featured bar in Manhattan (or the third Wednesday in Brooklyn) where greens—professionals in a variety of environmentally focused businesses or environmentally conscious citizens—get together to socialize, interact, network, and talk all things green.

**Metropolitan Waterfront Alliance** (www.waterwire.net; 800–364–9943): The city's leading advocate for sensible development of the waterfront. See chapter 14 for more info.

**Natural Resource Defense Council** (www.nrdc.org; 212–727–2700): One of the nation's foremost environmental lobby and advocacy organizations, with offices here in New York.

**Neighborhood Open Space Coalition** (www.treebranch.net; 212–228–3126): Calling itself "NYC's internet portal for environmental and urban quality of life issues," the NOSC uses the Treebranch Network to connect like-minded activist and advocacy organizations with concerned citizens.

**New York League of Conservation Voters** (www.nylcv.org; 212–361–6350): NYLCV is the independent, nonpartisan political arm of the state's environmental community, headquartered in New York City.

**New York Public Interest Research Group** (www.nypirg.org; 212–349–6460): NYPIRG trains students to be future advocates of consumer, environmental, and social justice, with an emphasis on governmental reform and policy outreach.

## Expos and Conferences

Detailed info about these events can be found in chapter 15's "Green Events Calendar."

**BioDiversity Expo**
www.biodiversityllc.org
(718) 853-9344
Hosted by *BioDiversity* magazine.

**Earth Day New York**
www.earthdayny.org
(212) 922-0048
Hosted by Earth Day New York.

**ECOFEST**
www.ecofest.org
(212) 496-2030
Hosted by the West Side Cultural Center.

**Eco-Metropolis**
www.opencenter.org
(212) 219-2527
Hosted by the Open Center of New York.

**Verdopolis**
www.verdopolis.org
(212) 358-9516
Hosted by Earth Pledge.

## Publications

The following are some useful print and online publications relating to New York City and environmental issues.

**The Green Apple**
Coupons for Natural Living in New York City
www.thegreenapple.org
Includes more than 200 coupons and discounts worth over $2,000 for green goods and services in New York City and online—including clothing, food, gifts, health and beauty, home, pets, restaurants, travel and entertainment, and more!

**Green Apple Maps**
(212) 674-1631
www.greenapplemap.org
Published online and available in print, these maps project various environmental features of the New York City landscape, and are often created with the assistance of student and community groups involved in educational programs.

*Green Sheet New York*
www.envadvocates.org
Published online by Environmental Advocates of NY, the *Green Sheet* is a monthly report of statewide environmental news, issues, and activism.

*New York Spirit*
(718) 638–3733
www.nyspirit.com
A monthly magazine focusing on
natural, enlightened living in
New York City.

*Satya*
(718) 832–9557
www.satyamag.com
A monthly magazine of vegetarian, environmental, and animal
rights issues published here in
New York City, with many local
features.

 Energy

## General Info

**Energy Star**
(www.energystar.gov): The virtual
clearinghouse for energy-efficiency
products and conservation strategies. This government-backed
program offers certifications for
products, tips for residents and
businesses, home-improvement
advice, and loads of background
information about energy use and
conservation.

**Green-e** (www.green-e.org):
This renewable energy certification program provides information

about all Green Power electricity
options available to consumers.
With geographically specific listings, this site provides background
information about renewable
energy and listings of all certified
renewable energy providers in the
area.

**New York State Public Service
Commission** (www.askpsc.com):
The PSC's website provides infor-
mation about energy conserva-
tion, as well as links to Green
Power alternatives and resources.

**NYSERDA** (www.nyserda.com):
The New York State Energy
Research and Development
Authority's website is loaded
with information about energy
consumption and conservation
within the state of New York.
Information about various
consumer incentive programs for
renewable energy is provided.

## Solar

**altPOWER, Inc.**
(www.altpower.com;
212-206-0547): altPOWER is
one of New York City's best
authorities on solar power. The
company offers consulting

services, products, and construction assistance to clients in any level of the building industry—architects, engineers, contractors, general managers, residential homeowners, businesses, developers, institutions, and governmental facilities.

BASIC (www.basicsolar.org; 212-803-5868, 718-389-5357): See chapter 3 for more information about the Big Apple Solar Installation Commitment. The group's website contains information about why and how to bring solar power to your home, as well as descriptions of successful solar projects in NYC and links to solar installers in the city.

## Providers

**Community Energy, Inc.** (www.newwindenergy.com): Certificates for wind farms in New York State, Pennsylvania, and New Jersey. The site includes information about the environmental benefits of wind power and detailed info about the various wind farms your purchase supports.

**NYPIRG Fuel Buyers Group** (www.nypirg.org/fbg/wind): The New York Public Interest Research Group's Fuel Buyers Group offers discounted rates on Community Energy's NewWind Energy.

**Power Your Way** (www.poweryourway.com): This Con Ed website provides one-stop shopping for choosing an ESCO. The "GreenPower" link contains a list of all renewable energy options. As of spring 2005, the only two ESCOs providing Green Power to NYC are:

- **ConEd Solutions** (www.conedsolutions.com).

- **ECONnergy** (www.econnergy.com).

**Sterling Planet** (www.sterlingplanet.com): A certificate for "Green America" Energy buys solar (5 percent), wind (45 percent), and "new bioenergy" (50 percent). New bioenergy is produced by a combination of landfill gas emissions—a natural by-product of organic decay—and clean wood waste, or logging milling residues that would otherwise go unused.

## Coffee

**Equal Exchange**
(www.equalexchange.org): An online vendor of all FAIR TRADE CERTIFIED products, with a focus on coffees, teas, and chocolate.

**TransFair USA**
(www.transfairusa.org): Offers a FAIR TRADE CERTIFIED label to coffee from farm cooperatives that use environmentally conscious farming practices and invest directly into their communities. The site also allows you to search for Fair Trade coffee vendors in your neighborhood.

## Community-Supported Agriculture (CSA)

Want to find a CSA in your neighborhood? Use this list to help find a distribution site near you. If there isn't one yet, consider starting one and drop the folks at Just Food (see page 253) a line. (Listings are separated by borough, and then listed with distribution neighborhood, address, contact information, and information about the primary farmer serving the site.) Contact your local CSA to see what the specific terms are for their arrangement, as they vary from site to site.

**Bronx**

**Baychester**
2052 Tillotson Avenue
(718) 320-9111
Farmer: Amy Hepworth,
Hepworth Farm, Milton, New York

**City Island**
110 Bay Street
(718) 885-1104 (Caroline)
Farmers: Debby and Pete Kavakos, Stoneledge Farm, South Cairo, New York

**Mott Haven**
St. Benedict the Moor
281-283 St. Ann's Avenue
(718) 665-9693, ext. 12
(Deborah)
Farmer: Zaid Kurdieh, Norwich Meadows Farm, Norwich, New York

**Norwood**
Epiphany Lutheran Church
Bainbridge Avenue and 206th Street

(212) 229-7954
Farmer: Zaid Kurdieh, Norwich
Meadows Farm, Norwich, New
York

## Riverdale
Mount St. Vincent
6301 Riverdale Avenue
(718) 543-6627
Farmer: David Hambleton, Sisters
Hill Community Farm,
Stanfordville, New York

## Riverdale
Riverdale Neighborhood House
5521 Mosholu Avenue
(718) 549-8100, ext. 129
Farmers: Rachel and Steffen
Schneider, Hawthorne Valley
Farm, Harlemville, New York

## Brooklyn

## Bay Ridge
Lutheran Church of the Good
Shepherd
7420 Fourth Avenue
(718) 745-8520
Farmers: Ted and Jan Blomgren
and Thomas Christenfeld, Cooke
Hollow Farm, Valley Falls,
New York

## Clinton Hill
P.S. 56
170 Gates Avenue

(718) 907-0616
www.clintonhillcsa.org
Farmers: Ted and Jan Blomgren
and Thomas Christenfeld, Cooke
Hollow Farm, Valley Falls,
New York

## Cobble Hill
St. Peter/St. Paul Church
Congress and Court Streets
(718) 802-1061
www.cobblehillcsa.org
Farmer: Bill Halsey, Green Thumb
Organic Farm, Watermill,
New York

## East New York
ENY Farmers Market
Barbey and New Lots Avenues
(718) 649-7979 (Sarita)
Farmers: Cheryl and Mike
Rogowski, Walter Rogowski Farm,
Pine Island, New York

## Park Slope
Garden of Union
Union Street and Fourth Avenue
(718) 707-1023 (Judy Janda)
Farmers: Ted and Jan Blomgren
and Thomas Christenfeld, Cooke
Hollow Farm, Valley Falls,
New York

### Red Hook

Center and Clinton Streets
(718) 855-5531 (Jen)
Farmers: Cheryl and Mike
Rogowski, Walter Rogowski Farm,
Pine Island, New York

### Williamsburg

McCarren Park
North 12th and Driggs Streets
(718) 599-1953
Farmers: Cheryl and Mike
Rogowski, Walter Rogowski Farm,
Pine Island, New York

## Manhattan

### Chelsea

Hudson Guild
Fulton Center, 119 Ninth Avenue
(212) 924-6710, ext. 245
www.chelseacsa.org
Farmers: Debby and Pete
Kavakos, Stoneledge Farm,
South Cairo, New York

### East Village

6th Street Community Center
638 East 6th Street (between
Avenues B and C)
(212) 677-1863 (Howard or
Annette)
www.sixthstreetcenter.org/
csa_index.html
Farmer: Amy Hepworth,
Hepworth Farm, Milton, New York

### Gramercy

Phipps CDC
484 Second Avenue (at 27th
Street)
(212) 686-6533 (Dave)
Farmer: Zaid Kurdieh, Norwich
Meadows Farm, Norwich,
New York

### Harlem-Central

Thurgood Marshall Academy
135th Street and Adam Clayton
Powell Boulevard
(212) 694-8715
Farmer: Jean-Paul Courtens,
Roxbury Farm, Kinderhook,
New York

### Harlem

Community Food Resource
Center
252 West 116th Street
(212) 665-8747 (Vanessa)
Farmer: Jean-Paul Courtens,
Roxbury Farm, Kinderhook,
New York

### Hell's Kitchen

Hell's Kitchen Flea Market
39th Street (between Ninth and
Tenth Avenues)
(212) 967-5818 (Cindi)
Farmer: Len Pollara, Upper
Meadows Farm, Montague,
New Jersey

## Inwood

Isham Park
(212) 353-6842
inwoodcsa@hotmail.com
Farmers: Claudia Kenny and Willy
Denner, Little Seeds Garden,
Stuyvesant, New York

## Midtown

Prince George
14 East 28th Street
(212) 471-0858 (Jenny)
www.commonground.org/csa/
Farmer: Zaid Kurdieh, Norwich
Meadows Farm, Norwich,
New York

## SoHo

Lt. Petrosino Square
Spring, Lafayette, and Kenmare
Streets
(212) 219-2527, ext. 170 (Carrie)
Farmer: Guy Jones, Blooming Hill
Farm, Blooming Grove, New York

## Upper East Side

Church of the Heavenly Rest
90th Street and Fifth Avenue
(212) 502-8562
Farmers: Debby and Pete
Kavakos, Stoneledge Farm,
South Cairo, New York

## Carnegie Hill/Yorkville

Church of the Epiphany
York Avenue and 74th Street

(212) 502-8562
Farmers: Debby and Pete
Kavakos, Stoneledge Farm,
South Cairo, New York

## Upper West Side

Site to be determined
(518) 758-9079
Farmers: Dan and Tracy Hayhurst,
Chubby Bunny Farm, Stuyvesant,
New York

## Upper West Side

550 West End Avenue (at 86th
Street)
(212) 539-3826
Farmer: Jean-Paul Courtens,
Roxbury Farm, Kinderhook,
New York

## Upper West Side

Site to be determined
(212) 284-6812 (Rachel)
Farmers: Eve Kaplan and Chris
Walbrecht, Garden of Eve,
Riverhead, New York

## Washington Heights

New Leaf Café
Fort Tryon Park
(212) 928-1840
Farmers: Claudia Kenny and Willy
Denner, Little Seeds Garden,
Stuyvesant, New York

McBurney YMCA
125 West 14th Street
(212) 741-6375 (Judy)
Farmers: Debby and Pete
Kavakos, Stoneledge Farm,
South Cairo, New York

## Queens

### Astoria

Goodwill Industries
4-21 Twenty-seventh Avenue
Contact not yet available (call Just
Food at 212-645-9880)
Farmer: Bill Halsey, Green Thumb
Organic Farm, Watermill,
New York

### Astoria

Arrow Community Garden
35-38 35th Street
(718) 937-1264
www.queenscsa.org
Farmer: Bill Halsey, Green Thumb
Organic Farm, Watermill,
New York

### Douglaston

Alley Pond Environmental Center
22806 Northern Boulevard
(718) 229-4000, ext. 212
Farmer: Matt Kuszyski, Golden
Earthworm Organic Farm,
Jamesport, New York

### Forest Hills

Forest Hills Community House
108-25 62nd Drive
(718) 592-5757, ext. 286
Farmer: Matt Kuszyski, Golden
Earthworm Organic Farm,
Jamesport, New York

## Farmers Markets

Independently operated farmers markets—often connected
with local community gardens
or neighborhood alliances—
can be found in the following
locations. When available, contact information is provided.

### Manhattan

East Harlem/Union Settlement
East 104th Street and Third
Avenue
Thursday, 8:00-4:00
May-November
Maritza Owens: (212) 828-6000

Harlem Renaissance
Lenox Avenue (between West
111th and West 112th)
Saturday, 8:00-4:00
Mid-July-December
Bonita Lloyd Nettles: (212)
932-2141

La Marqueta
East 115th Street and Park
Avenue
Saturday, 9:00–4:00
Mid-July–October
Jose Arrero: (212) 534-4900

Tucker Square
Columbus Avenue and 66th
Street
Saturday, 8:00–5:00
July–December

**Bronx**

Bronx Terminal (wholesale)
Exterior Avenue (under I-87,
north of East 149th Street)
Monday–Saturday, 3:00–10:00 A.M.
Jack Hoeffner: (845) 457-3453

Casita's Marqueta at St.
Atanaisius Church
Tiffany Street and Southern
Boulevard
Wednesday, 8:00–4:00
May–November
Sandra Flecha: (718) 589-2230

Harvest Home 165th Street
Museum of Arts at Grand
Concourse and 165th Street
Sunday, 8:00–4:00
July–October
Maritza Owens: (212) 828-3361

Harvest Home Alexander Avenue
Alexander Avenue (between
142nd and 143rd Streets)
Thursday, 8:00–4:00
Mid-July–October
Maritza Owens: (212) 828-3361

Harvest Home Forest Avenue
Forest Avenue (between
Westchester Avenue and 156th
Street)
Wednesday, 8:00–4:00
Mid-July–October
Maritza Owens: (212) 828-3361

Harvest Home Mount Eden
Claremont Park at Mount Eden
and Morris Avenues
Thursday, 8:00–4:00
Mid-July–October
Maritza Owens: (212) 828-3361

Hunts Point/Longwood
Southern Boulevard and
Tiffany Street
Wednesday, 8:30–4:00
Mid-July–mid-November
Miriam Haas: (914) 923-4837

MBD Community Park
1710 Southern Boulevard
(between East 173rd and 174th
Streets)
Friday, 8:00–3:00
July–mid-October
Damien Kitt: (718) 378-0970

New York Botanical Garden
Mosholu Gate and Kazimiroff
Drive
Wednesday, 10:00–3:00
Late-June–October
Miriam Haas: (914) 923-4837

### Brooklyn

Coney Island
KeySpan Stadium Plaza on
Surf Avenue
Sunday, 9:00–3:00
July–October
David Niles: (718) 266-4653

Brooklyn Multiservice
Health Center
592 Rockaway Avenue
Saturday, 8:30–4:00
Mid-July–mid-November
Miriam Haas: (914) 923-4837

East N.Y. Farms!
New Lots Avenue (between
Barbey and Jerome Streets)
Saturday, 10:00–3:00
June–mid-November
Ojeda Hall-Phillips: (718)
385-6700, ext. 100

Graham Avenue
Cook Street and Graham Avenue
Saturday, 8:00–5:00
Mid-July–October
Ed Vaquero: (718) 387-6643

Metrotech
Lawrence and Willoughby Streets
Thursday, 8:00–5:00
Mid-May–November

Red Hook
Clinton and Center Streets
Saturday, 9:00–3:00
Late June–November
Ian Marvey: (718) 855-5531

### Queens

Flushing Mall
122–31 Thirty-ninth Avenue (at
College Point Boulevard and
Prince Street)
Friday, 8:30–4:00
Mid-July–mid-November
Miriam Haas: (914) 923-4837

Jamaica
160th Street and Jamaica Avenue
Friday and Saturday, 8:30–4:00
Mid-July–mid-November
Miriam Haas: (914) 923-4837

## Food Co-ops

**Flatbush Food Coop**
1318 Cortelyou Road (between
Argyle and Rugby)
(718) 284-9717
www.flatbushfoodcoop.com

**4th Street Food Coop**
58 East 4th Street (between
Bowery and Second Avenue)
(212) 674–3623
www.4thstreetfoodcoop.org

**Park Slope Food Coop**
782 Union Street (between Sixth
and Seventh Avenues)
(718) 622–0560
www.foodcoop.com

## General Info

**Eat Well Guide**
(www.eatwellguide.com):
Promising "wholesome food from
healthy animals," the Eat Well
Guide website offers background
information on factory farming
and provides an incredibly useful
search engine that directs you to
restaurants and stores or markets
serving sustainably raised meat,
eggs, and dairy within the selected
geographic region.

**Environmental Working Group**
(www.ewg.org/issues/
organicfood/index.php): The EWG
website provides information and
mobilizes advocacy efforts in all
sorts of environmental fields, but
particularly handy is its

"Shopper's Guide to Pesticides in
Produce"—a downloadable wallet
card that shows which fruits and
vegetables are most and least
likely to contain pesticides.

**Farm To Table**
(www.farmtotable.org): This Earth
Pledge campaign is committed to
bringing foods from local, sustainably operated farms to tables in
New York City. An extensive collection of information about food
production practices is well complemented by a search engine
that allows you to find nearby
farmers markets, CSAs, and
restaurants or stores that bring
local, sustainable food to New
Yorkers.

**The Green Guide**
(www.thegreenguide.com):
See page 231.

**Sustainable Table**
(www.sustainabletable.org):
An information clearinghouse of
food-related issues, Sustainable
Table provides elaborately
detailed descriptions of various
food-production maladies (such
as factory farming, pesticide use,
and genetic engineering) as well
as information about food label-

ing, ways to get involved in the sustainable food movement, and tips for finding the healthiest, most environmentally conscious meals.

## Greenmarkets

As of spring 2005, Greenmarkets run by the Council on the Environment of New York City were operating in these locations on the days and times provided. Check with the council (www.cenyc.org) for current information.

### Manhattan

Downtown PATH
Vesey and Church Streets
Tuesday and Thursday, 8:00–6:00
June 17–December

Bowling Green
Broadway and Battery Place
Tuesday and Thursday, 8:00–5:00
Year-round

South Street Seaport
Fulton, Water, and Pearl Streets
Tuesday, 8:00–5:00
June–November

Tribeca
Greenwich, Chambers, and Duane
Streets
Wednesday, 8:00–3:00,
April–December
Saturday, 8:00–3:00, Year-round

Tompkins Square
East 7th Street and Avenue A
Sunday, 8:00–6:00
Year-round

St. Mark's Church
East 10th Street and Second
Avenue
Tuesday, 8:00–7:00
Year-round

Abingdon Square
West 12th and Hudson Streets
Saturday, 8:00–2:00
Year-round

Union Square
East 17th Street and Broadway
Monday, Wednesday, Friday,
and Saturday, 8:00–6:00
Year-round

Dag Hammarskjold Plaza
East 47th Street and
Second Avenue
Wednesday, 8:00–6:00
Year-round

Rockefeller Center
Rockefeller Plaza and 50th Street
Thursday, Friday, and Saturday,
8:00–6:00
October

57th Street
West 57th Street and Ninth
Avenue
Wednesday and Saturday,
8:00–6:00
Year-round

Tucker Square
West 66th Street and Columbus
Avenue
Thursday and Saturday,
8:00–5:00
Year-round

77th Street
West 77th Street and Columbus
Avenue
Sunday, 10:00–5:00
Year-round

97th Street
West 97th Street and Columbus
Avenue
Friday, 8:00–2:00
Year-round

Columbia
Broadway and 114th Street
Thursday, 8:00–5:00, year-round
Sunday, 8:00–6:00, year-round

175th Street
West 175th Street and Broadway
Thursday, 8:00–6:00
Late June–November

Inwood
Isham, Seaman, and Cooper
Streets
Saturday, 8:00–3:00
July 10–November 20

**Bronx**

Poe Park
Grand Concourse and 192nd
Street
Tuesday, 8:00–3:00
July–November

Yankee Stadium
Grand Concourse and 161st
Street
Tuesday, 8:00–6:00
June 29–November

Lincoln Hospital
148th and Morris Streets
Tuesday and Friday, 8:00–3:00
July–mid-November

**Queens**

Jackson Heights
Thirty-fourth Avenue and 77th
Street
Sunday, 8:00–3:00
May–November

## Brooklyn

Greenpoint–McCarren Park
Lorimer and Driggs Streets
Saturday, 8:00–3:00
Year-round

Williamsburg
Havemeyer Street and Broadway
Thursday, 8:00–4:00
July–November

Bedford-Stuyvesant
Fulton, Stuyvesant, and Utica
Streets
Saturday, 8:00–5:00
July–November

Fort Greene Park
Washington Park, Dekalb, and
Willoughby Streets
Saturday, 8:00–5:00
Year-round

Borough Hall
Court and Remsen Streets
Tuesday and Saturday, 8:00–6:00,
year-round
Thursday, 8:00–6:00,
April–December

Grand Army Plaza
Northwest entrance of Prospect
Park
Saturday, 8:00–4:00
Year-round

Windsor Terrace
Prospect Park West and 15th
Street Northwest
Wednesday, 8:00–3:00
May–November

South Park Slope/P.S. 10
Prospect, Seventh, and Eighth
Avenues
Saturday, 8:00–3:00
July 10–November 20

Cortelyou
Argyle, Beverly, and Cortelyou
Streets
Saturday, 8:30–3:00
July–November

Borough Park
Fourteenth Avenue, 49th and
50th Streets
Thursday, 8:00–3:00
July–November

Sunset Park
Fourth Avenue, 59th and 60th
Streets
Saturday, 8:00–3:00
July–November

## Staten Island

St. George
Borough hall parking lot, St.
Mark's and Hyatt
Saturday, 8:00–2:00
May–November

## Local Advocacy

**Added Value**
(www.added-value.org): See page 270.

**Just Food** (www.justfood.org; 212-645-9880): The local authority for sustainable food and food justice issues and advocacy, Just Food offers a comprehensive tool kit for setting up a CSA in the city, and provides extensive logistical and inspirational support throughout the process. Just Food is also very active in the development of food-producing community gardens, or "City Farms," throughout the city. See chapter 8 for more information about Just Food.

**Northeast Organic Farming Association of New York**
(www.nofany.org): NOFA-NY is an organization of consumers, gardeners, and farmers dedicated to creating a sustainable regional food system that is ecologically sound and economically viable through education, advocacy, and information dissemination.

**Slow Food**
(www.slowfoodusa.org): The Slow Food movement was discussed in detail in chapter 8, and a vital resource for New Yorkers with a passion for food and a concern for ecological sustainability is its *Slow Food Guide to New York City*, which provides eloquent descriptions of New York's finest food purveyors.

## Natural Food: Local Retailers

It seems like you can't swing your canvas shopping bag these days without hitting a natural food grocer. The fortunate popularity of wholesome, organic foods has resulted in a burgeoning retail market for these goods. To list them all here would consume a lot of pages, and the goal is conservation, right? On top of these smaller, often independently owned stores, these larger chains have shown a commitment to providing organic and all-natural foods: D'Agostino, the Food Emporium, Fairway, Gourmet Garage, and, of course, Whole Foods Market. See the listings for the Eat

Well Guide and Farm To Table on pages 249–250 for Internet searches, or consult your local yellow pages.

## Natural Food: Online and Delivery Services

Here are a few online natural food retailers that stand out from the scores available over the web (and that are within 100 miles or so of New York City, ensuring relatively short distances from field or pasture to plate).

**Applegate Farms**
Bridgewater, New York
www.applegatefarms.com
(866) 587–5858
Applegate Farms is proud to produce wholesome, all-natural meat products raised at 250 local family farms. The animals are never fed antibiotics or hormones, are always fed 100 percent vegetarian feed, and the meat is never processed with MSG or any other preservatives or fillers.

**Bobolink Dairy and Bakeyard**
Vernon, New Jersey
www.cowsoutside.com
(973) 764–4888
The Bobolink Dairy is a grass-only family dairy farm occupying 200 acres on the New York–New Jersey border; it produces raw milk, artisanal cheeses, wood-fired hearth breads, and grass-only meat. Cows are only administered antibiotics as a last resort when they're sick and natural treatment alternatives have failed. The cows are never confined indoors.

**500 Farms Artisan Meats**
Stafford, Connecticut
www.500farms.com
(860) 684–0222
The group 500 Farms is a union of two nonprofit organizations and an alliance of farmers, all of whom work together to revitalize sustainable, healthy, and humane farming in the Northeast, and to reintroduce heritage breeds of livestock for the sake of biodiversity and as a means to help small farms prosper. All of the family farms involved have animals that are fed vegetarian diets, without processed-grain by-products, and without hormones or the routine use of antibiotics. Even with 500 farms, you'll always know the immediate source of your meat—

every package is labeled with the name and address of the farm where the meat was raised.

**Fresh Direct**
New York, New York
www.freshdirect.com
(866) 283-7374
Started by the founder of Fairway Uptown, this online supermarket has become a popular option for New Yorkers seeking convenience in the grocery hunt. For green New Yorkers Fresh Direct offers an "organic and all-natural" department with a great selection and variety of more sustainable foods. Browse through its offerings of antibiotic- and hormone-free meats, USDA certified organic produce, organic and rBGH-free dairy, and even all-natural and minimally packaged health and beauty products void of dyes, sweeteners, and preservatives.

**Urban Organic**
Brooklyn, New York
www.urbanorganic.com
(718) 499-4321
Urban Organic offers weekly delivery of fresh, organic produce in boxes of varying sizes to fit any size of household. Content of the boxes varies from week to week. See the profile in chapter 8.

## Restaurants

Here's a collection of restaurants that are committed in some way to serving ecologically sensitive meals. Some focus on serving local, seasonal produce; some don't cater meats bred on hormones, antibiotics, and factory farms; some do all this and more. All in all, these are some of the best places in town to find the green plate special.

**Manhattan**

**Abyssinia**
35 Grand Street
(212) 226-5959

**Alain Ducasse**
The Essex House
155 West 58th Street (between Sixth and Seventh Avenues)
(212) 265-7300

**Amy's Bread**
75 Ninth Avenue (between 46th and 47th Streets)
(212) 462-4338
and

75 Ninth Avenue (at Chelsea
Market)
(212) 462–4338
and
972 Lexington Avenue
(212) 537–0270
www.amysbread.com

**Angelica Kitchen**
300 East 12th Street (at Second
Avenue)
(212) 473–0305
www.angelicakitchen.com

**Artisanal Fromagerie and
Bistro**
2 Park Avenue
(212) 725–8585

**Aureole**
34 East 61st Street (between
Madison and Park Avenues)
(212) 319–1660

**Avenue**
520 Columbus Avenue
(212) 579–3195
www.avenuebistro.com

**Babbo**
111 Waverly Place (between
MacDougal and Sixth Avenues)
(212) 777–0303
www.babbonyc.com

**Bachue**
36 West 21st Street
(212) 299–0870

**Balthazar**
80 Spring Street (between
Broadway and Crosby Street)
(212) 965–1414

**Beacon Restaurant**
25 West 56th Street (between
Fifth and Sixth Avenues)
(212) 332–0500
www.beaconnyc.com

**Beppe**
45 East 42nd Street (between
Broadway and Park Avenue
South)
(212) 982–8422

**Bistro le Steak**
1309 Third Avenue

**Blue Hill**
75 Washington Place (between
Washington Square West and
Sixth Avenue)
(212) 539–1776

**Blue Smoke**
116 East 27th Street (between
Park Avenue South and Lexington
Avenue)
(212) 447–7733

**Bonobo's**
18 East 23rd Street
(212) 505-1200

**Bouley**
120 West Broadway (at Duane
Street)
(212) 964-2525

**Bright Food Shop**
218 Eighth Avenue
(212) 243-4433

**Candle Café**
1307 Third Avenue (at 75th Street)
(212) 472-0970
and
154 East 79th Street
(212) 537-7179
www.candlecafe.com

**Caravan of Dreams**
405 East 6th Street (at First
Avenue)
(212) 254-1613

**Chanterelle**
2 Harrison Street (at Hudson
Street)
(212) 966-6960

**Chow Bar**
230 West 4th Street
(212) 633-2212

**City Bakery**
3 West 18th Street (between Fifth
and Sixth Avenues)
(212) 366-1414

**Counter**
105 First Avenue (between 6th
and 7th Streets)
(212) 982-5870

**Craft and Craftbar**
43, 47 East 19th Street (between
Broadway and Park Avenue South)
(212) 780-0880

**Daniel**
60 East 65th Street (between
Madison and Park Avenues)
(212) 288-0033

**Danube**
30 Hudson Street (at Duane
Street)
(212) 791-3771

**D'Artagnan Rotisserie**
152 East 46th Street (between
Lexington and Third Avenues)
(212) 687-0300

**Eleven Madison Avenue
Restaurant**
11 Madison Avenue
(212) 889-0905

### Elio's
1621 Second Avenue
(between 84th and 85th Streets)
(212) 772-2242

### Esca
402 West 43rd Street (at Ninth
Avenue)
(212) 564-7272

### Etas-Unis
242 East 81st Street (between
Second and Third Avenues)
(212) 517-8826

### 50 Carmine
50 Carmine Street
(212) 206-9134

### Five Points Restaurant
31 Great Jones Street
(212) 253-5700

### Fleur de Sel
5 East 20th Street
(212) 460-9100

### Four Seasons
99 East 52nd Street (between
Lexington and Park Avenues)
(212) 754-9494

### Good Health Café
324 East 86th Street (between
First and Second Avenues)
(212) 439-9680

### Gotham Bar and Grill
12 East 12th Street (between
Fifth Avenue and University Place)
(212) 620-4020

### Gramercy Tavern
42 East 20th Street
(between Broadway and Park
Avenue South)
(212) 477-0777

### The Grange Hall
50 Commerce Street
(at Barrow Street)
(212) 294-5246

### Heartbeat
149 East 49th Street
(212) 407-2900

### Helianthus
48 MacDougal Street
(between Houston and Prince)
(212) 598-0387

### Herban Kitchen
290 Hudson Street
(at Spring Street)
(212) 627-2257
www.herbankitchen.com

### Honmura An
170 Mercer Street
(between Houston and Prince)
(212) 334-5253

**Il Buco**
47 Bond Street
(between Bowery and Lafayette)
(212) 533-1932
www.ilbuco.com

**Jean-Georges**
Trump International Hotel
1 Central Park West (between
60th and 61st Streets)
(212) 299-3900
www.allinfo.net/jg/
jean_georges.htm

**Josie's**
300 Amsterdam Avenue (at 74th
Street)
(212) 769-1212
and
565 Third Avenue (at 37th Street)
(212) 490-1558

**Judson Grill**
152 West 52nd Street (between
Sixth and Seventh Avenues)
(212) 582-5252

**Kate's Joint**
56-58 Avenue B (at 4th Street)
(212) 777-7059

**La Caravelle**
33 West 55th Street (between
Fifth and Sixth Avenues)
(212) 586-4252

**Le Bernardin**
155 West 51st Street (between
Sixth and Seventh Avenues)
(212) 489-1515
www.le-bernardin.com

**L'Ecole**
French Culinary Institute
462 Broadway (at Grand Street)
(212) 219-3300

**Le Pain Quotidien**
1131 Madison Avenue (between
84th and 85th Streets)
(212) 327-4900

**Life Café**
343 East 10th Street (at Avenue
B)
(212) 477-9001

**Lupa**
170 Thompson Street (between
Bleecker and Houston Streets)
(212) 982-5089

**March**
405 East 58th Street (between
First Avenue and Sutton Place)
(212) 754-6272

**Mary's Fish Camp**
64 Charles Street (at West 4th
Street)
(646) 486-2185

**Molyvos**
871 Seventh Avenue (at 55th
Street)
(212) 582-7500
www.molyvos.com

**Oceana**
55 East 54th Street (between
Park and Madison Avenues)
(212) 759-5941
www.oceanarestaurant.com

**Omen**
113 Thompson Street (between
Prince and Spring Streets)
(212) 925-8923

**Onju**
108 East 4th Street
(212) 228-3880

**The Organic Grill**
123 First Avenue
(212) 477-7477
www.theorganicgrill.com

**Ouest**
2315 Broadway
(between 83rd and 84th Streets)
(212) 580-8700

**Ozu**
566 Amsterdam Avenue
(212) 787-8316

**Payard**
1032 Lexington Avenue
(212) 717-5252
www.payard.com

**Pearl Oyster Bar**
18 Cornelia Street (between
Bleecker and West 4th Streets)

**Prune**
54 East 1st Street (between First
and Second Avenues)
(212) 677-6221

**Quantum Leap**
88 West 3rd Street (between
Thompson and Sullivan)
(212) 677-8050

**Quintessence**
263 East 10th Street (between
First Avenue and Avenue A)
(646) 654-1923

**RM**
33 East 60th Street (between
Park and Madison Avenues)
(212) 319-3800

**The Sanctuary**
25 First Avenue
(between 1st and 2nd Streets)
(212) 780-9786

**Savoy**
70 Prince Street
(at Crosby Street)
(212) 219-8570

**Share**
406 East 9th Street

**Soba Nippon**
19 West 52nd Street
(between Fifth and Sixth Avenues)
(212) 489-2525

**Spring Street Natural**
62 Spring Street (at Lafayette)
(212) 966-0290

**Strictly Roots**
2058 Adam Clayton Powell
Boulevard (Seventh Avenue at
123rd Street)
(212) 864-8699

**Sullivan Street Bakery**
73 Sullivan Street (between
Broome and Spring Streets)
(212) 334-9435

**Tabla/Bread Bar**
11 Madison Avenue
(at 25th Street)
(212) 889-0667

**The Tasting Room**
72 East 1st Street
(at First Avenue)
(212) 358-7831

**Terra 47**
47 East 12th Street (between
Broadway and University Place)
(212) 358-0141

**Tocqueville**
15 East 15th Street
(212) 358-7831
www.tocquevillerestaurant.com

**Town**
The Chambers Hotel
13 West 56th Street (between
Fifth and Sixth Avenues)
(212) 582-4445

**Union Square Café**
21 East 16th Street
(between Fifth Avenue and Union
Square West)
(212) 243-4020

**Verbana**
54 Irving Place
(between 17th and 18th Streets)
(212) 260-5454

**Wallse**
344 East 11th Street (at
Washington Street)
(212) 352-2300

**Washington Park**
24 Fifth Avenue
(between 9th and 10th Streets)
(212) 529-4400

**WD-50**
50 Clinton Street
(212) 477-2900

**Westville**
210 West 10th Street
(212) 741-7971

**Zen Palate**
34 Union Square East
(212) 614-9345
and
663 Ninth Avenue
(212) 582-1669
and
2170 Broadway
(212) 501-7768

## Brooklyn

**Bliss**
Williamsburg
191 Bedford Avenue (between
North 6th and North 7th Streets)
(718) 599-2547

**Blue Ribbon Brooklyn**
Park Slope
280 Fifth Avenue (between
Garfield and 1st Streets)
(718) 840-0404

**Café Melange**
Boerum Hill
444 Atlantic Avenue (between
Bonds and Nevins Streets)
(718) 935-1220

**Chestnut**
Carroll Gardens
271 Smith Street (near DeGraw)
(718) 243-0049

**Franny's**
Park Slope
293 Flatbush Avenue (between
St. Mark's and Prospect Place)
(718) 230-0221
www.frannysbrooklyn.com

**Goga Café**
Carroll Gardens
521 Court Street (between West
9th and Garnett)
(718) 260-8618

**The Greens**
Brooklyn Heights
128 Montague Street
(at Henry Street)
(718) 246-1288

**The Grocery**
Carroll Gardens
288 Smith Street (between
Sackett and Union Streets)
(718) 596-3335

**The Minnow**
Park Slope
442 9th Street (between Sixth
and Seventh Avenues)
(718) 832-5500

**Moustache**
Boerum Hill
205 Atlantic Avenue (between
Bonds and Nevins Streets)
(718) 852-5555

**Mr. Falafel**
Park Slope
226 Seventh Avenue
(between 3rd and 4th Streets)
(718) 768-4961

**New Prospect Café**
Park Slope/Prospect Heights
393 Flatbush Avenue (at Eighth
Avenue)
(718) 638-2148

**Second Helpings**
Park Slope
448 9th Street (at Seventh
Avenue)
(718) 965-1925

**Sparky's American Food**
Williamsburg
135-A North 5th Street
(718) 302-5151

**360**
Red Hook
360 Van Brunt (at Wolcott Street)
(718) 246-0360

**Vegetarian Palate**
Park Slope/Prospect Heights
258 Flatbush Avenue (between

Sixth and Seventh Avenues)
(718) 623-8808

**Queens**

**Buddha Bodai Vegetarian
Restaurant**
Flushing
42-06 Main Street (between
Franklin and Maple)
(718) 939-1188

**Health Nut**
212-03 Twenty-sixth Avenue
(718) 225-8164

**Linda's Natural Kitchen**
Kew Gardens
81-22 Leffers Boulevard
(718) 847-2233

**The Oneness Fountain-Heart**
Flushing
157-19 Seventy-second Avenue
(718) 591-3663

## Seafood

**Audubon Seafood Lover's
Guide**(http://seafood.audubon
.org/): A free downloadable wallet card that helps the consumer
make more conscientious choices
at the market or restaurant. It
divides many popular fish species
into three categories, ranging

from those that are sustainably harvested to those whose populations are endangered or are harvested in ways harmful to the aquatic environment.

**Seafood Choices Alliance** (www.seafoodchoices.com): "Bringing ocean conservation to the table" is the guiding credo of this website that also features a searchable database of where to find sustainable seafood in New York City.

 Health & Beauty

## General Info

**Environmental Working Group** (www.ewg.org/reports/skindeep): The seminal "Skin Deep" report by the EWG provides "a safety assessment of ingredients in personal care products," evaluating thousands of products for their threat to human health. Armed with a "Searchable Product Guide," this resource provides all you need to know about health and beauty products with regard to human health.

*The Green Guide* (www.thegreenguide.com): See page 231.

## Retailers

A number of safe and eco-friendly health and beauty product lines are listed in chapter 13. These can typically be found in the same natural food groceries that carry sustainable food products. Also, holistic health "drugstores" are very common around the city. Some reliable online retailers for these products are listed below.

**Burt's Bees** www.burtsbees.com

**Ecco Bella** www.eccobella.com

**Eco-Beauty Organics** www.eco-beauty.com

**GoodHumans Shopping** www.goodhumans.com/Shopping/Bath_and_body Carries multiple brands.

**Holistic Beauty** www.holisticbeauty.net

**InterNatural** www.internatural.com

**Natural Beauty Solutions** www.naturalbeautysolutions.net Carries multiple brands.

**Pangea Organics**
www.pangeaorganics.com

**Terressentials**
www.terressentials.com

## Salons

These hair salons and body spas use organic ingredients and take an all-natural approach to health and beauty treatment.

**Ayurveda's Beauty Care**
99 University Place, 5th Floor
(212) 529–3300
www.ayurvedabeautycare.com
Spa services featuring all-natural ayurvedic facials.

**Heights Hair**
91 Pineapple Walk
Brooklyn Heights
(718) 403–0301
A full-service unisex salon offering hair coloring, highlighting, and perms using only toxin-free, vegetable-, plant-, and mineral-based ingredients.

**John Masters Organics**
77 Sullivan Street
(212) 343–9590
www.johnmasters.com

Herbal-based, ammonia-free hair color, shiatsu scalp treatments, organic hair and skin care products.

**Pratima**
162 West 56th Street, Suite 204
(212) 581–8136
Ayurvedic natural skin treatment and care products.

## Household Goods

### Cleaning Supplies

Of the many eco-friendly cleaning supplies available, these reputable brands come highly recommended.

**Aubrey Organics**
www.aubreyorganics.com
(800) 282–7394
All-purpose soap, glass cleaner.

**Bon Ami**
www.bonami.com
Bath soap, oven cleaner, scouring cleaner.

**Dr. Bronners**
www.drbronner.com
(760) 743–2211
All-purpose soap, dish soap.

**Earth Friendly**
www.ecos.com
(800) 335-ECOS
Shower cleaner, toilet cleaner,
glass cleaner, drain clearer, oven
cleaner, furniture polish, dish
soap, laundry detergent.

**Ecover**
www.ecover.com
(800) 449-4925
All-purpose soap, toilet cleaner,
oven cleaner, dish soap and
detergent, laundry detergent,
nonchlorine bleach.

**Hope's**
www.hopecompany.com
(800) 325-4026
Furniture polishes, metal polishes.

**Mrs. Meyer's Clean Day**
www.mrsmeyers.com
(877) 576-8808
All purpose soap and detergent,
shower cleaner, toilet cleaner,
glass cleaner, oven cleaner, laundry detergent, furniture polish,
carper cleaner, nonchlorine
bleach.

**Seventh Generation**
www.seventhgeneration.com
(802) 658-3773
All-purpose soap, bath cleaner,
toilet cleaner, shower cleaner,

glass cleaner, oven cleaner, dish
soap and detergent, laundry
detergent, nonchlorine bleach.

**Vermont Soapworks**
www.vermontsoap.com
(866) SOAP-4U2
All-purpose soap.

## Cleaning: General Info

**Environmental Media Services**
(www.ems.org/household_
cleaners/alternatives.html):
Provides recipes for eco-friendly
alternatives to common and toxic
household cleaners. Also has
links to many facts and information about dangerous ingredients
in common household cleaners.

*The Green Guide*
(www.thegreenguide.com):
See page 231.

**Green Seal** (www.greenseal.org/
certproducts.htm): Green Seal is
an independent, nonprofit organization that offers certification to
environmentally friendly products.
The above link brings you to a list
of all of Green Seal's certified
products, with a special section
on cleaners. To see Green Seal's

recommendations for safe and eco-friendly general-purpose cleaners, check www.greenseal.org/ recommendations/CGR= GPCleaners.pdf.

**Washington Toxics Coalition** (www.watoxics.org): Features information about a number of toxic and chemically based environmental issues, including a "Toxics in the Home" section, where you can find specific information about the dangers of chemicals in the home. There is a specific report on "Safer Cleaning Products" with good reference information.

## Local Retailers

The following local establishments carry a variety of eco-friendly products, including housewares and various other lifestyle products. It's recommended that you call any store or visit its website (if available) to see what exactly it carries.

**Bettencourt Woodworking**
70 North 6th Street
(Williamsburg)

(718) 218-6737
www.bettencourtwood.com
Sleek bamboo and recycled wood furniture.

**Environment 337**
337 Smith Street
(Cobble Hill)
(718) 522-1767
Various eco-friendly home and lifestyle items.

**The Future Perfect**
115 North 6th Street
(Williamsburg, at Berry Street)
(718) 599-6278
www.thefutureperfect.com
Assorted home goods, contemporary design and sustainable style.

**gomi nyc**
443 East 6th Street
(212) 979-0388
www.gominyc.com
An interesting assortment of recycled products for the home.

**IIKH**
458 West 17th Street
(212) 675-9400
www.2kh.com
"Smart, stylish, sexy, green" goods for the home, body, baby, pet, and more.

**Organic Avenue**
23 Ludlow Street, Loft #2
(212) 334–4593
www.organicavenue.com
Men's and women's clothing,
footwear, accessories, housewares, health and beauty, food,
and media.

**Sublime**
26 Varick Street
(212) 941–8888
www.sublimeamericandesign.com
Carries a variety of urban-chic
furniture featuring many local
designers, some with an ecological sensitivity.

**Terre Verde**
120 Wooster Street
(212) 925–4533
A true eco-department store.

**3R Living**
276 Fifth Avenue
(Park Slope, between Garfield and
1st Streets)
(718) 832–0951
www.3rliving.com
Various items for the home and
life.

## Online Retailers

**Eco Wise**
http://ecowise.com
Your "earth-friendly everything
store."

**Green Feet**
www.greenfeet.com
Home and garden, personal care,
clothing, cleaning supplies, and
more!

**Green Home**
www.greenhome.com
An environmental superstore with
everything for the home.

**Kwytza Kraft**
www.kwytzakraft.com
Various housewares made with
single-use chopsticks collected
from restaurants around China,
which are then thoroughly sani-
tized and used in high-design
products.

**Loop Organic**
www.looporganic.com
Fine organic cotton bed and bath
linens.

**Real Goods by Gaiam**
www.realgoods.com
An extensive online and print catalog of environmentally sensitive

products for the house and home, workplace, personal care, and more.

**Resource Revival**
www.resourcerevival.com
Unique products for the home made of entirely recycled materials.

**Vivavi**
www.vivavi.com
An assortment of housewares and clothing products from ecologically advanced designers.

## Parks & Gardens

### Botanical Gardens

**Brooklyn Botanic Garden**
www.bbg.org
(718) 623-7200
Located in Prospect Park.

**Conservatory Garden at Central Park**
www.centralparknyc.org
(212) 310-6600
Located at Fifth Avenue and 105th Street.

**New York Botanical Garden**
www.nybg.org
(718) 817-8700
Located at Bronx River Parkway and Fordham Road in the Bronx.

**Queens Botanical Garden**
www.queensbotanical.org
(718) 539-5296
Located at 43-50 Main Street in Flushing, Queens.

**Staten Island Botanical Garden**
www.sibg.org
(718) 362-1010
Located at 1000 Richmond Terrace in Staten Island.

### Community Gardens

**Added Value**
(www.added-value.org; 718-855-5531): Added Value contributes to the sustainable development of Brooklyn's Red Hook neighborhood through urban agriculture programs. See chapter 8 for more information about Added Value.

**Green Guerillas**
(www.greenguerillas.org; 212-402-1121): Since 1973, Green Guerillas has helped citizen groups create, protect, and maintain community gardens throughout the city. It works with more than 200 community groups, providing an array of services from political advocacy to practical education.

**GreenThumb**

(www.greenthumbnyc.org):
Run by the New York City
Department of Parks and
Recreation, GreenThumb is the
largest community garden program in the country, with over
600 member gardens serving
more than 20,000 residents.
Providing assistance to community
groups in the form of materials,
grants, and technical and educational programs, GreenThumb
helps strengthen communities
and the urban environment
through gardening and open-
space management.

## Nature and Wildlife Preserves

Tucked away in the folds of
New York City are a number of
nature centers, wildlife preserves, and other outdoor
environmental facilities. Many
are on Parks Department or
state lands, but some are privately owned and operated.
The following listings are the
largest and most prominent
such preserves, but the Parks
Department has a full forty-
eight areas designated as

"Forever Wild" totaling more
than 8,700 acres, most of
which are hidden to even their
neighbors. For a full listing
check out the Forever Wild
website (www.nycgovparks.org;
search "forever wild").

### Bronx

**Crotona Park and Victory Garden**
Crotona Park
(718) 378-2061

**Orchard Beach Nature Center**
Section 2 of Orchard Beach
(718) 885-3466

**Pelham Bay Nature Center**
Pelham Bay Park
Bruckner Boulevard and
Wilkinson Avenue
(718) 885-3467

**Van Cortlandt Nature Center**
Van Cortlandt Park
246th Street and Broadway
(718) 548-0912

**Wave Hill**
Public Gardens and Cultural
Center
West 249th Street and
Independence Avenue
(718) 549-3200

## Brooklyn

**Jamaica Bay Wildlife Refuge**
Broad Channel (Brooklyn and
Queens) National Park Service
(718) 318-4340

**The Salt Marsh Nature Center**
Marine Park
(718) 421-2021
www.saltmarshalliance.org

## Manhattan

**Belvedere Castle Visitor Center**
Central Park
West 81st Street and West Drive
(212) 628-2345

**Dana Discovery Center**
Central Park
110th Street and Lenox Avenue
(212) 860-1370

**Inwood Hill Nature Center**
Inwood Park
218th Street and Indian Road
(212) 304-2365

## Queens

**Alley Pond Environmental
Center**
Alley Pond Park
228-06 Northern Boulevard
(718) 229-4000
www.alleypond.com

**Forest Park Nature Center**
Forest Park
(718) 846-2731

**Queens County Farm Museum**
73-50 Little Neck Parkway
Floral Park
(718) 347-3276
www.queensfarm.org

## Staten Island

**Blue Heron Nature Center**
Blue Heron Park
222 Poillon Road (between
Amboy and Hylon Boulevards)
(718) 967-3542
www.preserve2.org/blueheron/
blueheron.htm

**Clay Pit Ponds State Park
Preserve**
83 Nielsen Avenue
(718) 967-1976

**High Rock Nature Center**
High Rock Park
200 Nevada Avenue
(718) 667-6042

**William T. Davis Wildlife Refuge**
Travis Avenue
www.sigreenbelt.org/About/
WTDavis/wtdavis.htm
(718) 667-2165

## Parks: General Info

**New York City Department of Parks and Recreation**
(www.nycgovparks.org; 311):
The official and incredibly comprehensive resource for all things of or relating to city parks!

**New York State Parks**
(http://nysparks.state.ny.us):
The official state park website.

## Parks Advocacy

There are dozens of organizations—in a wide range of sizes and participation rates—that get involved with protecting, developing, programming, revitalizing, and basically bettering the thousands of acres of parkland here in New York City. Most of these organizations operate as not-for-profits and are often looking for volunteers and donations. All offer services and information to New Yorkers. The following list includes those that have proven particularly successful in making our open space nicer.

**The Battery Conservancy**
(212) 344-3491
www.thebattery.org
Rebuilding Historic Battery Park.

**The Bronx River Alliance**
(718) 430-4665
www.bronxriver.org
Protecting, improving, and restoring the Bronx River and Corridor Greenway.

**Bryant Park Restoration Corporation**
(212) 768-4242
www.bryantpark.org
Revitalizing and managing this popular Midtown park.

**Central Park Conservancy**
(212) 310-6600
www.centralparknyc.org
The gold standard for the public-private partnership in urban park fund-raising and management.

**City Parks Foundation**
(212) 360-1399
www.cityparksfoundation.org
Creates programming for parks, including athletic, cultural, arts and educational programs.

**Flushing Meadows Corona Park Unisphere, Inc.**
www.flushingmeadowscorona
park.org
Developing and revitalizing
Queens's flagship park.

**Friends of Hudson River Park**
(212) 627-2020
www.friendsofhudsonriverpark.org
Works with the city and state
government and the Hudson River
Park Trust to facilitate the
development of the West Side
waterfront.

**Friends of Van Cortlandt Park**
(718) 601-1460
www.vancortlandt.org
Protecting, promoting, and
preserving Van Cortlandt Park as
a natural resource.

**Greenbelt Conservancy**
(718) 667-2165
www.sigreenbelt.org
Oversees the operation, administration, and public use of this
largest of New York City's flagship
parks, running through the heart
of Staten Island.

**Hudson River Park Trust**
(212) 627-2020
www.hudsonriverpark.org
Works with the city and state gov-

ernment and the Friends of
Hudson River Park to facilitate
the development of the West Side
waterfront.

**New Yorkers for Parks**
(212) 838-9410
www.ny4p.org
An independent advocacy organization serving as a watchdog for
people of New York and their
parks and committed to attaining
a higher level of park services in
every New York City community.

**New York Restoration Project**
(212) 333-2552
www.nyrp.org
Focuses on raising money for,
revitalizing, and restoring many of
the city's under-resourced parks,
primarily in economically disadvantaged neighborhoods.

**Partnership for Parks**
(212) 360-1310
www.itsmypark.org
A joint program of the DPR and
the City Parks Foundation, PFP
works primarily on reaching out
to communities to mobilize,
strengthen, support, and staff
local park groups with the goal of
getting the public more closely
involved with neighborhood parks.

**Prospect Park Alliance**
(718) 965-8951
www.prospectpark.org
Modeled after the success of the Central Park Conservancy, the Prospect Park Alliance helps maintain this flagship Brooklyn park as one of the finest urban parks in the world.

**Riverside Park Fund**
(212) 870-3070
www.riversideparkfund.org
Dedicated to preserving and improving the 4-plus-mile stretch of Hudson River waterfront above 68th Street on the West Side.

## ♻ Recycling

**Build It Green! NYC**
(www.bignyc.org): See page 234.

**Craigslist** (newyork.craigslist .org): Among many other features, this website has a section for "free" goods from others who no longer have any use for them. Less recycling-specific than Freecycle (see below), but a great place to find quality secondhand stuff, or a good venue to get rid of your own.

**Freecycle New York City**
(http://groups.yahoo.com/ group/freecyclenewyorkcity): A national resource with a New York City chapter, this site lets users sign up to either peruse the listings of free materials or post their own unwanted goods.

**Recycle This! NYC**
(www.recyclethisnyc.org): An activist-run waste-prevention and recycling organization formed in the wake of New York recycling cuts, and still running strong with materials exchanges, waste drop-sites, and more.

**We Can, Inc.**
(www.wecanny.org; 212-262-2222): A nonprofit organization that collects redeemable bottles and cans from various businesses around the city to raise money for the poor and homeless. Also provides venues for the city's less affluent to redeem unlimited amounts of bottles and cans in a hassle-free and convenient setting.

## Compost

**Lower East Side Ecology Center** (212-477-4022): LESEC runs a Compost Education Center and Collection Program. LESEC accepts organic material for composting (fruit and vegetable peelings, coffee grounds and tea bags, egg- and nut shells, cut flowers, and similar organic material). LESEC also sells red wiggler worms, potting soil, worm castings, and worm condos there.

**NYC Compost Project** (www.nyccompost.org): All the information you'll need to start composting at home through an indoor or outdoor system. Includes links to suppliers for start-up composting materials and a detailed guide through the entire process.

## Waste Reduction Info

**Reduce.org** (www.reduce.org): An information clearinghouse with waste-reduction tips, strategies, and motivations. Many useful features for dealing with waste in all aspects of life.

## Waste Reduction Services

**Direct Marketing Association** (www.dmaconsumers.org/privacy.html): Get your name off of mass-mailing lists by signing up for this service offered by DMA.

**Earth 911** (http://newyork.earth911.org): A wonderful and comprehensive resource that features recycling and waste management information on the community level. Search by zip code for services—ranging from recycling to hazardous waste disposal to computer and large-item disposal—in your area.

**Lower East Side Ecology Center** (212-420-0621): Helps communities develop recycling or composting programs for reusable waste that the city DoS doesn't collect.
Also see page 276.

**NYC Compost Project** (www.nyccompost.org): See COMPOST.

**NYC Department of Sanitation**
(www.ci.nyc.ny.us/html/dos/
home.html; 311): This DoS
website has links to all kinds of
critical information on waste
management in the city. It
includes free mail-order labels,
flyers, and decals for your home
or business's recycling center.

**NYC Wastele$$**
(www.nycwasteless.org): A great
resource to help navigate the
city's often confusing recycling
and waste management programs.
Practical tips for the individual,
the business, or governmental
organizations.

**Recycle This NYC** (www.recycle
thisnyc.org): See page 276.

**Wireless Foundation**
(www.wirelessfoundation.org/
donateaphone/index.cfm):
Recycle your old cell phone with
the Wireless Foundation and raise
money for honorable charities all
at once.

 **Transportation**

## Alternative Transportation: Advocacy and Info

**Auto-free New York**
(www.auto-free.org;
212-475-3394): Alternative
transportation information and
advocacy.

**Citystreets**
(www.citystreets.org): A New York
City–based pedestrian rights and
advocacy group.

**MTA** (www.mta.info): The Metro-
politan Transportation Authority's
website has it all. A one-stop
source for any of your mass tran-
sit needs.

**New York Climate Rescue**
(www.climaterescue.org):
Information about global warm-
ing's effect on New York City.

**Straphangers Campaign**
(www.straphangers.org;
212-349-6460): NYPIRG's mass
transit advocacy campaign, fea-
turing plenty of information about
the MTA's NY Transit system, and
featuring the "Subway Diversion"
e-mail notification service.

## TIME'S UP!

(www.times-up.org; 212-802-8222): A direct-action environmental and alternative transportation advocacy group. The site features information about ongoing environmental campaigns, group rides, repair workshops, and informative presentations programmed by TIME'S UP!

## Transportation Alternatives

(www.transalt.org; 212-629-8080): The authoritative source for all elements of alternative transportation in New York City. An extensive resource with information and strategies for traffic calming, safe streets, car-free parks, sensible mass transit, bicycling, and pedestrianism. Any question relating to any of the above has doubtlessly been answered by TA.

# Alternative Transportation: Services

## CityRacks

(http://www.nyc.gov/html/dot/html/bikeped/bikerack.html; 311): Explains how to get the city to install a bike rack in front of your home or business—for free!

## Recycle-A-Bicycle

(www.recycleabicycle.org): This unique program teaches students bicycle mechanic skills, refurbishing old abandoned bicycles and donating or reselling them. Two public shops in the East Village (75 Avenue C, between 5th and 6th Streets; 212-475-1655) and Dumbo (55 Washington Street, between Front and Water Streets; 718-858-2972).

## TransitChek

(www.transitchek.com; 800-331-CHEK): Save money on mass transit by getting your employer to sign up for TransitChek. Employees and businesses alike save at tax time with this unique program.

## Zipcar

(www.zipcar.com; 866-4ZIPCAR): The "anti-car." This communal approach to car ownership in New York City lets you pay only for times you use a car, reducing hassle, headaches, and extra cars and traffic on the streets.

## Water

### Conservation

**Department of Environment Protection** (http://www.ci .nyc.ny.us/html/dep; 311): The city DEP offers lots of information about municipal water use, history, and conservation tips. Through this site you can also find the "Residential Water Survey Request Form" for a free water-efficiency survey by DEP workers, and free efficient faucets, fixtures, and showerheads.

**H2ouse** (www.h2ouse.org): A remarkably comprehensive resource for information about and strategies for water conservation. Take the "Home Tour" and find out how to save water throughout and even outside your home.

 ## Workplace

### General Info

*Green@Work Magazine* (www.greenatworkmag.com; 561–627–3393): A bimonthly periodical replete with profiles of companies effectively using green business practices, how-to resources, case studies, and special opportunities and services for most fields of work.

**GreenBiz** (www.greenbiz.com): Heralded as "the resource center on business, the environment, and the bottom line," GreenBiz provides information and services to help businesses incorporate ecologically sustainable operations while minding profitable business practices.

**The Natural Step** (www.naturalstep.org): Provides services to companies to help integrate principles of sustainability into their decisions, operations, and core strategies. From executive briefings to design consultation to sustainability assessments, The Natural Step offers quite a bit to the business looking for the green edge.

### Local Services

**Greg Barber Company Environmental Paper & Printing** (www.gregbarberco.com; 201–727–0400, ext. 105): Specializing in eco-friendly paper and printing work, from small-scale, personal jobs to large industry orders. Business cards, letterhead, print-runs, and more.

**Waste-Free NYC**
(www.wastefreenyc.org):
A nonprofit organization that researches the effects of business practices on environmental and human health. The website offers a wealth of information about waste management practices and policies.

# Abbreviations

| | |
|---|---|
| BASIC | Big Apple Solar Installation Commitment |
| BIG NYC | Build It Green! NYC |
| BTU | British thermal unit |
| CEC | Community Environmental Center |
| CEI | Community Energy, Inc. |
| CENYC | Council of the Environment of New York City |
| CFL | Compact fluorescent lamp |
| CPC | Central Park Conservancy |
| CSA | Community-supported agriculture |
| CSO | Combined sewage overflow |
| DEP | Department of Environmental Protection |
| DMA | Direct Marketing Association |
| DOS | Department of Sanitation |
| DOT | Department of Transportation |
| EPA | Environmental Protection Agency |
| ESCO | Energy service company |
| FDA | Food and Drug Administration |
| GE | Genetic engineering or genetically engineered (as in crops) |
| GMO | Genetically modified organisms |
| kWh | Kilowatt hour |
| LESEC | Lower East Side Ecology Center |

| | |
|---|---|
| MTA | Metropolitan Transportation Authority |
| NOFA-NY | Northeast Organic Farming Association of New York |
| NSN | Neighborhood Streets Network |
| NYC PSC | New York City Public Service Commission |
| NYPIRG | New York Public Interest Research Group |
| PANNA | Pesticide Action Network of North America |
| PFP | Partnership for Parks |
| PV | Photovoltaic (solar panels) |
| PVC | Polyvinyl chloride |
| rBGH | Recombinant bovine growth hormone |
| TA | Transportation Alternatives |
| USDA | United States Department of Agriculture |
| VOC | Volatile organic compounds |

# Index

# About the Author

Ben Jervey writes about environmental topics, music, travel, and the green building industry for print and online magazines and newspapers and has worked with a not-for-profit organization dedicated to the development and care of the city's parks. He lives in Brooklyn, New York.